Locating gender

Cambridge Studies in Work and Social Inequality

Series editors
R. M. Blackburn, Ken Prandy, Jenny Jarman

Locating gender

Occupational segregation, wages and domestic responsibilities

Janet Siltanen

Carleton University, Ottawa

Routledge
Taylor & Francis Group

LONDON AND NEW YORK

First published 1994 by UCL Press

Reissued 2020 by Routledge
2 Park Square, Milton Park, Abingdon, Oxon OX14 4RN
605 Third Avenue, New York, NY 10017

Routledge is an imprint of the Taylor & Francis Group, an informa business

British Library Cataloguing in Publication Data.
A catalogue record for this book is available from the British Library.

Library of Congress Cataloging-in-Publication Data
Siltanen, Janet.
    Locating gender : occupational segregation, wages, and domestic
responsibility / Janet Siltanen.
        p.   cm. – (Cambridge studies in work and social inequality, 1)
    Based on the author's thesis (doctoral).
    Includes bibliographical references.
    ISBN 1-85728-253-1 : $65.00. – ISBN 1-85728-254-X (pbk.) : $24.95
    1. Sexual division of labour–Great Britain. 2. Equal pay for equal
work–Great Britain. 3. Work and family–Great Britain.
I. Title. II. Series.
HD6080.65.G7S67   1994
308.31615.0051–dc20   94 0047
                                                                 CIP

Typeset in Palatino.

ISBN 13: 978-0-367-53237-6 (hbk)
ISBN 13: 9780-367-53239-0 (pbk)
ISBN 13: 978-1-003-08107-4 (ebk)

Contents

Acknowledgements

This manuscript has had a long gestation period, and many people have provided support, encouragement and intellectual grist along the way. The core of the work is my doctoral research, during which I was supervised by Sandy Stewart. His commitment to research as the creative foundation of sociology was inspiring then, and has been so since. I am indebted to all those who helped to arrange interviews, and who provided background and historical material. For reasons of confidentiality, most can not be named, but I can thank two people who were especially helpful: Barbara Duffner from (what was then) Post Office Headquarters and Kim McInlay, from the Union of Communication Workers. My thanks too to all those I interviewed. In discussing and presenting their experience and views, I have tried to respect the integrity of the former and the considered nature of the latter. I hope that my efforts are seen to be a positive return on theirs.

The manuscript contains material which goes a considerable way beyond the parameters of the original doctoral thesis. The preparation of the material on wages in Chapter 4 was facilitated by information received from the Low Pay Unit. Some people have read all, or parts of, this new material. My thanks to Helen Corr, Julia Brannen, Angela Dale, Jenny Jarman and Gill Jones. Others have been through it all, more than once: a special thanks to John Holmwood, Sandy Stewart and Bob Blackburn. The presentation of this work has benefitted from the advice, information and comment received, but of course the interpretations offered should be taken to reflect my own views only.

Finally, a very special acknowledgement for David Dean who has lived through "parenting and employment" in more ways than any human being should be subjected to.

JANET SILTANEN

Introduction

The main aim of this research is to contribute to the task of isolating the power of gender as an explanatory category, and to help specify the concept of gender in a manner that resonates fully with social experience. In doing so, I understand the primary job to be one of locating gender as a social process within a more general framework of social organization and inequality. This direction of thinking necessarily leads one to examine patterns of change and continuity in social arrangements, and, as part of this exercise, to identify the significance of variation in the salience of gendered experience.

The research addresses four areas of current interest in the study of gender and employment. First, it seeks to contribute to the growing interest in the *diversity* of women's employment experience, and the larger project of disaggregating gender categories in social analysis. The object here is not only to identify complexity in women's employment experience, but also to ascertain the major social processes and patterns that structure these complex relations. In the pursuit of the twin objectives of recognizing diversity and isolating major processes, two questions arise that require serious attention. How is the diversity in experience within gender categories located in terms of social phenomena structuring relations of employment and domestic responsibilities, such as inequalities in general social resources, age, "race", and life-course trajectories? And, how does the diversity within gender categories connect with aggregate patterns of gender inequality? The arguments presented in this text inform aspects of these two questions. One central focus of the research – the phenomenon of occupational segregation by sex – provides an interesting case for the examination of these issues, since it consists of a strong aggregate pattern of gender inequality within a hierarchy that also stratifies both women's and men's employment.

The second area of interest is occupational segregation by sex itself, particularly at the level of individual jobs or employment establishments. National patterns of gender distributions in employment are useful in establishing the prevalence of occupational segregation by sex as a phenomenon in the dynamics of employment structuring, and in examining aggregate trends in gender inequality. But, as many commentators have observed, aggregate patterns underestimate the degree to which women and men work in segregated employment environments and, most importantly, cannot sufficiently illuminate the social practices involved in the reproduction and transformation of gendered employment distributions. Case studies of well defined jobs, or within identifiable employment settings, are required in order to uncover the history and social circumstances of gender-segregated employment. As the current study indicates, detailed research of this sort suggests a more specific role for gender processes in the structuring of employment than is often presented in the explanation of aggregate patterns.

One feature of this examination of the forces creating and transforming patterns of occupational segregation by sex is an assessment of the impact of the 1975 Sex Discrimination Act in a specific place of work. The gender segregation present in the workplace surveyed in this study was underpinned until 1975 by *formal* restrictions on, and distinctions between, women's and men's employment. Examining attempts to maintain and eradicate formal sex discrimination at the level of employment establishments provides insights into the dynamic of social change and the factors enhancing or inhibiting that dynamic. Although the main focus of this analysis concerns events and circumstances primarily over the decade of the 1970s, some earlier historical material is provided in order to understand better the forces creating sex discrimination as official employment policy. The process of negotiating the equalization of employment conditions to meet the conditions of the 1975 Act, and the circumstances in the jobs at the end of the decade, provide further clues that help to locate the issue of gender in patterns of occupational segregation.

In examining patterns of change and continuity in gendered employment distributions, it became clear that occupational segregation "by sex" was an imprecise description of the relation between jobs and the social circumstances of job incumbents. More general processes of relations of employment and domestic responsibilities were at work, and an elaboration of these processes is the third area of interest addressed. In the general literature on the relations of household circumstances and the structuring of employment, two separate developments can be observed. On the one hand, there is considerable support for attention to household circumstances and strategies in the study of stratification

2

and, more narrowly, employment, and the place of gendered experience in these areas. On the other hand, there is growing support for the idea that gender processes operate within employment independently of factors associated with the domestic setting. The argument developed in this research seeks to identify the significance of variations in the structuring of household and employment relations, and to locate gendered experience as a component of wider processes. A more complex understanding of household and employment relations helps to address the explanatory gap that arguments about the "gender embeddedness" of employment have sought to fill. The importance of relations to household financing, and of differentiations between jobs in terms of the social capacities facilitated by wage levels, is captured in the formulation for divisions in employment experience used in this research; that is, a distinction between full-wage and component-wage jobs. In developing this distinction, the focus shifts to the decade of the 1980s where increasing inequalities in wages, and persistent wage inequalities between women and men, are shown to have significant consequences for the potential social capacities available to wage earners.

The fourth area of interest is the understanding of the relation between conceptions and experience. Many argue that conceptions of gender are general and slow to change. They suggest further that certain understandings of gender relations persist despite variation and change in the significance of gender in the structuring of experience. Areas where this persistence is identified include the impact of parenting and domestic experience on women's understandings of employment, and the potency of an ideology that grants employment priority to a male breadwinner. Are gender conceptions so impervious to the nature of experience, or have we simply not approached the problem with sociological categories sufficiently meaningful to allow variation and change to be observed? The interests in identifying diversity and complexity are important components in the attempt to answer this question. The significance of gender in the structuring of experience and understandings is undeniable, but, as this research shows, there is considerable variation in the extent to which gender is a meaningful component of understandings. When variation in the salience and nature of gendered experience is identified, variation in the salience and nature of gender conceptions can also be observed.

During this century, women have constituted at least 30% of the labour force. By no stretch of the imagination have they had proportional representation within the sociology of employment. Reasons for this have now been fully elaborated, critically appraised, and rarely justified as current practice. Yet there is more to be done. The legacy of the emphasis on "workers and their wives" is a wealth of misconceptions

3

about, and faulty explanations of, experiences and understandings of employment. The job of constructing an adequate account of employment is in progress and the current study will, I hope, be of assistance. This process of construction is not a simple one. A number of sociology's cherished explanations rest on questionable assumptions – for example, that gender patterns in employment are labour market outcomes, that the financial support of dependent children is primarily a male responsibility, and that "the family" is a permanent filter through which women experience their working lives. To face up to the reality that challenges these assumptions is to face the necessity for new explanatory frameworks.

The development of new explanatory frameworks is towards explanations that address more adequately the complex patterns of social experience, both over time and at particular points in time. The major focus of this research presentation is a task necessary for the development of new explanations: an assessment of the explanatory potential of "gender" in the analysis of women's and men's employment experience. This task is a substantial and difficult one, for constructing an adequate understanding of variations in employment experience requires rethinking the conventional "gender biased" theories of employment, and the more recent theories of the "gender embeddedness" of employment.

Reading the literature on women and men in employment, I find myself unconvinced by statements made about women's incapacity to understand their experience, dismayed by the lengths sociology has travelled in order to protect "accepted" theory against inconvenient discoveries of the importance women attach to employment, unconvinced of several categorical distinctions drawn between the interests of female and male workers, and generally puzzled at the connection between the women and men who appear in "theory" and the women and men who appear in the research on which this book is based. To some extent, the women and men I interviewed are not typical. They are employed in a public corporation; they work together, in the same jobs; and, within each job, the women and men work full time at the same rates of pay. Many work night shift, or a six-day week, on a permanent basis. In other respects, the women and men in this study are not atypical. They work in jobs that do not employ an equal proportion of women and men. They are single, married, separated or divorced. Some have no children, others are supporting children, or have children who are no longer dependent. The majority of them are white; a minority are black, and have emigrated to Britain from various countries. There are aspects of their jobs, workmates, supervisors and union that they like, and aspects they dislike. As a group, their views on equality between the sexes range from agitation at its slow realization, to hostility towards the very idea.

4

When I began to try and make sense of their views and experiences, I found that the distinctions of job and gender did not very often, in themselves, correspond with undifferentiated social groups or forms of understanding. Other factors – for example, whether or not women and men were married or currently supporting dependent children, the length of time women had spent as full-time mothers, and the relation of a person's current job to past and likely future employment – emerged as important features that were more productive in clarifying patterns in social circumstances and locating understandings. Distinctions by job title or job task were very quickly abandoned as too crude to encompass variations in employment relations and conditions. Gender, either alone or in combination with job distinctions, proved a problematic explanatory concept because the wages, domestic responsibilities, work histories and employment attachments of women and men did not always divide in neat, "gender appropriate" ways. Although some variations were more consistent with divisions by age or "racial" group, these divisions did not completely neutralize patterns related more directly to, for example, education, household circumstances, work history patterns or access to household resources. It became obvious that a number of accepted explanations of women's and men's employment, in both sociological and feminist literature, were at odds with the patterns and understandings of experience in the group of people I was studying. After examining data from other larger and better known sources, it is my view that the social features and processes established in the central research project of this report can be traced through the community more generally.

A primary concern of this research, then, is to further the understanding of employment by assessing the relevance of gender distinctions in employment, and by proposing an explanation of employment experience that locates those gender distinctions found relevant. This involves extending the framework of explanation to include employment relations that are and are not differentiated for women and men, and conditions of employment that do and do not involve gender divisions and conflict. In doing so, the appearance of "women" and "men" in theoretical statements of employment is transformed and variations in their understandings will be seen to be intimately tied to variations in the nature of their experience. In addition, and in large part a consequence of locating and specifying gender, issues concerning the relations of employment and non-employment circumstances will be clarified. This will be the case especially for employment and parenting relations.

The book is presented in seven chapters. Chapter 1 reviews problems in explanations of gender and employment, and presents issues pursued in more detail throughout the text. It also introduces the study that forms the core of the research – the investigation of gender segregation in the case of two occupations: postal workers and telephonists. Chapter 2 examines the historical background to the creation and abolition of sex discrimination in the employment conditions of the telephonist and postal jobs. In each job, hiring practices and conditions of service became formally distinguished by sex owing to changes in the working conditions of the jobs that altered their relation to standard aspects of women's and men's employment. The enactment of the Sex Discrimination Act was the main reason for the abolition of distinctions by sex in the formal conditions of employment, although in both cases moves in this direction had been afoot for some time. In the postal job, the conditions of men's employment had suffered a relative decline, thus bringing the job into a closer relation to jobs typically done by women. This was the job in which men opposed the equalization of employment conditions most strenuously. When employment conditions for women and men in the telephonist and postal jobs were equalized, the jobs continued to have a highly skewed distribution of female and male employees, and reasons for this are presented in Chapter 3. There it is argued that the distribution of women and men in the different jobs is structured by general social resources and relations to household maintenance. Concerning the latter pattern, a distinction between full-wage and component-wage jobs is proposed as the major profile of the structuring of household and employment relations. Women and men with similar relations to household maintenance are shown to be similarly employed in either component-wage or full-wage jobs. Together Chapters 2 and 3 shed significant light on processes structuring occupational segregation. While a gender pattern is prominent in this process, it is shown to be a specific feature of a more general structuring of employment and domestic relations.

In various ways, the next three chapters explore the potential sociological significance of the full-wage and component-wage distinction. In doing so, however, they also address other issues and debates. Chapter 4 alters the focus on full-wage and component-wage jobs, by sharpening definitions and examining their prevalence among men and women in full-time employment. It concentrates on the adequacy of wages as a source of household income by setting out minimum levels of full-wages for two types of household: those composed of one man, one woman and two children; and those composed of a single adult below retirement age. Component-wages are then defined as wages insufficient to support a single adult household at a minimum standard of living. The chapter concludes by assessing the adequacy of women's and men's full-time earnings in Britain in relation to these levels of full-wages and component-wages over the 1980s.

Chapter 5 also pursues the relationships between domestic responsibilities and employment inequalities from a broader perspective. It begins with a discussion of the relationships between occupational gender segregation, wages and work histories. There is considerable difference of opinion in the research literature about the nature of these relationships, and the discussion concentrates on particular issues fuelling these debates. The relationships between employment in gender-skewed jobs, wage levels and patterns of work histories were very clear for women in the case study of this research. The chapter moves on to present these, and to cement further the distinction between full-wage and component-wage job incumbents, in terms of lifetime patterns of work. It presents detailed information on the work histories of women with children, and establishes marked differences between women in full-wage and component-wage jobs in their lifetime negotiation of domestic and employment relations. Where possible, these patterns of experience are traced into the wider population by referring to other more general studies of women's work histories and of the consequences of work history variations for employment positions and inequalities.

Chapter 6 supports further the salience of the data patterns observed in the earlier chapters by demonstrating their close connections with variations in understandings of employment and non-employment experience. The chapter considers relations between variations in experiences of parenting and employment, and understandings of these relations. The notion that family and employment experiences have a different general salience for women and men in full-time jobs is shown to be an inappropriately gendered and static view. Not only did most of the women and men in this study consider both to be important, but the circumstances in which they give either priority were identical, and had a strong family life-cycle dimension. This part of the argument concludes with an analysis of conceptions of inequality in parenting and employment, and interesting contrasts in perceptions of inequality between those in full-wage and component-wage jobs are presented. The chapter then pursues relations between gendered divisions in experience and gendered conceptions from another angle. The focus here is on priorities in the allocation of employment, and on the relative importance people give to gender, marital status and household circumstances in terms of entitlement to a wage. The presence and substance of gender distinctions regarding claims on employment are shown to be linked to variations in gendered experiences of parenting and employment, particularly as these are embodied in the full-wage and component-wage jobs.

The final chapter summarizes the arguments and discusses their implications for explanations of employment.

Chapter One

The location of gender in explanations of employment

Introduction

Difficulties in explanations of employment direct attention to the way in which central concerns are conceptualized. Two related conceptual problems are of primary importance in locating gender as a social process. One problem involves how gender categories – women, men and divisions between them – appear in theory. Difficulties in this case are a part of larger questions of explanation, occasioned by the abstraction of theoretical categories from their social context. The other problem involves theories of employment more directly and stems from the unsatisfactory understanding of the relation of employment to more extensive social experience. The interplay of employment and non-employment experiences has been a matter of dispute in sociology for many years. The problematic nature of this relation is acute in studies of gender and employment. The influence of gender-related processes on employment and in employment is of special concern, for it raises crucial questions about the meaning and generality of gender categories. This chapter introduces issues raised by the conceptual status of "gender" in attempts to explain women's and men's employment experience. This presentation foreshadows more extensive discussions within subsequent chapters.

Gender divisions and categories

If "gender" is to have explanatory force, its use in sociological research requires reconsideration. Two practices have been especially detrimental to the development of a full appreciation of women's and men's employment experience: the *a priori* judgement that gender is a meaningful component of the social circumstances being investigated; and the assumption that the meaning of gender will be of a pre-specified form. These practices are related, but each can be associated with specific difficulties in the analysis of employment and its location in wider social processes.

The burden of the case for the consideration of gender as an important feature of social relations, and sociological explanations, rested on the demonstration that "gender matters". In the face of uninterest, or opposing positions, those who argued the case for the incorporation of gender into sociological analysis were obliged to document the operation of "gender" across a wide spectrum of social activity. The case for the consideration of gender has been widely accepted and the burden of the contemporary task is to demonstrate not only how gender becomes a meaningful component of social life, but also when it is meaningful and when it is not. Having won the argument for the importance of gender, there is now a need to assess the quality of gender as an explanatory concept and to locate its importance. Calls for caution in the use of gender categories in explanations of social experience and for the "deconstruction" of gender categories have been heard within the social sciences for some time now.[1] Despite these expressions, gender categories often continue to appear in accounts of inequality, power and oppression, as if they had general validity as categories of social experience. It is significant that many recent discussions of gender as an aspect of social explanation are compelled to reiterate arguments against the "essentialist politics", "polarized thinking", "false universalism" and "categoricalism" of some contemporary views, including some versions of modern feminism (cf. Connell 1987, Eisenstein 1984, Segal 1987). It is equally significant that contemporary guidelines to research practice of a gender-sensitive but non-sexist kind warn against the tendency to "assume gender to be a key variable in the analysis of data and field material" (Morgan 1986:48), and warn against practices such as the overgeneralization of gender-significant findings, and "sexual dichotomism" (Eichler 1988).

The project of adequately specifying gender is not sufficiently encompassed, however, by a process of deconstruction, for the question here is *how* gender is deconstructed. Typically the procedure is to examine how gender definitions and social practices vary according to other significant aspects of social experience like age, "race" and class, or how they vary through history. But, even when particularized in this way, we cannot assume that each of the cross-classified categories is an autonomous, coherent entity of identity and social experience. The analysis of gender has typically fetishized variations in social experience as categories of identity. In such circumstances it is impossible for gender not to have

9

meaning, not to be a significant aspect of social experience. In other words, these forms of analysis rarely pose the salience of gender as a question, and consequently social change involving the neutralization of gender salience is difficult to identify.

Arguments against the use of unspecified gender categories have been especially slow to take in the areas of stratification and the sociology of work. Here, debates about the sociological significance of women's employment for structures of employment and inequality still rage. The recalcitrant conventional position of some influential figures has worked against the development of theories of inequality and employment that can locate the salience of gender and develop statements of inequality that adequately address the social experience of all members of British society. For those who accept the significance of gender in studies of employment and inequality, there are perhaps three reasons why gender categories continue to appear to have general validity. One is that strong patterns of difference between "women" and "men" in paid and unpaid work reinforce the tendency to use gender categories as mutually exclusive terms of analysis. The second reason is that certain distributions within employment are discussed and examined routinely in relation to gender categories when in fact the distributions concerned may not be as clearly divided as the use of gender categories suggests. A prime example of this is "occupational segregation by sex". The third reason is that although the advantages of deconstructing gender categories have been recognized, the interest in explaining aggregate differences in, for example, pay or occupational distribution usually coincides with a resurrection of gender categories as a general dimension of analysis.

Many contemporary accounts of employment continue to *assume* that divisions between women and men will be a fundamental aspect of analysis. Presupposing the import of gender divisions, and using "women" and "men" as pre-theoretical terms of analysis, have produced the related problems of gender-differentiated explanations and a reliance on gender-differentiated attributes as explanation.

The need to take the salience of gender as an issue in the analysis of work, rather than an assumption, is supported by two main observations: alterations in the typicality of gender divisions in work patterns; and the significant variation in experiences of domestic life and employment within gender categories. Several believe that gender retains an overall salience despite such complexities of experience, that evidence of change or variation is more apparent than real. They believe that meaningful changes are hindered, and conceptions of experience distorted, by continuing ideological, though not practical, attachments to gendered forms of social life. It is certainly the case that gender distinctions remain an important feature of contemporary conceptions of social relations and

10

social practices. Nevertheless, variations from standard gender patterns raise questions concerning the quality of explanations for those standard patterns. Further, even though some changes may be marginal, or some variations slight, they present problems of explanation that are central to the understanding of social processes of employment and the gender distinctions they involve.

Changes and variations in the salience of gendered experience force a reconsideration of theories of employment that do not locate gender distinctions in wider social processes. As previously noted, this reconsideration is not simply a matter of examining gender divisions within other major axes of inequality such as "race" and class. As categorical distinctions, and even as distinctions specified by each other, they have not offered the degree of complexity needed to isolate and explain patterns of inequality sufficiently. The reconsideration of theories of employment required is one that aims to explain aggregate patterns in terms that address the variety in disaggregated experience.

The conceptual difficulties surrounding gender in studies of employment have had considerable influence on the identification of practical and sociological problems and on the understanding of social processes involved in patterns of stability and change. A concern that has been prominent in the literature for many years is the gendered experience of parenting and employment relations, and how this experience structures women's and men's commitment to, and understanding of, waged work. In addition, there has been growing attention to the operation of "gender" as a direct organizing force within employment itself, along with the observation that the strength and depth of this structuring are significant obstacles to social change. The problems with the conceptual status of gender that have been discussed are present in these concerns, as the following sections suggest.

Conceptions of women's relations to employment

In the latter part of this century, the economic activity rate of married women steadily increased. While this development sent ripples across the surface of sociological understandings of employment, it is the phenomenon of the increasing employment of women with dependent children that has disturbed sociological explanations most deeply. As households with dependent children are increasingly supported by both women and men, the conventional gender distinction between breadwinning and childrearing becomes more limited as a portrayal of women's and men's adult lives. This form of gendered experience has played a very strong role in both mainstream and some feminist explanations.

11

To the extent that it recedes as a feature of social experience, its explanatory facility must be re-examined. A problematic feature of contemporary explanations is the extent to which gendered experience is not placed within the full range of social arrangements and the course of experience over individual lifetimes.

Differences in work experience run within, as well as between, gender categories. For example, there are significant contrasts between women in the duration and circumstances of full-time parenting, as well as in the employment characteristics of their work histories. At the same time, some women have experienced the negotiation of employment and parenting relations in a manner that resembles the experience of many men – with minimal opportunity for full-time parenting, and with extensive wage earning responsibility. In the search for an explanation of the aggregate differences in women's and men's experience, the diversity within gender categories and instances of similarity between gender categories are frequently overlooked. Many current explanations isolate aggregate differences between women's and men's employment and address these as the major object of explanation. To the extent that these differences are abstracted from overall patterns in experience, not only are the latter ignored, but the processes structuring the former may be misidentified.

Although relations of women and men to paid work are changing as more women contribute financially to the support of households and dependent children, many women are, of course, wholly dependent on a male wage while their children are of pre-school age, and partially dependent when in part-time, or other low-waged, employment. The concern here is how specific occasions of gender differentiation are located in relation to the wider course of social relations. There has been a tendency to interpret the interruptions in women's employment and their financial dependence at particular times, as the determining features of parenting and employment relations. Over stressing the periodic absence of women from waged labour or the periodic engagement in part-time work, and arguing that these produce and represent a partial commitment to employment, has led to misconceptions of women's relations to employment and their experiences within it. That women are less committed to waged work or value its "social" over "economic" importance are two examples of statements that rely on anything less than a full-time, continuous employment history as evidence. Although such statements may reflect specific circumstances during women's working lives, they certainly do not reflect the whole range of women's relations to employment. Women's experience varies, both between themselves and over the life cycle, as to whether, or to what degree, they are dependent on a male wage. To appreciate fully how employment interruptions or part-time work figure in women's employment, these facets of employment circumstances must be set within a more comprehensive understanding of women's experiences throughout individual lifetimes. Recent evidence has shown that some features of women's work histories are tightly connected to inequalities in employment, while others have immediate but no long-term consequences.[2] Given this, it would be more appropriate to take the dynamic characteristics of work histories as the basis of analysis, and to place specific details in relation to overall work history patterns.

Insufficient attention to the variability in women's and men's parenting and employment experiences and to similarities in some circumstances has also led to misconceptions of understandings of employment. While the forces sustaining gendered experience are a major component of employment structuring, how particular experiences can alter or undermine, rather than reinforce, conceptions based on these divisions needs to be thoroughly appreciated. There is a kind of ecological fallacy in many discussions concerning the importance of a gender division between parenting and employment in conceptions of experience. This particular gender division exists as a relatively stable aspect of contemporary developed societies. Full-time childrearing, although taking up less of a woman's lifetime, is still primarily women's work. Because of this social stability, there is a mistaken assumption that women's relations to childrearing and to male financial support are equally stable in individual conceptions of social experience. To assume, for example, that the social relations and identity of motherhood shape the understandings of a woman facing 20 years of employment after her children are independent, is to take an unduly static and certainly misleading view of the importance of family life in women's conceptions of themselves and their social circumstances. The importance of domestic responsibilities must be an issue in the analysis of conceptions of employment, rather than assumed initially as a gender-specific component. As an open-ended feature of analysis, conceptions of domestic and employment relations can be analyzed in relation to variations in parenting and employment experience for both women and men. For variations in experience to be identified exactly, it is crucial to set immediate or particular social circumstances within the context of lifetime experiences, and understandings need to be examined in relation to both.

Critics of conventional analyses have questioned the gendered use of non-employment experience in explanations of relations to employment. Several stress the merit of overcoming gender-differentiated forms of explanation by examining employment and domestic relations as experienced by men as well as women.[3] While few would disagree with this suggestion, there remains the question of how these relations, and their connection with understandings, are conceptualized. At the moment, the research question is often posed as one of the "interaction" between two or more sets of circumstances. Rather than focusing on social relations as the objects and means of explanation, analysis proceeds by drawing connections and tracing antagonisms between social positions or identities as relatively fixed and abstract entities. These entities have a problematic relation to social experience in that, typically, their substance is taken from particular circumstances. When used as general theoretical categories, they allow only a limited grasp of the nature of social experience. The conceptually discrete form of these positions and identities cuts them off from the circumstances of their production, and they contain no conception of social relations as such. Consequently, their relation to understandings is doubly problematic: whether understandings appropriate to a position or identity are present becomes an "empirical" question; and problems arise concerning the nature of understandings when positions or identities that are conceptually antithetical are experienced simultaneously. Explanations of relations to employment in terms of the positions and identities associated with gender divisions are a case in point.

Within feminist analysis, for example, there is an ambivalent attachment to the male breadwinner/female childcarer division. On the one hand, the fact that men are the sole breadwinners for most married couples is challenged. On the other hand, the widespread acceptance, or "ideology", of men as breadwinners is argued to operate in the structuring of resources within the home and waged work and within understandings of women's and men's relations to both. It is not surprising, therefore, that the "feminine dilemma" of the dual roles literature has reappeared under a new guise in more contemporary considerations of understandings of parenting and employment relations. Participation in both family life and employment is argued to act against the coherent development of women's consciousness (cf. Beechey 1986, Edwards 1979, Pollert 1981, Porter 1982). When in employment, it is suggested, women view themselves as others view them – as not male breadwinners – and their dual identification as supported mothers and independent waged workers results in a fragmented, contradictory consciousness. These statements regarding the incoherence of understandings must certainly be questioned. Rather than problems in women's understandings, they reflect problems with explanations that present experiences in static, discrete terms, or that present experiences of specific kinds, and at particular times, as dominant and continuous aspects of understandings.

Problems in the explanation of employment and non-employment

14

relations are exacerbated when insufficient attention is paid to wider patterns of social relations within employment itself. The question here is whether explanations of women's and men's employment take adequate account of how these are structured socially and of the implications of differentiated experience within a highly segregated pattern of work. One difficulty is the relatively undeveloped sociological understanding of relations between the circumstances of jobs and the circumstances of people in jobs. Several misconceptions of "women" and "men" as paid workers can be traced to an insufficient attention to the segregated nature of the waged work women and men do. Characterizations of women as waged workers and assessments of women's capabilities within paid work have all suffered from the practice of de-emphasizing the importance of structured employment circumstances and taking "women" to be a social entity with unique characteristics.

Attributes that have been used to characterize women as waged workers – for example, low commitment, lack of militancy, flexibility, low interest in wages and promotion – have been interpreted as being a consequence of prior orientations, values or attributes that women import into and express within their waged work. The crucial point implied by, but not developed in, dual labour market theory is that differences in aspects of employment circumstances are often mistakenly regarded as outcomes of the preferences or commitments of women and men as distinct categories of employees. It is the case, of course, that employment in a particular job does not imply an identity of interests or understandings among job incumbents (Stewart et al. 1980). Nevertheless, evidence of similarity between women and men similarly placed in employment challenges the practice of locating differences in women's and men's understandings of employment in pre-given dispositions associated with women and men as pre-defined social groups. This should alert us to the importance of ascertaining variations in women's conceptions of employment, as well as warn against accepting statements that attribute women's conceptions to pre-given attributes of "women as women". The point to be made here is a very important one. The severely segregated nature of the jobs employing women and men facilitates the assumption and conclusion that women and men are distinct groups with characteristic preferences and understandings of employment. When differences in women's and men's understandings of employment are dislocated from the social circumstances of their production, the result is explanation by means of an atheoretical conception of sex/gender differences.

The foregoing has outlined ways in which over-generalized, unlocated and pre-specified gender categories distort the representation

and explanation of women's experiences and conceptions of employment. Similar explanatory issues can be identified when these research
practices are extended to the analysis of the structuring of employment
itself.

Gender and the structuring of employment

The fact that women and men are employed in jobs highly skewed in
their gender composition, and the fact that the highly rewarded jobs are
those in which men predominate have led many to argue that "gender"
operates to shape the character of occupations and labour force distributions. The "gender saturation" of work tasks has been designated a substantial dimension in the social definition of skill and a substantial factor
in maintaining the identify of, and inequality between, "women's work"
and "men's work". As I have argued elsewhere (Siltanen 1986), this formulation cannot adequately address the employment inequalities
between women and men, or the employment inequalities within each
gender. Explanations highlighting the characteristics of sex-typed jobs
and a process of allocation emphasizing the "gender appropriateness" of
job incumbents reproduce at a more aggregate level the explanatory
problems outlined previously. The analysis of differences between
"women's work" and "men's work" in employment involves distortions
similar to those identified in the study of "sex differences". Attributes
associated on average with the employment of women and men are
reified as differences between two categories that are taken to be inter-
nally undifferentiated and mutually exclusive. These reified categories
are then used to explain, or are assumed to correspond with, women's
and men's employment experiences. As a result, important variations in
the employment of both sexes are not seriously attended to, and similarities between them are not fully considered.

Attempting to understand variations in employment circumstances in
terms of an opposition between "women's work" and "men's work"
involves the use of categories that do not correspond adequately with
the nature and complexity of either women's or men's employment
experience. Further, the distinction itself is difficult to sustain in terms of
both labour content and labour supply. The strength of comparable
worth arguments is testimony to the lack of differentiation in the labour
content of many "female" and "male" jobs. These views must confront
the significance of the gender skewed, rather than mutually exclusive,
distribution of occupational segregation. Although there are some jobs
that employ men only, there are none in which men are not employed. In
addition, research has demonstrated that jobs that are exclusively male

16

in one workplace can be exclusively female in another. Given this, there is a major problem for attempts to explain the occupational distribution of women and men by a conception of "gendered" allocation processes in which the substance of job tasks plays a crucial part. The problem is providing an explanation for the presence of "gender-inappropriate" job incumbents. They are, from the outset, outside the territory on which the attempted explanation is based. That this is so reflects necessarily on the adequacy of the type of argument constructed to explain the employment of the "gender-appropriate" job incumbents.

The popularity of arguments designating "gender" as an intrinsic feature of waged work and the "gender construction" of jobs as the major process underlying occupational distributions of women and men must be seen in part as a retreat from the perceived inadequacy of earlier explanatory efforts. In particular, a number of commentators emphasize the limited explanatory potential of relations of domestic and employment experience (cf. Beechey 1983, Curran 1988, Walby 1986). Again we must allow the possibility that the limitations of explanatory frameworks are a function of the conceptual distinctions they employ. Earlier attempts to explain the occupational distributions of women and men in terms of domestic circumstances focused on "sexual divisions" in the home. It was assumed that "women" have relations to domestic circumstances and employment that are distinct from the relations of "men", and that "sexual divisions" in households were definitive for women's and men's waged work. For "women", the division entailed disadvantages in waged work in both the short term (for example, the accommodation of hours of waged work to domestic responsibilities) and the long term (for example, lower occupational attainment and income). For "men", the division entailed advantages in waged work in terms of claims that could be made as wage earners with domestic responsibilities as husbands and fathers (for example, claims for a family wage). The fact that these explanatory attempts appear inadequate is not because of the limited impact of domestic responsibilities in the structuring of employment. The reason lies, rather, in the limitations of the theoretical categories and data used to approach the matter.

In the form outlined above, we have an imprecise and insufficient statement of relations of domestic responsibilities and employment. It is insufficient because it considers marriage and parenting to be the only features of domestic life that may impinge on employment experience. It is imprecise because it takes "sexual division" as the general form of relations between domestic circumstances and employment. With such blunt conceptual instruments, the significant distinctions that mark social processes are bound to elude us.

The attempt to conceptualize women's employment in terms of the

17

reserve army of labour is a case in point. A review of this attempt illustrates the need to reassess the explanatory status of gender categories and the significance of non-employment circumstances in theories of the structuring of employment.

The rise and fall of the reserve army of labour

The explanatory power of the reserve army concept is now widely questioned (Beechey & Perkins 1987, Dex 1985, Rubery 1988, Walby 1986). Tracing the development of the disenchantment with the reserve army of labour as a means of explanation demonstrates the need to specify gender categories and gender divisions in explanations of employment, and to take their precise meaning as a problem to be addressed. This example is an especially poignant one because the issues leading to the rejection of the reserve army of labour as an appropriate concept are left unresolved in prominent forms of explanations offered as more promising conceptions of the place of gender in employment processes. The focus of currently favoured explanations is occupational segregation by sex, and many discussions of this phenomenon reproduce the problematic form of gender formulations that led eventually to the dissatisfaction with the reserve army of labour concept.

Initially, women as a group were argued to form a reserve pool of labour for the dominant male labour force. Ideas concerning the appropriate activities for women and men were sufficiently potent, it was argued, that, regardless of individual requirements for waged work, women's employment could be conveniently manipulated to meet fluctuations in the demand for labour. Benston was among the first to articulate this position:

> Women function as a massive reserve army of labor. When labor is scarce (early industrialization, the two world wars, etc.) then women form an important part of the labor force. When there is less demand for labor (as now under neocapitalism) women become a surplus labor force – but one for which their husbands and not society are economically responsible. The "cult of the home" makes its reappearance during times of labor surplus and is used to channel women out of the market economy. This is relatively easy since the pervading ideology ensures that no one man or woman, takes women's participation in the labor force seriously. Women's real work, we are taught, is in the home; this holds whether or not they are married, single or the heads of households. (Benston 1982:199, originally published 1969)

The view of the female labour force as a reserve army of labour achieved a high profile when propounded by Braverman (1974). At the same time, amid the greater publicity for this characterization, qualifications and limitations were making their appearance. Braverman himself stressed the occupational specificity of the phenomenon, arguing that newly proletarianized female workers "formed a reserve for the 'female occupations'" (1974:386). The reserve army argument was refined further and regarded more critically in the latter half of the 1970s. Beechey (1977) designated married women as a preferred source of reserve labour. They are, she argued, a flexible population of waged workers, and offer the additional advantage of their low cost. The support married women receive from husbands means they can be paid lower wages, and they have little claim on the resources of the welfare state, or employers, when unemployed. While it was married women who were regarded as "semi-proletarianized", the expectation that single women would marry was argued to affect their employment opportunities substantially. Although Bland et al. (1978) continued to consider all women as a reserve of labour, they also identified the need to be more precise, and argued that at different stages of the family life cycle, and within different domestic circumstances, women may form different types of reserve labour targeted for identifiable types of jobs.

Two criticisms of the conception of women as a source of disposable and flexible labour drew attention to the importance of certain characteristics of the structure of employment. Women's lower wages, relative to men's, were argued to act against any tendency to expel female labour (Gardiner 1976). The severe degree of segregation between jobs women and men do was identified as a significant factor inhibiting the substitution of female and male wage labour (Milkman 1976). These considerations led to a further refinement of the concept of the reserve army of labour as applied to women's employment position relative to men's. Up until this time, no empirical investigation of relative fluctuations in women's and men's employment in Britain had been undertaken. When this analysis was performed, a group of women in very specific social circumstances were identified as especially vulnerable to job losses during periods of recession in the late 1970s.

Bruegel (1979) distinguished two ways in which women may cushion men against the full force of recessions and unemployment: women's employment as a whole may deteriorate relative to men's; or an individual woman, compared with a man in an equivalent situation, may be more likely to suffer redundancy or unemployment. Her analysis of the employment experiences of women in Britain between 1974 and 1978 showed variation in women's relation to the reserve army process. Some women were cushioned from the worst effects of job cut-backs owing to their concentration in a relatively buoyant service sector. In contrast, women in manufacturing suffered a proportionally greater job loss than men, but women in manufacturing were not all equally affected. Women employed part time in manufacturing were disproportionately hit by redundancies compared with women and men in full time employment. Judging by her own analysis, Bruegel's attempt to delimit precisely how the employment of women may be thought of in terms of the operation of a reserve army of labour does not cover the circumstances in which women were shown to be more vulnerable to job losses. Women's employment on the whole had not deteriorated relative to men's; in fact the opposite seemed to be the case. Moreover, women employed part time are not in an "equivalent situation" to women and men employed full time.

Later research developments further specified and queried the applicability of the reserve army concept to women's employment by establishing variations in job losses among part-time workers in manufacturing (Perkins 1983); by identifying male part-time labour as equally vulnerable (Dex & Perry 1984); and by examining significant differences in the extent to which female employment is more cyclically volatile (Joshi 1981; Rubery & Tarling 1988). Overall, the relatively more buoyant position of female labour in aggregate terms has been traced into the 1980s (Beechey & Perkins 1987, Dex & Perry 1984, Martin & Wallace 1984, Rubery 1988, Walby 1986). The irreversible nature of women's entry into employment was also noted as a challenge to the flexible and disposable characterizations inherent in the reserve army concept (Yantz & Smith 1983). Subsequent challenges have extended the investigation to examine employment categories at a more disaggregated level; to include secular as well as cyclical variations; and to attempt an argument integrating reserve army observations with other major features of women's employment. These views have emphasized that if the reserve army of labour is appropriate at all as a conceptualization of women's employment, it is so only in historically specific terms in relation to women's absorption into the labour force (Humphries 1983), or only in a very specific set of circumstances, which are neither constant across recessionary periods nor relevant to all areas of female employment (Rubery 1988).

It is instructive to review the direction taken by attempts to conceptualize the female labour force as a reserve army of labour. We have moved from an original conception of "women" as a reserve army of labour to the specification of particular workers in particular industries at particular times as among those especially vulnerable to job losses. Those arguments that characterized "women" as a form of flexible and disposable labour as a result of a conventional configuration of domestic relations, or as a group of reserve workers in a competitive relation to a primary workforce, or as a group of workers more subject to the vagaries of public pressure and opinion, were shown to have mischaracterized the employment experiences of significant groups of women. In the end, the employment characteristics of the reserve army of labour that were argued to apply to women as a group were found to apply to a very specific range of experiences that at times were also relevant to some men.

The explanatory problem can be identified as one of attempting to theorize "women" as an unspecified category within the structure of employment and non-employment relations. The appeal of the reserve army conception was its apparent capacity to explain aggregate differences between female and male employment. The initial case was built upon an opposition between female and male labour, with unique characteristics attached to each grouping. Such characteristics were in fact inconsistent with variations within the female and male labour force, and these contradictions eventually undermined the reserve army as a plausible statement of the structuring of aggregate gender differences.

It is significant that at the time of the first empirical investigation into whether or not women's employment in Britain could be conceptualized in terms of a reserve army of labour, the first major study of occupational segregation by sex in the British labour force was also conducted (Hakim 1979). This study has had a tremendous impact on the understanding of the structuring of women's and men's employment. It has, in particular, helped to consolidate the criticism of reserve army formulations and the promotion of containment rather than competition or disposability as the major feature of women's employment position relative to men. Several recent contributions to this area cite evidence of high levels of occupational segregation by sex as substantial evidence for the gender embeddedness of employment processes. In fact, in some of the major discussions occupational segregation is now being marshalled in a manner similar to early formulations of the reserve army of labour – to explain the relatively disadvantaged position of "women" in employment. For example, Walby (1986:88) judges that the "most perceptive argue that women have not functioned as a reserve army of labour but that their patterns of employment are a consequence of employers preferring to employ women who can be paid low wages and given worse conditions of employment than men because of occupational segregation". Similarly, Curran (1988:349) suggests that "the distinctive position of women within the labour market arises because they get jobs that are gendered as 'women's jobs'".

What has not happened in the move from disposability and competition to containment as a major research focus is the preservation of the recognition that the early formulations failed because of variation in the female labour force itself. The problem was less one of a generalization of a certain sort, than one of an unspecified characterization of "female labour", "women's work" and "sexual divisions" per se.

Researchers have demonstrated the diversity in women's employment experience (e.g., Crompton & Sanderson 1986, Dex 1987, Martin & Roberts 1984, Purcell 1988, Rubery 1988), and have established the significance of variations in women's understandings of employment and unemployment (e.g., Coyle 1984, Dex 1988, Hunt 1980, McNally 1979, Martin & Wallace 1984). However, as attention has shifted to questions of "occupational segregation by sex", the tendency towards over-generalized and unlocated gender categories has reasserted itself. Despite the interest in socially locating gender, explanations of gender segregation too frequently present, for example, "women" as dependent on men in the family and under normative pressure to give priority to the family over employment (Beechey 1986:119, Scott 1986:162), and "men" as successful in organizing around their long-term self-interest and excluding women from more advantaged jobs (Cockburn 1986:80, Walby 1986:248).[4]

The perspective adopted and developed in the current research does not deny the contemporary salience of gendered experience and conflict; it seeks the specification of this salience. In pursuing this objective, I shall argue that the apparent strength of the pattern of "occupational segregation by sex" has inhibited questioning the ability to generalize gender categories. The validity of these unspecified categories appears to be confirmed by a pattern of employment organization that seems to be defined primarily by a gender division. This investigation challenges the apparent simplicity of occupational segregation by sex as a representation of the structure of employment. Perhaps if the pattern of segregation can be shown to require more refined conceptualizations, the project of specifying and locating gender can be recovered and advanced.

If problematic gender formulations have been retained in the move to occupational segregation by sex as a focus for explanations of employment inequalities, an important dimension has been lost. This dimension is the integration of processes of allocation and wage determination in explanations of employment. For all its faults, the reserve army of labour as discussed by, for example, Beechey (1977) is a statement of the convergence of wage determination and allocation processes. Conceptions of occupational segregation by sex typically involve patterns of allocation only, and as the focus of attention has shifted to this area of analysis there has been a tendency to separate statements of allocation from those of wage determination. The connection between occupational segregation by sex and the gender gap in wages is, therefore, rendered problematic and requiring explanation. Although many take the relationship between occupational segregation by sex and wage inequalities almost for granted, the connection between variations in female representation in occupations and variations in wages has not been, in fact, easy to establish. The research to be presented proposes an alternative structuring of occupational segregation, wages and gender by reassessing the relation of occupational segregation to gender and the relation of occupational segregation to wages. It establishes patterns in domestic and employment arrangements that locate variations in gendered experience, and identifies processes that do and do not reproduce gender as a salient component of relations to jobs and wages. Once these patterns of experience are clarified, interesting connections can be made to variations within and between women's and men's understandings of employment and its relation to wider aspects of social circumstances.

A number of questions in explanations of employment and the social circumstances of women and men have been raised and related to the underlying problems of explanation on which they rest.

The limitations in explanation that have been identified are problems in our general understanding of women's and men's relations to, and within, employment. Categories of sociological explanation that need to be particularized have been noted and the progress in explanation to be gained by such a procedure will be demonstrated as details of the current research are reported. Although some of the questions that have been raised relate to current debates within the literature, all are more intimately connected as issues confronted in the analysis of the data collected for the research that forms the core of this study.

The research to be presented will assist in establishing relations of structured employment experience and the broader social circumstances of those engaged in employment. It is organized around two sorts of jobs – one traditionally employing a majority of men and one traditionally employing a majority of women. Although skewed in terms of the female/male composition, both jobs have official employment conditions that do not distinguish between women and men. This has not always been the case, as in the past both jobs employed women and men under different conditions. Of especial interest in this regard is the relatively unique history of one job: it officially defined its female labour force as a reserve pool of labour, to be taken on and let off as the supply of men altered. The processes by which gendered employment conditions were created and eradicated reveals interesting information about the reproduction and transformation of gender inequalities in employment. Differences do exist in the employment conditions between the jobs, and between shifts within each job. Thus, the study can contrast and compare experiences of women and men employed, under official conditions of equality, within gender skewed areas of employment that entail variations in employment conditions that are not specifically tied to the gender of incumbents. Ironically, it is by looking at circumstances of official equality in employment that general processes of inequality may be better understood.

The research

The research was designed in order to explore aspects of women's and men's employment experience within the context of occupational segregation. The selection of jobs was of crucial importance. Although a gender skew was an essential criterion differentiating the jobs chosen, common features between the jobs were also important, in order to highlight interests central to the research. The two jobs selected are frequently presented as a "woman's job" and a "man's job" (cf. Oakley 1981, Hakim 1979). The former is telephone operators and the latter goes by the standard occupational title of "postmen and mail sorters". What contributes to the comparability of the two jobs is their location in the same public corporation, their representation by the same trade union and their classification as the same grade of job.

The telephonists and postmen/women interviewed worked for what was then the largest employer in the country – the Post Office.[5] At the beginning of the 1980s, the Post Office employed 420,156 people and 24% of these were women. Just over a quarter of the full-time Post Office staff were employed as postmen/women, and 8% as telephonists. The female and male labour forces were not similarly distributed across the two areas of employment. Of the full-time men, 29% were employed as postmen, and 2% as telephonists. For full-time women, the distribution was reversed; just over a quarter of full-time women were telephonists, whereas only 3% were employed as postwomen. There were about 40 times the number of full-time postmen as full-time postwomen, and full-time telephonists were predominantly female. However, the gender composition of the telephonist job varied by shift. Women were in the majority on the day shift, whereas men were in the majority on the night shift.

Telephonists and postal workers were both classified as belonging to the "manipulative" grade and were organized by the same union, the Union of Post Office Workers (UPW).[6] Both jobs were quite dramatically affected by the Sex Discrimination Act of 1975. Before this time, telephonists were officially classified as male or female and this corresponded with a restriction on employment on the night and day shift respectively. After 1975, women and men were allowed equal access to full-time day or night work, although both shifts continued to have a gender skewed composition. The official employment conditions of postmen were unaffected by the Sex Discrimination Act. They are hired now, and were hired prior to 1975, on "permanent" contracts that offer the usual benefits and protection for full-time workers. The conditions of postwomen's employment have altered substantially. Prior to 1975, full-time postwomen were hired only on "temporary" contracts. This meant they did not accumulate seniority, did not get a pension or maximum sick leave benefits, and had no job security. Postwomen were, as a condition of their employment contract, a reserve labour force, to be hired when the supply of postmen was low, and fired when the supply of postmen improved. After 1975, full-time postwomen were allowed access to "permanent" employment contracts with the same employment conditions as men.

As a public corporation, the Post Office was under especial pressure to eradicate the sex discrimination existing in these two jobs, in accordance with the 1975 Act. Before the Act was to come into effect, negotiations between the UPW and the Post Office managements took place over the process of equalization. The UPW had quite a different attitude towards the equalization of employment conditions for telephonists and for postmen/women. The equalization of the telephonist job was smoothly handled and quite progressive in the terms set for those women and men wishing to transfer into the shift previously barred to them. The equalization of conditions between postwomen and postmen was a matter of disagreement between the union and management, and a postwoman was eventually to lodge a complaint against both parties, arguing that the compromise they reached over how the new legislation was to be enacted was still discriminatory. She won her case, and by the end of the decade not only were new postwomen hired on equal terms as men, but existing postwomen received some redress for past discrimination against them.

At the end of the 1970s, the formal conditions of employment within the two jobs were the same for women and men. There remained, however, significant differences between the jobs and across shifts within each job. Day telephonists were the only group to be employed during standard office hours. Night telephonists and postmen/women all worked unsocial hours on a permanent basis. Pay varied by shift within both jobs, and on the whole postmen/women and night telephonists received the highest pay, and day telephonists the lowest pay. Those jobs in which men predominated, in other words, were also those jobs receiving higher pay.

A number of the features of the two jobs in the Post Office suited the interests of the research especially well. Telephonists and postal workers were classified as the same grade, organized by the same union, and essentially employed by the same employer. The employment conditions for postwomen and for both women and men telephonists were clearly discriminatory under the conditions of the Sex Discrimination Act, and both jobs were restructured to equalize employment opportunities and conditions for women and men. Women and men working together, under official conditions of equality, was for some period of time a possibility that was debated, contested and eventually realized as a practical change in the conditions of the two jobs. Although formal employment policy was no longer based on gender distinctions, the jobs continued to employ women and men in different proportions. By examining jobs skewed in their gender composition, we can assess the employment experiences of women and men in jobs typical and atypical for their sex. Variations between the jobs, in terms of pay, hours of work, shift duties and so on, facilitate an examination of how combinations of employment and non-employment experience are, and are not, differentiated for women and men, and how their understandings vary according to particular locations within the structured relations of employment and domestic responsibilities. Further, that women and men can, or should, work together as equal workmates was an issue within both jobs that can shed light on how relations between women and men are expressed in, and structured by, the social conditions of their experience.

In total, 144 interviews (75 men and 69 women) were conducted within one sorting office and one telephone exchange in the London area. Details of the sample are reported in Appendix I. Interviews with union officials, union executive members and various local and regional management officers also took place. Files containing historical information on the two areas of employment were made available from both union and management records. The process of collecting data from all Post Office sources was completed in the early 1980s. The women and men interviewed were given an hour off their regular duties to participate in the study. The interviews were recorded on tape and conducted in private. This form of data recording facilitated the use of qualitative material to elaborate and understand responses to questions during the interviews. Quotations from the interviews are listed in Appendix II. Questions were asked according to a standardized interview schedule, which was supplemented by additional questioning as points of interest arose. The questionnaire was a mixture of fixed-choice and open-ended questions, and included some experimentation with the form of asking questions. Aspects of the questionnaire used in the current presentation are reproduced in Appendix III.

Although research that has consumed so much of one's time and energy seems to the researcher to be almost self-evidently convincing, others may more reasonably find grounds for caution or doubt. The patterns in the data to be presented are often strong and usually consistent. In smaller samples, it is perhaps consistency that is often more convincing. However, to support the findings of the case study material, research based on larger and more representative data sources is reviewed where possible, and is argued frequently to reveal patterns resembling those documented more precisely here.

Notes

1. Influential early commentators include Edholm et al. (1977), Mathieu (1978a & 1978b), Rubin (1975) and Tresemer (1975). More recent discussions address the importance of disaggregating both gender categories, and include Connell (1987), Eichler (1980), Eisenstein (1984), Morgan (1986) and Segal (1987).
2. For relevant British research see, for example, Dex (1984), Joshi (1987) and Main (1988).
3. For example, Beechey (1986) and Feldberg & Glenn (1984).
4. See also a number of articles in Walby (1988).
5. The Post Office became a public corporation in 1969. At the beginning of the 1980s, it was run as two separate businesses with distinct management structures, although both businesses were ultimately under the control of the Central Headquarters of the Post Office. In 1981, the Post Office corporation became two separate corporations, the Post Office and British Telecommunications. For convenience, I shall sometimes refer to both as the Post Office, consistent with the organizational designation at the time of the interviews. Recent events in this sequence are, of course, that in 1984 British Telecommunications ceased to be a public corporation and in 1985 the Post Office became the Royal Mail (with divisions between mail delivery, counter services and parcel delivery later in the decade).
6. Now called the Union of Communication Workers.

Chapter Two

Occupational segregation:
a case of sex discrimination

Very few occupations employ women in a proportion equivalent to their representation in the labour market as a whole. Typically, women are employed in jobs that are characterized by a high concentration of female labour. The same situation is, of course, true for men, and the segregation of jobs by sex indicates that, for the most part, women and men do not compete for the same jobs. There has been considerable controversy over the genesis and maintenance of gender-segregated employment. One aspect that has hindered resolution of the controversy is a lack of information about the relation of job characteristics and job incumbents and, as a necessary component of this, a detailed picture of the social circumstances of incumbents in gender-segregated employment situations. The analysis of occupational segregation by sex is especially in need of a broader understanding of the social conditions of women and men in particular jobs.

Studies of occupational segregation by sex usually examine outcomes of social processes in that they are concerned with the distribution of the female and male labour force across and within occupations. From these analyses, a clear picture has emerged of the disadvantaged position of many women in waged work. We are less clear about the processes that reproduce and transform occupational segregation by sex. Traditionally, the analysis of job segregation has focused on the relationship between occupations, ordered by skill, position or pay, and their sex composition. Beyond these general associations, little is known of the relations between the material and social circumstances of jobs and the more general circumstances of the women and men employed within them. In the absence of fuller and more detailed information, the salient social feature of incumbents in the allocation of employment and the determination of wages has been assumed to be their gender. As the following analysis

28

shows, a more complex understanding of relations to employment helps clarify both the standard patterns in women's and men's employment and variations from the standard patterns. This chapter and the one that follows attempt to identify processes involved in the reproduction and transformation of occupational segregation in the telephonist and postal jobs, and the significance of gendered experience within these processes.[1]

The initial interest in this study of occupational segregation is the structuring of women's and men's employment before and after the introduction of the Sex Discrimination Act in 1975.

Of the two pieces of legislation introduced in the 1970s to promote equality between women and men in employment, it was the Sex Discrimination Act that had the most impact in the Post Office. Equal pay for women and men had been a condition of employment long before the Equal Pay Act came into effect (Boston 1980, Grint 1988). By contrast, before the Sex Discrimination Act, it was common practice for the Post Office to distinguish by sex in job grades and employment conditions (Clinton 1984, Cohn 1985, Daunton 1985). The "gendered" terms and conditions of employment for women and men in the postal and telephonist jobs were typical in this respect, although each area of employment discriminated by sex in a unique manner: men were officially defined as the preferred source of workers for the postal job and the exclusive source of full-time night telephonists. Thus the sex segregation by shift in the telephonist job and differences in women's and men's conditions of employment in the postal job were official employment policy. This chapter highlights the social changes that occurred in the postal jobs during the decade of the 1970s, and begins with a description of the two areas of employment at the end of the decade. This is followed in each case by details of the nature of sex discrimination that existed prior to 1975. We shall consider how it came about, how it was changed, and the immediate aftermath of the change. After access to and conditions of employment within the postal and telephonist jobs were equalized, the sex composition of the jobs altered, though not very dramatically. To explain the continuing differences in the sex composition of the jobs we need to examine more extensively the relations between the circumstances of the jobs and the people employed within them. This will be the subject of the next chapter.

The telephonist and postal jobs were broadly similar in terms of entry requirements and job training. As jobs within the Post Office, both were within the "manipulative" grade and neither required applicants to have any educational qualifications. After a preliminary interview that assessed basic aptitudes and skills (such as hearing, sight, and reading and writing ability, and for the postal job a rudimentary intelligence assessment), new recruits to both jobs passed through a training period lasting from 8 to 10 weeks. Throughout their first year, telephonists and postal workers were required to perform aptitude or proficiency tests that, if passed, confirmed employment in the job. Although these were relatively easy jobs for anyone to enter, women and men did not do so in equal numbers. The postal and telephonist jobs had a proportional distribution of female and male labour characteristic of many jobs. At the London Sorting Office, 90% of postal workers were men, and at the London Telephone Exchange 73% of telephonists were women.[2] However, an immediate qualification concerning the gender profile of telephonist employment is necessary. While the day telephonist labour force was predominantly female, most night telephonists were men. In the London Telephone Exchange, women constituted 89% of the day shift and 23% of the night shift. We are, therefore, dealing with two jobs – night telephonist and postal worker – in which men predominated, and one job – day telephonist – in which women were in the majority.[3] The significance of this three-way distinction will become apparent as the following analysis unfolds.

The postal job

For most postal workers, their current employment compared favourably with previous jobs. Those who had experience of redundancy, stagnant wages or the insecurity of wages based on piece rates found the security of employment in the postal job, its stable wage and abundant overtime possibilities major advantages. The positive characteristics of the postal job were more widely recognized as particularly desirable at certain stages of the family life course.

> You come in for the security. My wife kept on at me ten years ago, before we had our first child, to get a secure job first, before we went into a baby. That's why I joined the Post.
> (Postman, *The Guardian*, "Postman's Knocks", 28/11/73)

Typically, postwomen were previously employed in routine manual jobs, for example as sewing machinists, electronic assemblers or packers, and for them the autonomy and variety of the postal job were especially valued compared with the experience of factory work.

> You've not got anyone breathing down your neck. You're free to get on with your job and no one worries you. Whereas if you're in a factory you've got all those foremen telling everyone what to do and you're under everybody's eyes. Well this job, you get on with

> your job and no one bothers you providing you do your job prop-
> erly.   (Postwoman, 103)

> I like getting out of the building and going out on delivery. I get
> bored so easily but here you do so many different things. It's not
> like going into a factory, sitting at the same bench all day, doing
> exactly the same thing. You are on the move. (Postwoman 195)[4]

Although it was a manual job requiring the lifting and carrying of
mail bags, some women found postal work less taxing than their previous jobs doing "women's work", with the added benefit of decent
wages.

> I started here because I wanted as much money as I could get for
> the work that I did. I've worked jolly hard and I've worked harder
> outside the Post Office as a woman getting women's pay than I do
> in here. It's the truth. At the jeans factory, the job I did was so
> heavy and so hard, really heavy work, heavy bundles being
> picked up.

> [Was it heavier than in here?]

> Oh my goodness yes and for half the money. See the men were the
> cutters and they were on a bonus, so they were working as fast as
> they could to get as much bonus. And the women weren't on a
> bonus and they had to keep up with them. This is why you
> worked so hard. And I think this is what first decided me that if I
> was going to work hard again, I may as well get the most I could.
>   (Postwoman, 109)

Postal workers did three main shifts: earlies, lates and nights.[5] Within
each shift, a number of duties were allocated for a period of time on the
basis of seniority and personal choice. When there was a "general re-
sign", all duties were reallocated. People submitted their names for a
particular duty (and shift) and the most senior person of those applying
was allocated the job. Postal workers on the early shift worked six days a
week. Starting time for all days was 6am. Finishing time on weekdays
was 1:30pm and on Saturdays 11:30am. Most of the work was outdoors
and consisted of the collection and delivery of mail. Some early duties
involved a double delivery (at 8am and 11am) and were highly
regarded. Not only did they mean you were on your own and outside
for the majority of the time, they also were known as "get away" jobs.
The faster you did your second delivery, the sooner your duty was fin-

ished. The late shift was the least liked. It was a shift that split time for family and social life into two parts. Starting times varied from 10 am to 2 pm and finishing times varied from 7 pm to 11 pm. The duties were mostly indoors and involved sorting as well as the loading and unloading of mail from collection and delivery vehicles. An advantage of the late shift was having the weekend off. Most night shift duties were also indoors and the tasks were similar to the late shift. The night shift was based on a five-night week and began between 10 pm and midnight, ending between 6 am and 8:30 am.

The shifts also differed in terms of the degree of supervision. One of the advantages of the early shift was that for most of the time "you're your own gov'nor". Since later shifts primarily involved indoor work, supervision was more apparent – especially on sorting duties when supervisors were frequently stationed at the end of a row of sorters. Supervisors largely assisted the postal job by answering queries and sorting out difficulties, but many postal workers felt their presence was unnecessary. The most common complaints about supervisors on the postal job had to do with charges of interference and incompetence. The main disciplinary responsibility of supervisors seemed to be the monitoring of timekeeping and making sure people were actually doing their job rather than off having a quick smoke or a cup of tea. While reprimands occurred, in general supervision had a low profile.

Within the Post Office, there were few avenues of improvement for postal workers. Counter work as a clerk selling stamps and so on to the public was one avenue that, for internal recruitment, required the passing of a numeracy test. Promotion from the postal job was more usually towards a supervisory post and was very much a double-edged affair. The first step towards a supervisory post was to become a "postman higher grade" (PHG). This option was open to those over the age of 21 who had an acceptable performance record and who had been employed as postal workers for over one year. As one might expect given the minimal entry requirements, there was no great incentive to move to this job and, if the move was not made while the postal worker was at a fairly junior level, it was rarely made at all. On taking promotion to PHG, seniority was lost and, in the first years, PHGs did not work a permanent shift. There was no opportunity to leave the sorting office on deliveries – all the work was indoors and most of it was highly mechanized. Finally, potential overtime was less and the pay increase at the higher grade did not compensate for this loss. As many people said, "promotion" to PHG was not worth the bother or the cost.

> Everyone got offered it. I turned it down because I didn't want to
> do all the shifts again. I was tired of being pushed and shoved

about and I would lose all my seniority again.   (Postwoman, 126)

I got the option after three years but by then I got the permanent early job that I wanted. Had I taken PHG, you immediately become junior again. You got to work shift work again and for that reason, and my family were young, I refused it. That's the unfortunate thing here. Every time you take a step up, you step backwards in your seniority. So, if you took every grade, you'd never get a job you wanted.   (Postman, 141)

They keep asking me but I can't really make up my mind because I like to go out, you know. You feel good when you go out delivering letters, having a jaw with the public.   (Postwoman, 131)

The only difference in pay is about 5 pounds in a week and I thought to myself, well if I'm doing this walk I get every afternoon off, whereas if I'm a PHG I'm going to be messed about from pillar to post. It's going to be lates one week, earlies the next and why should I do all this for 5 pounds a week? If I want 5 pounds, I'll do overtime.   (Postman, 159)

Attracting and keeping sufficient numbers in the postal job was a chronic problem. The London Sorting Office lost about one-fifth of its postal workers a year and, of every 20 who were trained, two were expected to remain. Although wages and employment were secure, the basic wage was low and this, combined with unsocial hours on all shifts and a six-day week on the early shift, contributed to working conditions that many were unable or unwilling to accept.

Pay varied by shift according to different allowances for night work and other unsocial hours. The main variation in earnings was the number of overtime hours. Overtime was usually plentiful since sorting offices were often understaffed, and it was used to top up the weekly wage. Of the postmen interviewed regularly, 68% did overtime on top of their 43 basic hours, averaging 14 extra hours per week. Among all postmen in the Post Office, overtime earnings comprised 22% of their gross average earnings.[6] The average weekly earnings for postmen were below the average for male manual workers: they earned 82% of the average male manual wage (see Table 2.1). When overtime earnings are taken into account, the relative position of the postmen's wages rises, but only to 90% of the average male manual wage.[7]

The majority of postwomen who were interviewed also worked overtime hours on a regular basis, although they were somewhat less likely to work overtime than postmen (56% did overtime regularly). Post-

Table 2.1 Average gross weekly earnings for full-time postmen/women expressed as
a percentage of the average in selected occupations.

	Excluding overtime		Including overtime	
	Women	Men	Women	Men
Postmen/women	100	100	100	100
Supervisors of clerks	79	70	90	86
General clerks	108	90	123	108
All manual	115	82	128	90
Processing, making, repairing and related – metal and electrical	100	76	111	83
Painting, repetitive assembly, product inspecting, packaging	108	81	120	91
Transport operating, materials moving and sorting	110	86	119	90

Sources: Earnings for postmen/women are for 1979 and are as supplied by the Post
Office. Other earnings are from Table 99 and Table 100, Part D, *New Earnings Survey*,
1979 (London: HMSO, 1979).

women who did work overtime put in the same number of overtime
hours on average as postmen. Among all postwomen in the Post Office,
overtime earnings comprised 13% of their gross average earnings. In
contrast to the men, postwomen's average earnings compared favourably with women's earnings in other manual occupations and they were
much higher when overtime earnings are considered. Excluding overtime, postwomen earned 115% of the average female manual wage, and
128% when overtime is included. The boost they got from their overtime
pay is even more dramatic when postwomen's earnings are compared
with those of women general clerks: they earned 108% of the latter's
basic earnings and 123% of earnings including overtime. Postwomen
were also better placed than other female manual workers in terms of
pay relativities with male workmates. Whereas female manual workers
in general were earning 67% of the male manual worker's basic wage,
and 59% of the wage including overtime, postwomen were earning 94%
of postmen's basic earnings, and 85% of postmen's earnings including
overtime.[8]

The earnings of postmen have not fared well during this century.
Although comparisons of aggregate job categories over such a timespan
are difficult, it appears that, on the whole, semi-skilled occupations have
very slightly improved their earnings position from the beginning of the
century relative to average male incomes. By comparison, the income
trend for Post Office postmen in London relative to other semi-skilled
jobs was a general decline. In 1906, postmen were earning 119% of the

average earnings of semi-skilled men. Their position then declined steadily so that by 1955 they were earning 85%. They remained at this position into the next decade. The more general category of postmen, mail sorters and messengers shows some gains in pay, in relation to all full-time men, in the middle of the 1970s, but these were lost during the latter half of the decade (Routh 1980:107ff).

The decline in the relative wage of postmen was accompanied by difficulties in recruiting men for the job. The UPW and the Post Office management have a long history of disagreement as to the appropriate solutions to recruitment problems. While shortages of postmen made women an attractive source of reserve labour for the Post Office, struggles over wage rates and the necessity of overtime resulted in employment practices that severely restricted women's employment opportunities in the postal job until 1975.

A job proper to men

To understand the debates that took place over equal opportunities in the 1970s, it is necessary briefly to review the history of gender divisions and conflict in the postal job. Since its formation in 1919, the Union of Post Office Workers has battled with the Post Office over the wages and recruitment of women.[9] The Post Office used a strategy of employing women at lower wage rates as a cheap answer to shortages in male labour. In turn, the UPW supported a variety of measures to protect the employment opportunities and conditions of its male members. At its inaugural conference, the UPW adopted the demand for equal pay, a policy adamantly opposed by the Post Office until the mid-fifties.[10] While the UPW boasts of its role, together with the Civil Service unions, in "pioneering" equal pay for women, positions within the membership and among executives were divided on the matter, and equal pay was incorporated into wage claims with varying degrees of commitment (Clinton 1984, Daunton 1985, Grint 1988). Although some definitely argued for equal pay on the grounds of social justice and the advancement of women's employment in the Post Office, it is clear from debates over the issue that the more influential interest supporting equal pay coincided with a concern to limit the employment of women.[11]

The fact that demands for equal pay were often accompanied by demands to limit or halt the recruitment of women suggests that the UPW pursued equal pay as a strategy to protect the interests of its male members against what they saw as the consequences of employing cheaper female labour. Such a two-pronged strategy for protecting the employment interests of incumbent men was used by other influential groups in the labour movement. Male compositors, for example, opposed the employ-

35

ment of female compositors while at the same time insisting on equal pay for them. Although Cockburn (1983) interprets this as a "contradiction" in the position of the male printers, this can be the case only if support for equal pay is interpreted as support for female employment. In the case of postal workers, there is ample evidence to the contrary.

During the inter-war years, the pay position of postal workers deteriorated and the employment of women expanded, so that by the mid-1930s General Secretary Bowen was attributing "most of our present ills" to the "policy of employing less men and more women". The 1935 conference responded by passing two motions, one calling for the immediate introduction of equal pay "as a measure to counter the influx of women earning less pay", the other insisting that increases in women's employment be stopped.[12] The official position of the union was neatly summarized in the mid-1940s by General Secretary Geddes who claimed that the "UPW was not 'for equality between women and men' but for 'equal pay for equal work irrespective of sex'" (Clinton 1984:431). Events around the introduction of equal pay in 1955 highlight this distinction.

From its formation, the UPW was in favour of the marriage bar operating in the Civil Service.[13] After the abolition of the marriage bar in 1946, the UPW continued to debate its desirability. At the 1953 conference, supporters of the marriage bar succeeded in winning a motion calling for its re-implementation. Although the motion was couched in terms of the negative effects of unemployment on the careers of single women (and supported strongly by some women telephonists on this basis), the discussion of the motion revealed the strategic convenience of rhetoric affirming the proper position of married women – out of the Post Office and in the home. The success of this strategy, however, was short lived, as the decision was revoked the following year (Clinton 1984:432-3).[14]

Shortly after, other measures were proposed to limit the employment of postwomen. In 1955, when equal pay was introduced into the Civil Service, and consequently into most grades organized by the UPW, the long-standing demand from the union was realized.[15] With the Post Office forced to employ women and men at equal rates, women could no longer be used as a cheap alternative to men. Nevertheless, they could still be used as an alternative to increasing wages in order to attract adequate numbers of male postal workers and, as discussed previously, the relative wages of postmen were at a low point in 1955. As far as postmen were concerned, a shortage of male staff always carried the threat of increased numbers of postwomen rather than an increase in wages. It also meant plenty of overtime, which would otherwise be reduced if more postwomen were hired.

I think over the years in here, because the wages have been poor,

36

there's been discrimination against women. And I'll be honest with you, I was one of them. In my eyes, years ago because the wages were so poor, the Post Office tried to bring women into the job to fill the gaps. The Post Office was trying to blackmail us into the situation where they could keep the wages poor and bring women in here. And see there was a certain amount of overtime going and the men would do this overtime and boost their income. Well what the staff were finding in here was that the women coming in here would do away with the overtime and they would be going on the flat rate.   (Postman, 226)

In the same year that equal pay was introduced, the union success-fully negotiated conditions for postwomen's employment that limited the recruitment of postwomen and defined them as a supplement to the male labour force. Postwomen could be recruited only against a male vacancy, and would be fired when a male became available for the job.[16]

For postwomen, 1955 was a step forward on a rug being pulled from under their feet. They gained equal pay and many lost their jobs. By 1961, the number of postwomen was 20% less than in 1951.[17]

I started in '54 and worked two years. Then we got equal pay, and the unions got us equal pay, but when we got it, they got us out. They gave us the push and all the postwomen here, some of them had been here donkey's years, all had to go. We got equal pay and we got the sack within a few weeks of getting it.(Postwoman, 222)

Staff shortages were again acute towards the mid-1960s, and in 1965 the UPW agreed to a limited recruitment of temporary full-time female and part-time labour into the postal job (CH/BE/2 – Part 2; A&PRD 184/65). The union was pushing for a pay rise at that time, and in 1964 had staged a one-day strike followed by an overtime ban. The 1965 agree-ment to the limited recruitment of full-time female and part-time postal staff was compensated for by a rise in wages. The postmen's objections to the employment of postwomen were overcome by a "10 bob rise".

They were very short of staff. They couldn't get men because they paid very poor wages then. I think when I first started they paid about 5 pound a week. So the men were promised a rise, I think it was about 10 shillings, if they would have women in the office and they agreed. So they got us in here on a 10 bob rise.
                                              (Postwoman, 172)[18]

Both postwomen and postmen report that when postwomen were

taken on again at the London Sorting Office in 1965, a number of post-men communicated their objections to the women's presence, and engaged in activities that undermined the women's ability to do their job properly.

> We didn't want to work with them. I was on this walk and we always had a very good team, my mates and I, and we didn't want them. We tried to refuse them cause we didn't want them working with us but after a while we got lumbered with one.
>
> (Postman, 141)

> The men made it very unpleasant for us. They wouldn't show us anything or help us. And if you said to them "I don't know this walk, I've never done it," they'd say, "Well here's your chance to learn it then," and then they'd disappear.   (Postwoman, 222)

> They used to insult us. They used to tell you straight, "Go home and cook your husband's dinner," "Go home and do the ironing and the cooking, we don't want you here". They wouldn't show us what to do. They were really horrible to us when we first started.   (Postwoman, 172)

> Oh, it was terrible. I was going to pack up the first night. It's only that it was so near Christmas and we had no money and nothing for the kids, presents or anything like that, that I decided to stay on and it's funny because it became a challenge then. The men didn't want us and they got my back up so much I just wouldn't pack up. When we first came here nobody would help us. When I first started I did the southeast dispatching and I was the only one on it and on the southwest dispatching there's about 11 loads, on the southeast there's 28. And there were three men on the south-west and there's only me on the southeast and I done it all. And on the second night I thought to myself there's something very pecu-liar going on here and I just stopped work and the gov'nor came up – cause if you stop work you might as well go and get your cards – and he said, "What do you think you're doing?". And I said, "I'm not working no more," and he said, "Oh, you're pack-ing up?" and I said, "No I'm not packing up". I said, "First of all I want to know why the southwest division can have three men whereas the one I'm on has only me and it's twice the work". Cause then I knew they were pulling a planker you see. The men that was supposed to be there with me weren't there.
>
> (Postwoman, 126)

The hierarchy of preferred labour was outlined in the *Head Postmasters' Manual* (1968), which stipulated the conditions for the employment of persons in the "postmen's" job. These conditions operated until the introduction of the Sex Discrimination Act.

> Although it is recognized that Postmen's work is proper to men, when there is inability to recruit Postmen because of a shortage of male labour women may be recruited and temporarily employed on work proper to Postmen provided they are replaced by men when they become available.

In the London region, similar conditions regarding recruitment were specified for both full-time female and part-time labour. A specific vacancy quota was set to ensure a supply of jobs for men.

> In the London Postal Region conditions will be considered to justify the recruitment of postwomen or part-time staff at offices where the number of full-time vacancies is 5 per cent or more of the authorized postmen establishment. This means that a 5 per cent vacancy ratio will be maintained in each office in the London Postal Region where part-time staff or postwomen are employed, and that where such staff have been recruited, and the vacancy ratio falls below 5 per cent, they will be discharged.[19]

Postwomen were liable for the full range of postmen's duties, but not the full range of employment benefits or conditions. Full-time postwomen were employed with temporary status, which gave them inferior sickness benefit, no promotion rights, no pension and no seniority. Since duties and times of annual leave are determined by seniority, postwomen usually found themselves with the jobs and holiday times that the men didn't want. As full-time temporaries, postwomen could be fired at any time with statutory notice, and with local quotas on part-time and female labour within the postal grade, their employment was not secure. Postwomen found their job frequently threatened by calls to "get rid of the women".

> When we were temporary, we'd always get a period in the year when someone would say they're going to get rid of the women. Whether it was done to keep us on our toes or to let us know we weren't wanted I don't know. But we used to get periods of this.
>
> (Postwoman, 101)

There is a hard core of men even today that don't want women in the job. When the women were temporary staff, any time we had a fight on the lads would say, "Well, here's our opportunity, we'll get rid of the women".   (Union official)

Several of the women interviewed had had the experience of being fired when men became available.

When they sent out for women to come in full time, some went to Sorting Office A and some went to Sorting Office B. I went to B but they got rid of the women up there. They didn't like the women working there I suppose. The men thought we was taking their jobs away from them or they weren't getting their overtime. I don't know why, but they just didn't want women in the Post Office. Cause the men – I mean we got the same money as men see, and we had to do the same work as a man, but the excuse, whether it was true or not, the why they got rid of us from there, was that they had their full quota of men. They only took the women when they couldn't get the men. When they got their full quota of men, they didn't want you no more.   (Postwoman, 102)

Yet acute recruitment difficulties undercut many local agreements restricting part-time and female labour. In 1972, the largest increase in employment was of part-time postwomen and there was a net decline in the number of postmen. In the following year, the only increase in the postal job was of full-time postwomen. In this year there was again a drop, this time more substantial, in the number of postmen.[20]

The employment of full-time postwomen and part-time labour was the issue of an emergency motion at the UPW's 1973 annual conference. Emergency motion "310. E" read as follows:

Conference agrees that re-emergence of difficulty with Postal Staffing . . . cannot be dealt with in terms of the 1965 Postman Staffing Agreement. A new agreement that takes account of Pay, Conditions and Contract of employment, Redundancy and Industrial Relations Legislation shall be urgently negotiated. Until such agreement is reached any increase in part-time and female labour over current levels and agreements shall be strenuously resisted and the Executive Council is instructed accordingly.[21]

The discussion of the motion focused on part-time labour. The employment of full-time postwomen, while included within the motion, was a less prominent part of the debate. The mover of the motion declared the situation an emergency one that could lead to the escalation of part-time employment unless immediate action was taken to improve the ability of the Post Office to compete in British labour markets. The seconder noted that staffing levels in his region were as much as 26% below requirements, and that if postmen received better pay and had more decent hours and conditions of employment, there would be no need to employ part-time labour. In all supporting statements, improvements in pay, hours and conditions of employment were stressed as the strategy needed to cope with staffing shortages. Those opposing the motion rarely did so on behalf of full-time postwomen or part-time staff. They expressed concern that the effect of the motion would be a reduction in services (which might reduce overtime and hence take-home pay) and perhaps a reduction in jobs or the loss of the second delivery. When it came to the vote, the motion was "carried overwhelmingly". Not surprisingly, motions at the same conference dealing with the equal employment of full-time postwomen were given short shrift. A motion from Birmingham proposing equal employment conditions for postwomen, including the recognition of seniority, was defeated. Another proposing the aggregation of women and men in the postal job was lost. A more general motion calling for the recognition of the parliamentary bill on equal rights for women and men, and instructing the Executive Council to provide the membership with a report on its effects within the Post Office and on current staffing agreements, was withdrawn.[22]

In 1973, the UPW was clearly opposed to the recruitment of, and equal conditions for, postwomen. Yet, this was also the year in which the Post Office decided it would have no choice but to equalize postwomen's and postmen's employment should legislation against sex discrimination be introduced. The Post Office, in October 1973, approached the union with a proposal that women should be equally eligible with men for recruitment to full-time vacancies and on a long-term pensionable basis (CH/ BE/2 – Part 2; *The Post*, 28/2/74, p. 21). The union executive responded by informing the Post Office "of the Union's traditional policy that the Postman grade is a male grade and further that only improvements in the pay of the grade will cure the recruitment policy". The union indicated its intention to abide by the 1973 conference decision and its "traditional attitude". It reiterated that until there was a modification of staffing agreements and an improvement in the pay and conditions of postmen, it would resist any attempts to employ part-time and female labour. If equal opportunities legislation became law, the union acknowledged it would have to re-examine its situation, but in the meantime the union hoped that the Post Office would "recognize the strength of feeling which exists" and "not run the risks involved in forcing this issue".

The 1973 conference decision to oppose further recruitment of postwomen and part-time labour was reaffirmed at the 1974 conference (UPW Annual Conference Agenda Pad 1974). A proposed amendment to the union's position, which called for a review of the union's policy on full-time postwomen, fell. The agenda for the 1974 conference included a report on the pending legislation against sex discrimination, and the views submitted by the Executive Council to the Department of Employment in October 1973 were presented. The union's position was that there was no discrimination on the grounds of sex in any of the grades organized by the UPW and, indeed, it maintained that the union had been in the "forefront of the struggle for equal rights for women ever since its formation" (*The Post*, 28/2/74, p.30). Despite such protestations, difficulties with respect to the proposed legislation were noted in almost all the jobs organized by the UPW – postmen, postmen higher grade, telephonists and doorkeepers. In such cases, the UPW expressed the hope that since current staffing agreements were made with the "full agreement" of the union membership, the legislation would allow these agreements to stand until the membership consented to modifications.

The UPW delayed any further action in anticipation of a change of government in 1974. However, the new Labour government, it discovered, intended to pursue legislation that the union thought was "tighter and more far ranging" than that previously proposed (UPW Annual Conference Agenda Pad 1975). After examining the government White Paper, the Executive Council decided to await draft legislation. By March of 1975, the UPW finally admitted it could procrastinate no longer. It acknowledged the need to modify its traditional policies in the light of the impending equal opportunities legislation and the "adverse comment" it had received regarding its 1973 conference decision.

In 1973 Motion 3.10E laid down a clear embargo on the employment of postwomen and part-timers. The Executive Council has not deviated from that decision. Since that time the union has been subjected to considerable adverse comment on the grounds that we are pursuing an anti female policy. We have been criticized for this throughout the labour movement. We have argued that Motion 3.10E was no more than a protective device designed to improve the pay and conditions of our members. Although there has been some understanding of our situation it is still generally held that as a union we are opposed to equal opportunities for women. We are now called upon to face up to our responsibilities in this respect. The Equal Opportunities legislation will outlaw our continued opposition to the employment of Postwomen.

(*The Post*, 21/3/75, p.19)

Thus, a new agreement between the Post Office and the UPW concerning the employment of postwomen was negotiated. The union stressed three points (*The Post*, 21/3/75, p.17). The General Secretary presented an objection to a proposal that postwomen's seniority be dated from the beginning of their current continuous service, proposing instead that postwomen's seniority begin accumulating from a common and contemporary date. The necessity was noted for an agreement regarding the fact that existing postwomen had not been required (as were permanent male staff) to take the aptitude tests to confirm their employment. The union also stressed its continued objection to any increase in part-time labour.[23]

At this point, the union's executive found itself in a difficult position. The argument it had been presenting to the Post Office on behalf of postmen – that the "postmen's job" was a job proper to men – now had to be argued in reverse to its male members. The postal job could no longer be considered a job in which men had priority and it was up to the Executive Council to secure postmen's assent to this change. The Executive Council presented the draft agreement with the Post Office to the membership, proposing that in future postwomen and postmen be recruited on the same terms and conditions, and recommended its acceptance. It felt it could recommend the agreement in good faith since it had been able to meet the terms of Motion 3.10E. An increase in pay and extra payments for Saturday work, in addition to earlier final collections, it argued, had improved the conditions and pay of the postal job. While its views regarding part-time labour had not changed, the Executive Council felt that:

> Postwomen should be recruited in the same way as are men and ... they should have the full liability for the total range of postmen's work and progression to PHG. We are convinced that to stand out against this development is to try and turn back the tide of history. We have no reservations about our attitude and we urge conference to adopt a similar view. (*The Post*, 21/3/75, p.19)

The membership did adopt the proposed agreement, although not without opposition. For example, one unsuccessful amendment proposed to pursue the exclusion of postwomen from the scope of the legislation in view of the manual work associated with the job (*The Post*, 30/4/75, p.18).

The final agreement, effective as of 1 September 1975, stated that postwomen be recruited to cover full-time duties on the same terms and with the same conditions as postmen. Women would be liable for the full range of duties and conditions applying to long-term (established) postmen and previously not applying to temporary full-time postwomen (CH/BE/57; *Branch Officials Bulletin* 1975: 385).[24] Existing postwomen with more than 12 months' service were to be given long-term status immediately; those with less than 12 months' service would be offered long-term status at the completion of one year. Neither was required to pass the aptitude test. Postwomen with less than 6 months' service would be required to pass the aptitude test to qualify for long-term status. Postwomen were to begin accumulating their seniority from the date of the agreement.

In the case of postwomen, the Sex Discrimination Act enabled a change in the conditions of their employment that until 1975 had been blocked by the union. The postmen had for years pursued a strategy of social closure in order to protect their priority in the postal job. By restricting access to the grade on the basis of sex, the postmen sought to control the labour market for the postal job as a means of maintaining or increasing wage rates in the face of labour shortages. Support for equal pay for postwomen did not in all cases correspond with support for women's employment. For an influential component of the union, it represented an attempt to curb the demand for female labour. Agreements restricting the conditions and levels of recruitment of postwomen were a direct attempt to control the supply of female labour and to keep the postal job a male grade. The two strategies to contain female employment converged dramatically in 1955 when many women received equal pay shortly before losing their jobs.

Postwomen were in a weak position both in terms of their employment contract and in terms of their representation within the union and the job. However, once the principle of equal opportunity was established as law, the postwomen were able to use the law to improve the conditions of their employment further. The agreement negotiated for the equal employment of postwomen and postmen did not count the years of postwomen's service before 1975 as part of their seniority. It was this situation that a postwoman contested by charging the union and the management with sex discrimination.

Postwomen and the fight for seniority

While postwomen were by no means passive observers of the negotiations over the conditions of their employment, they were a small minority within the union and their attempts to have their opinions heard were often unsuccessful. Women officers at branch level were few in number and their opposition to the position the union had adopted against postwomen was difficult to voice.

44

The union weren't behind the women, I'll tell you that for a fact. And there wasn't a great deal you could do. Cause you know one or two women on their own with about 20 men – there isn't much you could do. You could say your piece and get shouted down. That's all. That's all you could do. (Postwoman, 101)

At the London Sorting Office, the meeting to decide on the issue of women's seniority was well attended, and the women were outnumbered.

We called a meeting of women to discuss seniority and the men made sure they all showed up. There was 95 per cent turn-out at that meeting and we were only 200 so the men won cause there were so many of them. (Postwoman, 127)

The only union meeting I've been to was about women and seniority, whether women should get all their seniority or just back to 1975. We voted against giving them all their seniority but it meant nothing in the end because they got it anyway. (Postman, 153)

The position of the union was clearly not in the interests of the postwomen, and many felt the union had been operating in bad faith in relation to its postwomen members. With the implementation of the Sex Discrimination Act, the union "got it in the eye" and, to many, the real credit for gaining the postwoman's full equal rights belonged to a woman in Birmingham who fought the union and the Post Office on their behalf.

They really shouldn't have taken our union money. They wasn't fighting for us to get our seniority, our equal rights. Really they took that money under false pretences. They didn't do much for us. If they'd done anything, why did it have to be a woman up north that fought for our seniority? Why didn't they fight for it? They didn't mind taking our union money did they? When the equality came in they got it in the eye didn't they?
(Postwoman, 102)

We got our equal rights in 1975, they couldn't call us temporary no more. When the law came out, we were established and a woman up in Birmingham, she fought for us and she got us our seniority from 1969. I got only 9 years' seniority although I've got 13 years' service. But it wasn't even our union that got us that. It was a woman up in Birmingham, she fought for us. (Postwoman, 126)

Following the defeat of the motion from Birmingham at the 1973 conference, and considering the support from the conference to limitations in the employment of postwomen, postwomen in Birmingham set up a more general campaign to obtain their equal employment rights (CH/BE/2 – Part 2). They took action against the UPW, and pursued a case in the National Industrial Relations Court. Referring to union rules that say the objective of the union is to protect and promote the interests of its members, the postwomen argued this was not being done in the case of their interests. The women intended to seek equality in terms of conditions of seniority, promotion and pension rights. The union appealed to the women to drop their action and offered a special local agreement. The special offer would allow women onto the seniority lists, but they would not be considered for promotion or transfer. The offer was conditional on the women dropping their claim in the Industrial Relations Court. The women replied that the offer was not sufficient as it was not a basic change to their "second-class position" both in their employment and in their union as evidenced by the 1973 conference decisions. They continued their claim (CH/BE/5).[25] Their application was heard on 22 October 1973, but was dismissed owing to ongoing negotiations between the UPW and the management on postwomen's permanent status.

After the 1975 agreement reached by the union and the management, Birmingham was again the focus of the postwomen's attempts to achieve equal terms of employment. The issue was the effective date of postwomen's seniority. Mrs Steel had been employed as a full-time postwoman since November 1961. According to the 1975 agreement, her seniority was dated from September 1975. In March 1976, she applied for a vacant walk. On the basis of the seniority rule, the walk went to Mr Moore who had started working as a postman in 1973. Mrs Steel originally complained to an industrial tribunal, stating that her complaint was against the union and not the Post Office. Her case was dismissed on the grounds that matters such as seniority were "entirely for the union, its members and the General Post Office" (*Industrial Relations Legal Review [IRLR]* 1977:288-91). The Equal Opportunities Commission (EOC) supported Mrs Steel's appeal against this decision and the Employment Appeal Tribunal allowed an appeal against the Post Office, though not against the union. The Employment Appeal Tribunal agreed that Mrs Steel had been indirectly discriminated against and considered the seniority agreement as it applied to Mrs Steel and other postwomen could be justified only if it was a matter of business necessity. The Tribunal concluded:

In effect the attitude of the Post Office is the not uncommon one of supporting sex equality – but not yet. The attitude of the union is similar, and it is probably fair to suppose that their reluctance to give postwomen added seniority . . . is not unconnected with the fact that so many of their members are men who would suffer a loss in seniority if women were to gain.   (*IRLR* 1977:289-290)

The tribunal re-hearing Mrs Steel's case did not find the seniority rule to be a matter of necessity and recommended that Mrs Steel's seniority be backdated to 1969, the year when the temporary grade was abolished for men. As many similar cases against the Post Office were pending (*EOC News,* March 1978, p.3), this was recommended as a national, not merely local or individual, arrangement (*Industrial Relations Review and Report [IRR & R]* 1978).

As of September 1978, all postwomen had their full-time seniority backdated to 1969. This meant postwomen were able, for the first time, to have some choice in the type of duty they would do and to have a chance of picking up a better job. They could also put in for promotion to PHG, the first step towards a supervisory position.

After the employment conditions of postwomen were brought into line with postmen's, objections to their presence continued to be expressed. Often, those referred to as the "hard core" refused to assist postwomen in any way on the grounds that, with their seniority recognized and their pay the same as the men's, they had to live up to their equal status in the job. Several postmen still believed women should be excluded from the job since it was at times very heavy work, and complaints that the men "carried" the women were a source of conflict.

> It's funny 'cause we were arguing with the women about this the other day. My mate was saying that we were carrying them and that's what the argument started over. The two women we were working with were arguing against my mate saying this and they were disagreeing with it. This one was saying she could do as much work as he could. I don't think she could, I mean he's a lot younger than her. It was just an argument over nothing, you know, I think they were just trying to be mean to him.
>
> (Postman, 202)

While many postwomen accept that they require more help with some of the heavy work than some men, they do not accept that on balance postmen perform the job better than postwomen.

> It's the same in any job isn't it. You get those who don't like women and the others they're okay. There's only one here I've had a barney with and I put it down to jealousy. He's jealous because I

47

don't think he thinks that a woman's able to do the job as well as
he is, and when he finds out she can, he don't like it.

(Postwoman, 131)

The women carry the men. When we first came here we had a
rough time because we'd get all the hard jobs, and I'm not joking,
it's true. We keep telling them all the time that it's us been carrying
them. (Postwoman, 109)

The telephonist job

Whether a telephonist was employed on the day shift or the night shift
was a significant indicator of the social and material conditions of her/
his job. Although the job tasks were the same on both shifts, there were
differences between them in terms of the pace of work, the number of
hours worked, the social environment of the workplace and pay. The
general characteristics of the day shift are presented first. This is followed by a discussion of the differences between the day shift and the
night shift. In the London Telephone Exchange, telephonists were hired
to do one of two types of job. Either they worked in the auto-manual
centre (AMC), where their main function was to assist persons having
difficulty making a telephone connection, or they worked in directory
enquiries (DQ), where they searched through telephone directories to
obtain a listed number requested by a caller.[26] New recruits were trained
for one of these jobs, but could in principle transfer to, and be trained for,
the other at a later point. Many of the features of AMC and DQ work were
similar. In both types of telephonist work, headsets connected the
telephonists to a panel of machinery and they responded to and dealt
with calls according to a standard procedure. There were "standard
expressions" that had to be used in addressing a caller and executing a
call. Deviations from standard procedure were reprimanded. Because
telephonists were plugged into a piece of machinery, they were
restricted in their movements and, in addition, had to ask permission if
they needed to leave their position at any time outside scheduled breaks.
In its statements on morale problems in the telephonist job at this time,
the UPW declared its view that "switchrooms are still institutionalized in
character with discipline in telephone exchanges being more rigid than
in most other work areas" (*The Post*, 21/3/75, p.28). Telephonists in the
AMC and the DQ were heavily supervised and continually monitored
electronically. The time to answer, and the time to complete, a call were
electronically recorded for every telephonist position. Telephone

exchanges had productivity targets, which, along with the actual monitored productivity, were posted on a board in the telephone exchange on
a regular basis. As noted during a UPW conference:

> Of all the workers in the land, the Telephonist in the Post Office
> was the most time-studied, work-measured, record-taken, looked-
> at grade in the trade union movement. The digits they dialled, the
> tickets they logged, if they went to the toilet, broke their legs,
> dropped their pencils, looked at a file, adjusted their chairs, sat,
> coughed, sneezed or blew their noses – there was a record for it
> from the time they started to the time they finished their duties.
> (*The Post*, July/August 1976, p.4)

The telephonist's demeanour and efficiency were also periodically
checked by a supervisor, who sat at a type of large control desk. The
electronic facilities of this desk allowed the supervisor to listen in on any
telephonist's headset without warning or detection.[27] The ratio of supervisors to telephonists, at the London Telephone Exchange, was 1 to 10
according to the staff complement, and much lower in practice. Supervisors were usually stationed behind a row of telephonists, and sometimes
walked up and down the length of a row answering queries, discourag-
ing gum chewing or too much talking, and telling telephonists in the
AMC to "take the lights". This urging to maintain a good productivity
level – being told to "take the lights" – was a major difference between
the AMC and the DQ job.

At the London Telephone Exchange, the AMC switchboard was operated by means of plugging cords into a panel of sockets. A call waiting to
be answered was indicated by a flashing light. When the telephonist
plugged into the call, the light went off. At any one time, an AMC
telephonist could be handling up to six calls and she or he controlled the
connecting and disconnecting of calls. In the DQ, the system was different and more akin to the cordless switchboards that were replacing the
AMC system. In the DQ, telephonists dealt with one call at a time and had
no control over their pace of work. Calls automatically "dropped" into a
telephonist's headset. DQ telephonists operated one switch only, to dis-
connect a call when it was completed. As a call was disconnected,
another was immediately directed into the headset. Although telephonists in the DQ had virtually no control over the pace of their work, the
substance of their job was often somewhat of a guessing game, making
the work at times more absorbing, and a few DQ telephonists described
their telephonist work as interesting. One needed a good knowledge of
London, of the location of shops, streets, the functions of government
departments and so on, in order to obtain the correct number for the

caller. The occasional use of practical knowledge was a relief from the pre-programmed method of receiving and dispensing information.

On the other hand, there was, in general, no variety in the type of work done in the DQ, whereas in the AMC there was a system of job rotation between a number of different sorts of calls or tasks. For example, one task involved moving from one telephonist position to another collecting the tickets telephonists fill out for particular calls, and another involved taking emergency calls. The main bulk of AMC telephonist work consisted of dealing with callers who had lost money in coin boxes or who were having difficulty reaching a number. Often, the annoyance of the caller was vented on the telephonists. Insults and abuse from callers were a common and frustrating experience for the telephonist, who was required to maintain an apologetic and deferential manner as part of their service to the public. The main skill telephonists often cite as required for their job was, as a result, one of temperament: patience.

Keeping staff in the day-shift job was a real problem in the London Telephone Exchange, where the numbers employed on the days were 75% of the numbers needed. Day telephonists were being trained about as fast as existing telephonists were leaving. Problems of recruitment and staffing levels did not exist on the night shift.

While a day telephonist, in either the AMC or DQ, sat in the same chair, faced the same switchboard and performed the same series of tasks as her/his night-shift counterpart, the day- and night-shift environments were completely different. The number of calls dealt with during the day shift at the London Telephone Exchange was substantially higher, and the number of staff required about four and a half times greater, than during the night shift. The pace of night work was, as a consequence, much more relaxed. As with the day shift, night telephonists were monitored electronically, but in contrast, personal supervision was less rigorous. Because the pace of work was less taxing, the demands of the job were more easily met and supervisors assumed more of a facilitating role – answering queries and dealing with especially difficult customers. A certain amount of discipline existed, although it was much less obtrusive than on the day shift. Many of the night telephonists and night supervisors met socially during breaks throughout their shift and often outside the telephone exchange. No such contact existed between the day telephonists and the day supervisors. Although classified as an unsocial job because of the hours, the night shift was, nevertheless, a more sociable job. It allowed more personal contact with workmates and callers than did the day shift. The complaint from the day staff that "you're not a person" was not heard from the night staff, and indeed several value the night shift because it enabled the expression of their individual character. Standard expressions were used less frequently, and seating arrangements and working styles (e.g., standing up) were variable. Night telephonists looked after their own canteen arrangements for their evening meal, and there was flexibility in the scheduling of breaks.

Both day and night telephonists were paid on the basis of a 41-hour week. Day telephonists actually worked the full 41 hours over a six-day week. Attendances were usually five days a week including roughly one Saturday in every six. Day telephonists worked hours similar to office work. Starting times on the day shift ranged from 8 am to 10 am, and finishing times ranged from 4 pm to 6 pm. At the London Telephone Exchange, there was a 45-minute lunch break on the day shift (a situation causing much dissatisfaction) as well as a morning and afternoon break. No telephonist was scheduled to work more than two and a half hours at the switchboard without a break. Night telephonists regularly worked on Sundays, and the higher valuation of Sunday hours reduced the number of hours they actually worked to about 32 per week. Duties were arranged so that no operator worked more than three through-duties per fortnight (12–13 hours at a time). A through night had to be followed by a rest night, and the remainder of the night telephonist hours were made up of "shorts", which started at approximately 6 pm and ended no later than 11 pm.

The average earnings of day telephonists were similar to those of women employed as general clerks (96%; see Table 2.2) or in the more highly paid service jobs (99% of catering supervisors' earnings). They did not earn much more than the average for women in manual jobs (102%). Day telephonists were least likely of all the sample to do overtime. Since the day shift was so understaffed, a lot of overtime was available for those who regularly worked the night shift, whereas the availability of overtime hours for the day shift was restricted mainly to working extra Saturdays. On average, 25% of day telephonists worked overtime and did 8 hours per week. In contrast to the relative wage position of their day sisters, women on the night shift earned more than the average wage for female general clerks, catering supervisors and women in manual jobs (118%, 123% and 126%, respectively; see Table 2.3). Even so, about 50% of women night telephonists did overtime regularly, averaging 21 hours per week. When overtime earnings are considered, women night telephonists earned substantially more (154%) than the average wage for female general clerks and an even higher percentage of the average wage for female manual workers (161%). Their earnings position relative to women clerical supervisors improved considerably (from 86% to 113%). They also did much better than women day telephonists in relation to men's wages, coming very close to the average for male manual workers (95%) and exceeding the average wage of male general clerks (115%).

51

Table 2.2 Average gross weekly earnings for full-time day telephonists expressed as a percentage of the average in selected occupations.[1]

| | Excluding overtime | | Including overtime | |
	Women	Men	Women	Men
Day telephonists	100	100	100	100
Supervisors of clerks	70	58	73	56
General clerks	96	75	99	74
Catering supervisors	99	69	101	67
Cleaners	112	87	112	77
Salesmen/women, shop assistants, shelf fillers	124	76	130	78
All manual	102	69	103	61

Sources: Earnings for telephonists have been supplied by British Telecommunications. All other earnings are from Table 99 and Table 100, Part D, *New Earnings Survey*, 1979 (London: HMSO, 1979).

Table 2.3 Average gross weekly earnings for full-time night telephonists expressed as a percentage of the average in selected occupations.

| | Excluding overtime | | Including overtime | |
	Women	Men	Women	Men
Night telephonists	100	100	100	100
Supervisors of clerks	86	72	113	92
General clerks	118	93	154	115
Catering supervisors	123	86	157	104
Cleaners	138	107	174	119
Salesmen/women, shop assistants, shelf fillers	153	94	200	121
All manual	126	85	161	95

Sources: see Table 2.2.

For men, day telephonist earnings were below men's average earnings in almost every job recorded in the New Earnings Survey. They earned 75% (Table 2.2) of the average wage for male general clerks and 69% of the average for male manual workers. Their income position was *reduced further* when overtime earnings are considered. The average earnings of male night telephonists inclusive of overtime, on the other hand, were roughly comparable with men's average earnings in manual jobs generally (95%; see Table 2.3), as well as the more highly paid supervisory clerical (92%) and service (104%) jobs. These similarities in the average earnings of male night telephonists were achieved, however, only with the addition of many extra hours of work. If overtime had not been available, male night telephonists would have been in a relatively poor position compared with these jobs (85% of manual, 72% of clerical supervisors, and 86% of catering supervisors).

In addition to the relatively poor basic pay of the telephonist job, career prospects were very limited. The structure of access to management positions was such that the highest position telephonists could attain was chief supervisor in an exchange, a sub-management position. As in the postal job, promotion in the telephonist job was greeted with ambivalent feelings. Before entering the lowest level of the supervisory grade, telephonists were placed on a "substitution list". This option became available after a few years' service and only if attendance and performance reports were in good order. Deliberately running up the number of days taken off for sick leave was not unknown as a way of avoiding being offered a position as a substitution supervisor. Being a subbing officer meant working some days as a telephonist and others as a supervisor, as required, often within the same exchange. It also meant being prepared to be sent to other exchanges as a substitution supervisor, for varying periods of time, and with varying amounts of prior notice. Often, it could be several years before a subbing officer was "picked up" for a permanent supervisory position. Promotion from the telephonist job could, in addition, take the form of a move to a clerical position within the telephone exchange – a job that handled traffic and financial records. But here there was a catch. A telephonist could not retain a clerical position if she or he turned down an offer to become a substitution supervisor. Another option for advancement within the Post Office, which was especially attractive to the younger telephonists, was a move to an international exchange. Handling international calls was considered to be a better quality, less tedious and more exciting telephonist job.

Prior to the introduction of equal opportunities in the telephonist job in 1975, the full-time day and night telephonist shifts were segregated by sex. Full-time telephonists and supervisors on the day shift were women; those on the night shift were men.[28] Women and men could work either telephonist shift on a part-time basis, although in practice most part-time workers were women on nights (until 11 pm). A union executive recalled the consolidation of the night shift as a male job:

Male telephonists only ever existed because women back in the thirties would not work beyond a certain hour at night. I think it was eight o'clock. The Post Office tried to force them to work later than that – through nights and all the rest of it, but they wouldn't do it. So what the Post Office then had to do was recruit a temporary casual man who could work for the night period. In the war, that all went and women went on nights. When the war ended, everybody reverted to the former conditions and it was at that time that the union made this agreement that formalized the employment of male telephonists and gave them this very advantageous attendance pattern.

Clinton (1984:374-6) confirms this interpretation of events. The night telephonist job was relatively insignificant numerically until the 1930s when cheap evening calls were introduced. As the job grew, so did pressure from the Post Office to take on women for a fuller range of night duties. At this time, both the UPW and the secessionist National Guild of Telephonists (NGT) had bargaining recognition and their rivalry focused on the night telephonist grade. To some extent both tried to win favour by supporting male priority in the grade. The UPW and the NGT campaigned against the efforts of the Post Office to extend women's employment past 8pm, though their strategy in doing so diverged somewhat. As Clinton reports (1984:428):

> There is no evidence that it has been possible to discover that any section of the workforce supported this change. The secessionist National Guild of Telephonists was able to portray the issue as largely one of women against men, but the Union mobilized large numbers of women in opposition.

Nevertheless, after the war, even as new male and female telephonist duties were being negotiated (UPW Handbook 1954), pressure was growing for equal pay, and with it came further pressure to abandon the distinction between "female" day and "male" night telephonists. We shall take up the history of the telephonist job in more detail from here and discuss the issues involved in equalizing the employment of female and male telephonists.

Integration and infiltration

There were three major stages in the implementation of equal pay and equal opportunities for telephonists (Hain & Stagg 1976). As with the postmen/women, equal pay was introduced into the telephonist job in 1955, to be achieved by 1961. In implementing equal pay, the Post Office management preferred a scheme whereby women would have equal wage rates with men only if they accepted the full range of telephonist duties, including night work. The union preferred a single wage rate and the existing division by sex between day and night staff, with special money and time compensations for night work. The Post Office offered the union a choice between two alternatives for the 1955 agreement: either all female telephonists would assume the full liabilities of the male telephonists and, on that condition, be paid equally; or, the present duties of female telephonists would stay the same and women would progress to a pay scale that was 95% of the men's. The settlement reached was a combination of these two proposals (*The Post*, 16/2/57; Post Office Circular, DF 658 Supplement). Existing female telephonists were offered a choice between the "95% option" and the "100% option". All new telephonists were recruited on the 100% option. Women would still be preferred for day work, and men for night work, but according to the 100% option both could be called to work the other shift "in the interests of the service". The agreement basically gave the Post Office greater flexibility in the deployment of its telephonist staff and was a move towards an undifferentiated 24-hour grade.

As the agreement got under way, problems emerged. The Post Office was finding it difficult to hire women willing to accept the range of attendances potentially required on the 100% option (Clinton 1984:434, Hain & Stagg 1976:3). Existing staff on the 100% option, both male and female, were also dissatisfied. Neither was pleased with the compulsory flexibility of their employment.

Further negotiations in 1960 resulted in the second stage of the progression towards equal conditions for women and men in the telephonist job (UPW Handbook 1961). The 95% option was abolished and all telephonists were placed on a single pay scale. A permanent night and Sunday work allowance was also established in 1961, and further enhanced in 1970. Recruitment to full-time employment on the day and night shift remained segregated by sex.

The third stage of equalizing the employment of female and male telephonists was the introduction of the Sex Discrimination Act, which focused attention on the restriction of the day and night shifts to one sex. Negotiations took place between the UPW and the Post Office over how the integration of women and men within the two shifts should proceed. One issue with high priority was whether the abolition of the "female" and "male" telephonist grades would mean the abolition of the distinction between the day and night shifts. The 1974 UPW conference accepted an amendment stating that "compulsory 24-hour integration of telephonists is not in the best interests of the membership" (*The Post*, Conference Edition 1974:8). The amendment was moved and seconded by two women who objected to the "round the clock" timetabling implications and stressed the potential disruption to people's lives outside their workplace. The executive was instructed to not consider any move towards a single 24-hour grade, and the agreement reached maintained the concept of a permanent day and night staff (TH/DC/9; *Branch Officials Bulletin* 1975:619–22). As of December 1975, full-time employment on the day shift and the night shift was opened to women and men. Special arrangements of transfer were insisted on by the union and covered all applications received for a six-month period, until June 1976. During this time, existing full-time telephonists (and supervisors) could apply to transfer to the shift previously barred to them and they could carry their full seniority. (Normally, only in compulsory transfers could seniority be carried into the new position.) Part-time staff could also transfer to full-time employment on the shift hitherto closed to them. Although part-time staff usually did not carry seniority when they transferred to full-time duties, the special offer of transfer stipulated that one-half of part-time service could be carried into full-time service. After the special transfer period, normal conditions of transfer again applied. For reasons to be discussed shortly, there was some delay in the special transfers taking effect, especially transfers from the day to the night shift.

Although approved by the UPW membership, the agreement was later objected to in a motion at the 1976 conference (*The Post*, Conference Edition 1976:5). The motion was moved by the Aberdeen branch of the UPW and called for part-time staff to be placed at the bottom of seniority lists, rather than acknowledging half of their part-time seniority when they transferred to full-time duties within the conditions of the special offer. The mover of the motion noted that the special agreement concerning the carriage of a proportion of part-time seniority was causing "anxiety and frustration" amongst full-time men and was discriminatory against them. The transfer agreement, it was argued, made full-time men more vulnerable to redundancy since long-service part-timers moving to full-time duties were becoming more senior to full-time men who had less service. The motion was defeated and the Aberdeen branch pursued its objection by other means. A year later, in May 1977, an industrial tribunal in Scotland heard the case of Mr Webster, who charged that the Post Office had committed an act of discrimination against him in terms of access to opportunities for promotion, transfer or training. Mr Webster had transferred from part-time to full-time night duties in June 1974 and had been placed at the bottom of the full-time seniority list. According to the usual rules regarding transfers from part-time to full-time duties, he was not allowed to carry any of his 10 years' service as a part-time employee. In the same Aberdeen exchange as Mr Webster, a woman who had worked as a part-time night telephonist for 12½ years applied for a transfer to full-time night duties under the conditions of the special offer and became a full-time night telephonist with 6 years and 3 months' seniority. She was placed ahead of Mr Webster in the seniority list. The tribunal decided that since the special offer of transfer was open to women and men, it was not discriminatory. In the tribunal's opinion, the special offer was discriminatory against part-time transfers before the special offer, although this discrimination was not based on sex. The tribunal dismissed Mr Webster's application.

Very few telephonists applied for transfers under the special offer (TH/DC/4, Hain & Stagg 1976:4): 1% of full-time male staff applied to transfer to days, and a slightly higher percentage of part-time male telephonists applied for full-time day duties; only 2% of full-time female telephonists applied for the night shift. The group to take most advantage of the special offer were part-time female night telephonists who applied for full-time night duties. Table 2.4 presents the number of transfer applications received by the end of the special offer, and the number of transfers still outstanding at the end of 1976. The practical realization of the special transfer offer was more difficult for women than for men. With recruitment generally a problem on the day shift, men wishing to transfer to days were more than welcome. The shortage of staff on days inhibited women's transfers to nights, since requests for transfer were to be dealt with "as soon as service considerations permit" (*Branch Officials Bulletin* 1975:619). In most cases, the proportion of transfers for women that were still outstanding at the end of 1976 was greater than that for men, although generally the movement towards the integration of

Table 2.4 Number of applications received for transfer by the closing date of the special offer (30 June 1976); number and percentage of transfers outstanding as of 29 December 1976.

	Transfer applications received[1]	Transfers outstanding Dec. 1976[1]	
	N	N	%
Telephonists			
Full-time to full-time transfer:			
Men on nights to day shift	96	11	11
Women on days to night shift	421	182	43
Part-time to full-time transfer:			
Men on nights to day shift	10	3	30
Women on nights to night shift	1049	516	49
Women on days to night shift	13	3	23[2]
Supervisors			
Men on nights to day shift	26	10	38
Women on days to night shift	17	9	53

1. Numbers do not include those who left the Post Office before their transfer applications could be effected. 2. Number outstanding does not include one woman who refused an offer of transfer.

Source: TH/DC/4.

telephonists had been greater on nights than on days. By the end of the decade, the proportion of women on full-time night duties in the central London area was higher (15%) than the proportion of full-time men on days (5%). In the London Telephone Exchange, no night-shift men transferred to the day shift. Four of the six night-shift women interviewed were previously on the day shift. Of the remaining two women on nights, one was a part-time to full-time transfer, and one was recruited to the night shift. All of the men working the day shift had been recruited subsequent to the Sex Discrimination Act.

Beyond the part-time seniority issue, additional opposition to the integration of women and men in the telephonist shifts came from the night-shift male staff. The UPW recorded a number of complaints from men on the night shift concerning "infiltration" by women. As one member of the union executive elaborated:

> It was the men who objected to women coming on nights. We had some appalling cases where men actually reduced the number of full-time duties to prevent women who were waiting to transfer onto nights from doing so. They had always had a large number of part-time women working the nights, the major reason being that they enabled the more sensible and satisfactory night men's duties to be introduced, but the through-nights were the full-time man's preserve. They felt that introducing women onto the full nights was an invasion of their male privacy. Because men had always been on duty alone at night in the exchange, it was a strange thing for a man to be sitting there along with a woman.

In the London Telephone Exchange, the male telephonists on nights were apprehensive about, though not hostile to, the possibility of women working full time on the night shift. The apprehension focused on the degree to which women would enter the night shift and the prospect of women supervisors from the day shift.

> First of all I think we were apprehensive. You see there's so many women in this place and they might just have taken over the night shift. I think the main thing that was causing apprehension is that so many girls would come on the night job and you'd finish up with female supervision, and they're inclined to be a little more officious than men.   (Night telephonist, male, 080)

As it turned out, the deluge did not happen and the general opinion was that the women and men worked together within the routine and environment of the night shift very well, and, for the women, the improved wages, easier atmosphere and escape from the hectic, heavily supervised day job were definite benefits.

Most of the men on the day shift had previous experience of working in a mixed-sex environment. Some women day telephonists were sorry to see the end of a single-sex working environment and the beginning of the social constraints they equated with mixed-sex environments. Generally, the women on the day shift welcomed the entry of men into their job, and indeed the success of the integration of the day shift was typically defined in terms of the men's happiness in, and acceptance of, a workplace in which they were in a minority. Any speculations about the extent to which employing men on the day shift would transform the nature of the job were soon quashed and the novelty of their presence was short-lived.

[What was it like when the men came on the days?]

It was a bit of a novelty really. Soon as we knew we had a man, everyone was looking to see what he was like, but it soon dies down really. At first it was "Oh no, I could never sit next to a man". Doing my work, you know, I didn't think I could work next to a man. But it doesn't make any difference now. They're just people.   (Day telephonist, female, 002)

The entry of women and men into both shifts following the enactment of the 1975 legislation seems to have favoured the promotion prospects of male telephonists. Since 1975, the ratio of male supervisors to male telephonists has increased while the ratio for women has stayed the same. At the beginning of 1975 there was one male supervisor for every five male telephonists. By the end of the decade, this ratio had risen to 1:4. For women, on the other hand, the ratio of female supervisors to female telephonists was 1:6 in 1975 and stayed at this level throughout the decade.[29] To some extent, this must be due to how the transfer offer worked out in practice at the supervisory grade.

This review of employment in the telephonist job suggests that, as with the case of postal workers, recruitment issues were also significant in maintaining sex segregation. On several occasions the Post Office failed in its attempts to expand women's regular duties, by incorporating night hours, and to create a 24-hour grade, in order to cover the increasing load of night work. Women were being urged to work hours conventionally regarded as unsocial. Although some may have welcomed this and the boost to earnings involved, the majority opposed the extension of their employment in this way. After 1975, when women and men had full access to day and night work, both shifts remained highly

59

skewed in their gender composition – an indication, perhaps, that previous arrangements largely reflected, rather than restricted, preferred options.

Conclusions

To date, the major studies of occupational segregation by sex have been conducted at a highly aggregated level of employment, and several commentators have identified the need for firm or establishment level analyses to identify fully processes underlying gender segregation. Of the case studies conducted, a significant number proceed from the premise that the designation of gender-appropriate employment inherent in gender stereotyping or gender ideology exerts a substantial influence on the creation and maintenance of "gendered" jobs.[30] One might think this premise would be confirmed by a case study of employment in the Post Office, where gender-segregated grades were official employment policy for many years and where overt sex discrimination severely limited women's access to equal conditions and opportunities of employment. It is clear from the material reported here, however, that perceptions of the appropriateness or otherwise of women and men doing certain *tasks* are less potent as an explanation of segregation than issues of hours and pay.[31]

Although the origins of sex discrimination and segregation in the Post Office are outside the scope of this study, the debates and issues that emerged over the dissolution of these circumstances provide an indication of the processes sustaining them. There is nothing intrinsic to the job tasks in the postal or telephonist jobs that explains why, before 1975, men were given priority in the postal job and employed full time exclusively on the night telephonist shift. A point made by Bielby & Baron is especially apt here (1986:791): "gender seems to be a very inefficient screen for attributes as easy to measure as physical strength and finger dexterity." Aspects of the postal job require a capacity typically associated with "men's work" – strength. Yet there are postwomen who find their current job no more physically demanding than some "women's work" they have done in the past, and tests of strength have never determined who is or is not hired for the postal job. There was, until 1975, a 7lb difference in the weight postwomen and postmen were expected to carry. Although for some postmen this was a source of grievance, it is also an indication that assumptions about women's and men's capacity for manual work did not threaten women's access to the job. Significantly, the postmen who tried to argue that owing to the manual tasks associated with postal work, the legal requirements of the Sex Discrimination Act might be evaded were unsuccessful in their attempt. Although the social and material circumstances of the day and night telephonist jobs vary substantially, the actual tasks performed are identical. It was, in fact, the recognition of this equivalence, along with the acknowledged advantages of the working environment and pay on the night shift, that stood at the heart of the men's fear that they would be inundated by women from the day shift when restrictions on their access to the night shift were abolished.

There seems good evidence to suggest that prior to 1975, discrimination by sex in both jobs was due to factors other than the nature of job tasks. Although at times stereotypes about gendered rights to employment and capacities for labour emerged as part of the rhetoric in discussions over pay, conditions and appropriate job incumbents, the essential issues involved established workers, most frequently but not exclusively male, protecting their access to and conditions of employment. In the case of the postal job, objections to the employment of women were conflated with objections to the employment of labour on terms threatening to current, or the possibility of improved, conditions. In other instances, women themselves objected to proposed changes because they were identified as a deterioration of their working circumstances. Thus, female day telephonists supported the idea of gender-segregated shifts to avoid the addition of unsocial hours to their own working day.

The persistence of the night telephonist job as a male job was due to difficulties in recruiting sufficient women willing, or able, to work night hours on a full-time basis. Attempts by the Post Office, in the 1930s and the 1960s, to extend women's hours into the evening duty failed, and there was equally strong objection to an integrated 24-hour telephonist grade during negotiations over the implementation of the Sex Discrimination Act. The declining income position of the postal job, and resulting shortages of full-time men applying for the job, were conditions within which the union attempted to protect wages and the availability of overtime by exerting control over the demand for, and supply of, all part-time and female full-time labour. The postmen had no job skills to safeguard, or to mobilize to their advantage as a means of closure, and their opposition to female labour was largely from a position of weakness. Appeals to women's proper place and to the compromise to femininity involved in manual labour were rhetorical icing on attempts to protect the postman's cake. The management and the union were often at odds regarding the solutions to recruitment problems, and this included disagreements over the recruitment of women. When postwomen were hired on different pay scales, the union pressed for equal pay in order to curb the recruitment of cheaper female labour. At the point when equal pay was achieved, the material position of the job had declined substantially. A shortage of postmen was a chronic feature of the postal job, and pressure from the Post Office to recruit women persisted. In an attempt to guard overtime hours and the claim for increased wages, the union negotiated conditions of service for postwomen that defined them as an official reserve labour force to be replaced when men became available for the job. The battle, from the postmen's point of view, was to keep the postal job a full-time job and, as we shall see in the next chapter, a "full-wage" job, and their strategy was to oppose categories of labour that were seen as a threat to these conditions – women and part-timers. The discomfort and hardship postwomen experienced as a consequence of the sex discrimination operating in their working environment cannot be minimized. Some of the hostility they faced from the "hard core" in the daily conduct of their job has been documented here. But it would be incorrect to give priority to this kind of macho posturing in the explanation of postwomen's disadvantaged employment conditions prior to 1975.

The continuing inequalities between women and men in waged work in Britain prohibits an enthusiastic assessment of the overall effectiveness of the Sex Discrimination Act. Nonetheless, changes in the formal conditions of employment in the postal and telephonist jobs in the Post Office count as one of its successes. Because of the legislation, access to both shifts of the telephonist job was equalized for women and men. The formal employment conditions and opportunities for postwomen were brought into line with those of postmen – partly because of the legislation per se, and partly because of the use to which the legislation could be put by the postwomen themselves. Since 1975, being female or male was of no consequence for the formal conditions of employment within the postal and telephonist jobs. In other words, sex discrimination as employment policy cannot explain why the jobs continued to have a skewed distribution of female and male workers.

Why did these jobs continue to employ more women or men? When respondents were asked for possible answers to this question, some did refer to aspects of their job tasks that they considered to be either coincident with "manliness" and, therefore, unattractive to women, or inconsistent with it and, therefore, unattractive to men. Others felt that more time was needed for past discrimination to work itself out of the system. At the same time, many of their accounts hit on two other factors that have always demarcated the day telephonist job from the night telephonist and postal jobs: hours and pay. Day telephonists are paid wages on which, it was said, a man could not support a family, and the other two jobs were described as ones in which it was possible for a woman to earn a man's wages. The hours worked by a day telephonist do not include unsocial hours as conventionally defined. By contrast, the night telephonist and postal job involve working unsocial hours on a permanent basis – hours that were described as atypical for women in employment.

The absence of dramatic change in the gender skew of the postal jobs after 1975 suggests the presence of a significant and relatively stable social process in the structuring of employment. The after-effects of previous hiring practices, or traditional definitions of appropriate employment for women and men, cannot account for one of the most striking features of the labour force employed in these jobs: the marked differences in the domestic circumstances of women and men employed as day telephonists, compared with women and men employed as night telephonists and postal workers. The jobs not only employed women and men in different proportions; they employed women and men in particular marital and family circumstances, with particular profiles of paid and unpaid work. In the next chapter, the relations between the circumstances of jobs and the wider social circumstances of the women and men employed within them are examined. This will include a consideration of a variety of features that place the postal and telephonist jobs, as well as postal workers and telephonists themselves, in a more general social context. By taking into account people's relations to domestic circumstances, as well as aspects of their social background, we shall be in a position to identify and explain the character of the continuing gender imbalance in the postal and telephonist jobs.

Notes

1. A condensed version of some of the information in these two chapters is presented in Siltanen (1986).
2. The London Sorting Office refers to the sorting office in which the study was conducted and is not the real name of that establishment. The same applies to the London Telephone Exchange.
3. As Treiman & Hartmann (1981) note, segregation studies at the level of "jobs" as opposed to "occupations" may find more intensive forms of gender segregation. They may also, as in this study, reveal predominantly male jobs within predominantly female occupations.
4. Following any quotations from transcriptions of interviews with respondents, the job, sex and interview number of the respondent are shown in parentheses. In cases where particular sorts of information would allow the identification of the person concerned, alterations have been made to details, but not to the overall sense of the quotation. Questions or interjections by the interviewer are contained in brackets and included in quotations in two circumstances only: when they are important to the sense of the quotation, and when they have directed responses in a particular way.
5. An earlier description of the postal job can be found in Young & Willmott (1973). Moran (1974) has done a study of the UPW and this includes an ac-

count of the jobs organized by the union. Less detailed, but more recent, descriptions can be found in Clinton (1984) and Cohn (1985).

6. The general figures for postmen's and postwomen's earnings were supplied by Postal Headquarters, Personnel Department, from the Post Office Earnings Survey. General earnings by shift were not available.

7. These correspond with Routh's figures for the general category of postman, male sorter, messenger. Men's wages in these jobs were approximately 85% of average full-time earnings throughout the decade, and 92% of the average full-time manual earnings from 1970 to 1973 (Routh 1980:175-6).

8. Postwomen and men were paid on the same scale. Gender differences in basic wages reflect differences in seniority and shift distribution.

9. See Clinton (1984) for a history of the Union of Post Office/Communication Workers.

10. UPW Research Department: Hain and Stagg, "Equal Pay Report", 1976; "Union History and Development – Points Re: Women", 1975.

11. Grint (1988:105) maintains that initially the UPW position was one of "resisting equal pay to inhibit feminization", changing later to support for equal pay for the same purpose. The account of events presented in this chapter differs from Grint in that it gives more emphasis to the UPW's direct attempts to halt or limit the recruitment of women to postal grades, and takes this as a major context for interpreting support for equal pay (see also Siltanen 1986).

12. Boston (1980:169); see also Grint (1988) for further details of the union's activities during this period.

13. Cohn (1985) over-emphasises the management interest in the marriage bar as a means of cost cutting by ensuring a "synthetic turnover". The UPW was equally supportive of the marriage bar as a means of protecting men's employment. Opinion amongst female members was divided on the issue (Clinton 1984:432), because abolition of the bar would mean the abolition of the marriage gratuity and greater competition for single women employees in gaining access to promoted posts.

14. The union continued, however, to use the marriage bar for its own staff until the mid-1960s (Clinton, 1984:433). Walby confuses this point when she argues that the UPW "ensured its operation in the Post Office until 1963" (Walby 1986:240).

15. Details of the agreement are set out in the "Package Agreement", volume 1, 1957.

16. The terms of this agreement stated that "females may be recruited and temporarily employed on work proper to postmen, provided they are replaced by males when they become available" (CHQ 89/55).

17. UPW reply to TUC questionnaire, 1961. Since there was recruitment of postwomen in the early 1950s, it seems reasonable to assume that the majority of the decrease happened after the 1955 agreement. There was no general decrease in the number of postmen over the same period.

18. There were in fact two pay rises, in May 1965 and again in January 1966. Between 1964 and 1966, the pay for the postal job improved from a range of £4 11s to £11 15s, to £5 17s with a top payment of £14 5s. (*Post Office Reports and Accounts 1963-64*, HMSO: 1964, and *1965-66*, HMSO: 1966).

19. Both quotations are from the *Head Postmasters' Manual B* (1968). Additional conditions were that the employment of either postwomen or part-time staff be confined to uncovered vacancies on full-time posts and that priority should be given to full-time postwomen over any part-time applicant of comparable quality.

20. From January to December 1972, the number of part-time postwomen increased by 985 (to 7682). There were also increases in the number of part-time postmen (by 352 to 2868) and full-time postwomen (by only 9 to 1155). During 1972 the number of postmen fell by 352 (to 94 031). From December 1972 to December 1973, the number of full-time postmen dropped by 3545 (as did part-time postmen by 314 and part-time postwomen by 18). The number of full-time postwomen increased by 279 (Post Office Manpower SBRD/M).

21. This, and following, information is from the *Conference Chronicle*, Union of Post Office Workers (1973).

22. Further discussion of these motions, and the debates that took place, can be found in Boston (1980:287-9).

23. The issue of part-time employment in the Post Office is complex. Part-time postal workers are paid the same rate as full-time workers and do not get paid overtime until they have worked the basic hours of a full-time worker. From the Post Office's point of view, therefore, part-time workers are a cheaper means of coping with staff shortages than either paying out overtime to full-time workers or increasing the basic wage to attract more full-time staff. The UPW's opposition to part-time labour is, in part, an attempt to protect the availability of overtime hours for full-time postwomen and postmen. As we have seen, overtime earnings are a substantial component of a full-time workers' average earnings. On the other hand, a policy of restricting part-time employment, and of making part-time workers redundant before full-time workers (as has been the case in some local agreements, see Counter Information Services 1976:15), is open to legal challenge under the Sex Discrimination Act (see *Industrial Relations Review and Report*, No. 186, 1978).

24. This included the condition that postwomen carry the same weight as postmen on deliveries. Previously postwomen carried 28 lb compared with postmen's 35 lb. This was a condition that some conference amendments attempted to head off by insisting that conditions be equalized to the most advantageous, but these were unsuccessful.

25. *Birmingham Post* of 2 August 1973 reported that Birmingham postwomen presented a petition in support of their claim signed by 400 Midland postwomen and postmen.

26. The mechanical work processes in the AMC were already quite outdated in the late 1970s. Over the 1980s both the AMC and DQ underwent technological innovation, principally the introduction of computerized systems.

27. Monitoring telephonists by "listening in" is practised in other countries. Langer (1972) discusses the supervision of telephonists in the US.

28. The exclusive access of men to night-shift work was not due to legislation, such as the Factories Act or its predecessors, which restricted the hours of women's employment in some industries. As a public corporation the Post Office was exempt. Cohn (1985) argues, however, that such legislation legitimated such arrangements.

29. In the earlier half of the 1970s, the ratio of male supervisors to male telephonists was also increasing but by a minimal amount. The ratio at the beginning of 1971 was 1:5.5, and by the end of 1974 it was 1:5.2. Absolute numbers of telephonists and telephonist supervisors declined during this period. Although the percentage decline in the male telephonist staff is greater than that for the female telephonist staff, the change in the supervisor to telephonist ratio for women and men is not just due to a differential decline in female and male telephonists. There was a greater absolute and percentage decline in female supervisors during this period. The number of female supervisors dropped by 978 (a decline of 23%) and the number of male supervisors dropped by 272 (a decline of 13%).
30. Examples of such case studies are in EOC (1985) and Walby (1988).
31. Those who have studied employment in the Post Office in earlier decades hold different positions on this point. Grint argues (1988:104) that occupational sex-typing did exist, "but its importance lay in its disaggregating consequences for women's participation in trade unionism, rather than in the construction of gender-related inequalities". By contrast, Cohn places great weight on "patriarchal management" and "legitimating ideologies". However, Cohn's evidence is weak and he himself admits (1985:130) that the "persistence of sex segregation in the Post Office is not easy to explain". He considers a number of factors but does not strongly endorse any of them, concluding (1985:133) that for "whatever reasons segregation survived, it nevertheless produced a small but real impact on women's economic opportunities".

Chapter Three

Occupational segregation:
full-wage and component-wage jobs

The creation and abolition of sexual divisions in the formal conditions of employment in the telephonist and postal jobs have been discussed. It is now time to widen the focus of this investigation and consider variations in employment experience in relation to respondents' social circumstances. In order to explain the existing distribution of women and men in the day telephonist, night telephonist and postal jobs, we need both a more precise understanding of the general social circumstances of the female and male labour force in each of the jobs and an appreciation of how variations in social circumstances are located as processes structuring relations to employment. We shall see that there are very clear patterns in relations between social circumstances and employment experiences, and that some patterns are coincident with differentiations in women's and men's experience while others are not.

This chapter is divided into three main sections. The first section begins the examination of the social profile of job incumbents, by outlining their position in the general structure of inequality. Neither postal workers nor telephonists are particularly well placed in relation to processes structuring the distribution of social resources. Yet, there were significant differences between them in the social background, of families of origin as well as past educational and occupational experience. There were also important distinctions within the two areas of employment in terms of social background and these will be outlined. Within the postal job, there was substantial variation by "race", particularly among postwomen. Within the telephonist job, certain groups of men were especially advantaged in terms of families of origin and education.

In the second section, a distinction is drawn between component-wage and full-wage jobs – a distinction that emphasizes the importance of domestic responsibilities in the structuring of women's and men's employment.[1] Here, the night telephonist job is aligned with the postal job in terms of the current domestic circumstances of incumbents and both stand in marked contrast to the circumstances of women and men in the day telephonist job. Particular attention is paid to the personal and domestic circumstances of incumbents when recruited to their current employment. The structure of financial obligation and household resources will be shown to correspond very closely with recruitment to component-wage and full-wage employment. The social circumstances of domestic life are not independent of social background or immediate claims on social resources. The relations between them will become apparent as the discussion in the chapter unfolds.

The final section provides a general overview of the data patterns discussed in the chapter and can be read as an alternative to the more detailed presentation.

Social background and employment

The postal and telephonist jobs involved the performance of routine tasks, the training for which was acquired after recruitment. Although specific types of pre-job experiences were not required for entry into either job, the social backgrounds of postal workers and telephonists were dissimilar in significant respects. As an employment option, the jobs stood in a different relation to general aspects of the structuring of social inequality such that the social background of postal workers was more disadvantaged than that of telephonists. The postal and telephonist jobs attracted, in short, a labour force with social backgrounds similar to those generally characteristic of non-skilled manual and routine non-manual workers, respectively. However, the social backgrounds of incumbents were more mixed than this strict division might suggest.

Before dealing with the social locations of telephonists and postal workers in more detail, it is necessary to introduce a major variation in the postal labour force. As discussed in the previous chapter, the postal job had a history of recruitment problems stemming largely from its declining income position and the inconveniences associated with shift work and a six-day week. Considering that it was also a non-skilled manual job, it is not surprising to find different "racial" groupings among its labour force.[2] Among the "racial minorities" in the sample of postal workers, women outnumbered men by over four to one. Thus, of the postal workers interviewed, racial minorities comprised 10% of the men and 46% of the women. No one in the racial minority groups was born in Britain. All had emigrated from their countries of origin, typically in their 20s. In contrast to the more diverse national origin of the men, all but two of the women emigrated from West Indian countries.[3] There was also some racial variation among the telephonists, but it was not as pronounced as in the postal job.[4] Racial difference was, then, a major feature of the social profile of postwomen and was much less prominent among the rest of the sample.[5]

The experiences of the black women and men, in terms of relations of social background and employment, diverged somewhat from those of the white women and men. Distinctions between postal workers and telephonists will, therefore, be established initially for the white sample, and the patterns relevant to their experiences will then be compared with those of the black sample.

Social background and employment: the white sample

The focus of this section is the locations of postal workers' and telephonists' social backgrounds within the general structure of social inequality. Father's occupation, mother's occupation, educational experience and previous employment are used as the principal measures of social background. Although the postal job employed more men than women, it drew both its female and male labour force from the same social stratum. Female and male telephonists were generally from a more advantaged social background than were postal workers. At the same time, there were important differences in social background within the telephonist labour force. The employment intentions of postal workers and telephonists are also presented as these clarify some aspects of relations between social background and current employment.

Postal workers and telephonists: general differences

Table 3.1 summarizes the main differences between postal workers and telephonists in terms of occupations of parents, education, and earlier employment experience. The relative disadvantage of postal workers can be seen in all three areas.

Whereas the majority of postal workers were from families in which parents held non-skilled manual jobs, telephonists were less likely to come from non-skilled manual backgrounds.[6] Indeed, close to one-quarter of telephonists had a parent whose main employment was in a professional or managerial job. Educational qualifications were not required for entry into the postal and telephonist jobs, and the largest part of both groups was unqualified. But telephonists were more advantaged with respect to education than postal workers. A larger percentage of telephonists had school qualifications, and they were more likely to have attended state selective or private schools.[7]

The postal job was rarely the first job held, and most postal workers

69

Table 3.1 Social background of postal workers and telephonists summary table (white sample).

	Postal workers	Telephonists
N	58	62
Father's occupation, % non-skilled manual	61	34
Mother's occupation, % non-skilled manual	89	57
Highest parental occupation, % professional/managerial	2	24
Education, % selective/public school	2	21
% qualified	24	39
First job, % non-skilled manual	79	44
Previous job, % non-skilled manual	86	54

had at least two previous jobs. Nevertheless, their current job was not dissimilar from the types of jobs held previously. For the vast majority of postal workers, both their first job on leaving school and their previous job, were non-skilled manual. For a significant number (one in six), their previous job was lost through redundancy. The employment histories of telephonists were characterized less by non-skilled manual work, although many had experience of such jobs. On leaving school, less than half of telephonists entered a non-skilled manual job, and of those who were employed prior to their current job, just over half held a non-skilled manual job.[8]

The social backgrounds of white postal workers were fairly homogeneous, and there were no notable differences by age or gender. This was not so for the telephonists. Although they were generally more advantaged than postal workers, there were important distinctions in the social backgrounds of telephonists that require discussion.

Distinctions among telephonists

The significant dimensions structuring social backgrounds of day and night telephonists are somewhat difficult to disentangle, in that the labour force of each shift is strongly patterned by age and gender. The day shift was generally younger as well as predominantly female. The sample is not up to sorting out the patterns definitively, but major groupings can be identified. Overall, two major groupings emerge. One group is composed of younger telephonists and older male telephonists on the day shift. The other group consists of night shift telephonists and older day-shift female telephonists. There are some noteworthy differences within these two groups, but generally they form two identifiable types of incumbents in the telephonist job.

The social background of telephonists is set out in Table 3.2, showing divisions by age, gender and, in some cases, shift. Younger male and

Table 3.2 Social background of telephonists by age, gender and shift (white sample).

	All telephonists	Under 30 Women	Men	30 and over Women	Men
N^1	62	10	11	19	22
N – day shift	38	9	7	15	7
N – night shift	24	1	4	4	15
Father's occupation					
% non-skilled manual	34	56	40	44	11
Mother's occupation					
% non-skilled manual	57	60	60	50	60
Highest parental occupation					
% professional/managerial					
Day shift	33	10	43	33	50
Night shift	17	0	0	25	23
Education					
% selective/public schools					
Day shift	26	0	57	15	57
Night shift	13	0	0	25	15
% qualified					
Day shift	53	67	71	27	71
Night shift	46	100	50	25	47

1. These numbers refer to the entire white sample. Percentages are sometimes based on smaller numbers owing to missing information.

female telephonists were from roughly similar family backgrounds in that non-skilled manual work was the main job for the majority of mothers and, to a lesser extent, fathers. There is a group of young male telephonists, however, who were from more advantaged non-manual families. They were on the day shift and 43% of them came from families in which the highest parental occupation was a professional or managerial job. This distinction in family background is carried into the type of education received. None of the younger female telephonists attended state selective or private schools, whereas over half of the younger day-shift men attended these schools. Yet the educational advantage of this group has not typically been realized. Those who attended state selective or private schools either attempted A levels and failed, or started but did not complete some form of career training or further education. Therefore, despite the disparity in schools attended, younger male and female telephonists were similar in terms of the percentage who were qualified and the level of qualification received.[9]

The younger male and female telephonists had more in common than their older counterparts. Differences between the older telephonists were most striking in the case of father's occupation and education. Compared with older men, older female telephonists were much more likely to come from a non-skilled manual background, to have attended state non-selective schools, and to be unqualified. In both attendance at more advantaged schools and achievement of qualifications, the older day-shift men resembled their younger day-shift colleagues, whereas the older day-shift women resembled night-shift workers.[10]

Employment experience immediately prior to the telephonist job was similar for women and men in the younger age group. Although young women were more likely than young men to enter the job straight from school, roughly two thirds of young women and men previously employed moved to the telephonist job from a routine non-manual job. It is again in the older age group of telephonists that substantial differences in previous employment experience appear, with older day shift women showing further similarity with the night shift staff.

Typically, older male telephonists had been employed full time continuously, and they entered the telephonist job from non-skilled manual employment (for example, milkman, security guard, hospital orderly). This was the case for almost two-thirds of the older men on both shifts. In addition, however, in the employment work histories of some older male telephonists there was movement up from routine non-manual employment (that is, to lower level professional or managerial jobs) prior to taking up the telephonist job. This was especially the case among older men with qualifications, particularly those on the day shift. Many of the older male telephonists had, as they put it, "retired" to their telephonist job. A large number of the older men recruited to the telephonist job said they left their previous job because they wanted a job with less responsibility and stress, or they left owing to work-related health problems.

The employment position prior to entering the telephonist job was very different for older female telephonists. One major difference between the older women and men was the general employment status of the women prior to their current job. Of the older female telephonists, 16% were not in paid employment immediately prior to taking up the telephonist job, 32% were employed part time and 53% were employed full time.[11] It appears that whereas some older men moved to the telephonist job from the peak of their occupational careers, many of the older women were resuming full-time employment following various accommodations to domestic circumstances. The previous job experience of the older female telephonists contrasted most sharply with the older day telephonist men, and there were similarities with the older night telephonists. As with the latter group, any non-manual experience of the older women was confined to routine levels. No one in either group matched the modest career advancement in non-manual jobs achieved by a number of the older day-shift men prior to their current job.

Employment intentions

Intentions with respect to current employment experience complete the picture of relations of social background and employment. The patterning of these intentions also foreshadows distinctions in domestic circumstances made at a later point.

Postal workers generally had no concrete plans to change their current employment situation by either leaving the Post Office or moving to another job within it. Their disadvantaged position in the general labour market and, as we shall see, their substantial financial obligations, both attracted them to, and kept them in, the relatively secure employment offered by the postal job. As described in the previous chapter, promotion possibilities from the postal job were limited and, in the case of PHG, involved losses that were often unacceptable. About 1 in 10 of postwomen and postmen planned to accept promotion to PHG and slightly fewer intended to try the numeracy tests required for internal recruitment to a "counter" job. Many dreamt of setting themselves up in their own businesses (fruit and veg stands, painting and decorating, or dressmaking), but a substantial number had been in their job for well over a decade (see Table 3.3) and it is highly probable that most were likely to see their postal job through to retirement.

Table 3.3 Number of years in current job by job, gender and recruitment age

| | Age at recruitment | N | Number of years in current job | | | |
			Under 5	5–9	10+	Mean
Day telephonist						
Women	Under 30	12	7	1	4	5.7
	30+	12	3	5	4	5.4
Men	Under 30	8	8	–	–	1
	30+	6	6	–	–	1
Night telephonist						
Women	Under 30	2	1	1	0	4.3
	30+	4	0	1	3	10.0
Men	Under 30	8	5	2	1	3.1[1]
	30+	12	1	2	9	12.9
Postal job						
Women	Under 30	5	1	4	0	5.7
	30+	34	6	16	12	7.9
Men	Under 30	21	8	7	6	9.4
	30+	20	3	4	13	12.8

1. Excludes one with 29 years' seniority.

73

Among the telephonists, older women on the day shift and night telephonists were also committed to their current employer. Very few were looking for employment with another employer. Indeed, a number were hoping to take advantage of the albeit limited career possibilities on offer from their current employer. For example, roughly one-third of older women on each shift were interested in becoming, or were already, substitution supervisors.

Those who were educationally advantaged in the sample – the younger telephonists and the older male day telephonists – had the least intention of staying either with their current employer or in their current job. Among the older male day telephonists, only one was not planning any employment moves at all. The most popular option pursued was a transfer to the night shift – a shift that offered a more congenial environment for those interested in a "retirement" job. The night shift also offered greater long-term security, since pension payments were calculated on the wage earned in the three years prior to retirement.

The group most actively seeking employment outside the Post Office were the young day telephonists. One-third of the young women and men were pursuing employment possibilities outside the Post Office to the point of formal enquiries or applications. In terms of options within the Post Office, the young telephonists were generally not interested in the supervisory career offered in the telephonist job. A telephonist job in an international exchange was a more attractive possibility for those intending to stay with their current employer, and many were thinking about this option. Considering all plans for changing employment, the majority of young male and female telephonists were not committed to their current job.

In short, the educationally advantaged groups in the sample had the least commitment to their current employment circumstances. Young day telephonists were the least committed to their current employer and older male day telephonists were the least committed to their current job. The older women day telephonists were highly committed to their current employment, as were night telephonists and postal workers in general. As we shall see later, these variations in relations to current employment are significant in interpreting aspects of employment experience and understandings.

Before moving on to further details concerning relations to employment in the postal and telephonist jobs, the social backgrounds of the black sample will be compared with those of the white sample.

Social background and employment: the black sample

Extensive comparisons between the white and black sample are not possible given the small numbers in the black sample.[12] The intention of the following discussion is to note several broad similarities with, and differences from, the social background of the white sample. Generally speaking, the social backgrounds of the black sample in the postal job were somewhat higher than those of the white sample, and among the higher social backgrounds in the night telephonist job.

Both black night telephonists had fathers and mothers who were employed in skilled manual or non-manual jobs. They were qualified and had an employment history that was similar to that of white night telephonists of equivalent social backgrounds. After leaving school, the first jobs in their countries of origin were non-manual jobs, as were the jobs they held in Britain prior to their current job. As in the white sample, the social backgrounds of the black postal workers were less advantaged compared with the telephonists.

In the families of origin of black postmen, the main occupation of half the fathers and half the employed mothers was a non-skilled manual job. All the black postmen were 30 years of age or over and, in contrast to the white postmen of this age, the majority had qualifications.[13] Typically, the first job held by the black postmen was in Britain and except for one case it was a non-skilled manual job. In short, the family background of white and black postmen was very similar and, despite differences in educational qualifications, so too were their respective employment histories.

The difference in family background was greater between black postwomen and white postwomen.[14] In terms of father's occupation, black postwomen were from a somewhat higher social background than that of white postwomen. Black postwomen were less likely to have fathers who were non-skilled manual workers. The largest proportion had fathers who were skilled manual workers, and several had fathers who were non-manual workers or came from farm-owning families.[15] There was no substantial difference between the white and black postwomen in terms of mother's occupation.

The ages of the black postwomen were even more homogeneous than was the case for white postwomen. With few exceptions, women in both groups were over 30 years old. However, whereas white postwomen were spread fairly evenly from 30 to 60, all black postwomen were in their 30s or 40s. This is important for locating differences in the proportion of each group that was qualified. In general, the number of black postwomen with at least school qualifications was double that of white postwomen. Comparing women in their 30s and 40s, the same proportion of the black and white postwomen had qualifications. The highest type of qualification in each group was also the same. In the age range under consideration, a small proportion of both groups of qualified women had minor professional qualifications. Although similarly qualified, reasons for not being in the profession they had trained for were different. The white postwoman had worked in her profession in Britain and left owing to particular financial pressures. The black women were employed in their professions in their countries of origin, but had not been able to translate this professional training and experience into a similar job in Britain.

Half the black postwomen held their first jobs in their countries of origin, and they were spread fairly evenly across non-skilled manual, skilled manual and non-manual jobs. After immigration to Britain, this group of black women had experienced a less advantaged occupational history. The jobs held in Britain before the postal job were, save one, non-skilled manual jobs, and of course they were all in a non-skilled manual job. The employment experience of the half whose first job was in Britain had not been substantially different from that of the white postwomen. Both groups had employment histories dominated by non-skilled manual jobs.

The social backgrounds of the black sample were, to sum up, somewhat divergent from those of the white sample in the postal and night telephonist jobs, but not dramatically so. The black night telephonists were from the higher types of family backgrounds found among white night telephonists – skilled manual or non-manual. Father's occupation for black postmen was, as for white postmen, primarily a non-skilled manual job. Family backgrounds of black postwomen were somewhat more advantaged, in that the majority of black postwomen were from families where fathers were less likely to be employed in non-skilled manual jobs than was typical for white postwomen. In line with what generally seemed to be the case among racial groups employed in Britain (Bruegel 1989, Brown 1984, Smith 1977), the black sample were proportionally more qualified than their white workmates. For postwomen, this appears to be a function of age differences. Although many of the black sample had an employment history similar in disadvantages to those of the white sample, some black postwomen who were initially employed in their countries of origin had experienced downward mobility when taking up employment in Britain.

Like most of the white sample in the night telephonist and postal jobs, the black women and men intended to stay with their current employer. The black postal workers were somewhat more likely to be considering a change of jobs within the Post Office. For example, about one in three black postwomen intended to apply for a counter job, especially women with school qualifications and previous experience of non-manual employment.

From this point onward, the black and white sample will not be distinguished except when experiences are divergent.

Domestic circumstances and employment: full-wage and component-wage jobs

We have seen how aspects of social background differentiate the postal and telephonist labour force, and some differences within each area of employment have been established. Further clarification of patterns of employment experience requires consideration of the domestic circumstances of the female and male labour force in the day telephonist, night telephonist and postal jobs. The domestic circumstances of the day telephonist labour force are distinctive. They contrast dramatically with the domestic circumstances of the labour force in the night telephonist and postal jobs. To characterize this contrast, the night telephonist and postal jobs will be referred to as "full-wage" jobs and the day telephonist job will be referred to as a "component-wage" job. This section begins with an explanation of the terms full-wage job and component-wage job, as well as a brief justification for using these terms to characterize the contrast between the day telephonist job and the night telephonist and postal jobs. This is followed by an analysis of the relations between domestic circumstances and the distribution of people in full-wage and component-wage jobs.

Full-wage and component-wage jobs

In Chapter 2, the jobs in this study were distinguished in terms of the sex composition of the labour force. Two jobs – night telephonist and postal worker – had a predominantly male labour force and one job – day telephonist – had a predominantly female labour force. Particular aspects of the jobs and the circumstances of their labour force will now be used to draw a distinction between the former as full-wage jobs and the latter as a component-wage job. These aspects are pay and relations to household maintenance.

Although one of the main differences between the full-wage and component-wage jobs was the higher pay of the former, the distinction does not rest solely on a quantitative difference in wages. The distinction is based on relations to household maintenance that individuals are able to sustain given the wages earned in the jobs. A full-wage job enables its incumbents to take sole responsibility for maintaining an independent

77

household, a responsibility that in some cases includes financial maintenance of other household members not in waged work. A component-wage job does not enable incumbents to be wholly responsible for the financial maintenance of a household. In other words, people in component-wage jobs contribute to the financial maintenance of households but do not have the resources to maintain an independent household single-handedly.

Three points should be clear from the outset. First, the designations full-wage and component-wage refer to the form of social relations enabled by the level of wages received. The full-wage designation implies the ability of incumbents to assume full responsibility as sole wage earners in their household. The standard of living at which they are able to do so is a separate issue, as full-wages could range from those just sufficient to support an independent household of a single adult to those more than sufficient for a household composed of a number of dependants. In principle it is possible, and it would certainly be desirable, further to differentiate types of full-wages. Some progress in this direction is discussed in the following chapter. The inability of component-wage earners to assume sole financial responsibility for their household also raises issues of social justice, as well as questions about definitions of low pay and minimum wages. These too are pursued in the following chapter. Secondly, as indicated above, some jobs may be more marginal as full-wage and component-wage jobs than others. This is certainly the case for the jobs considered here. The night telephonist and postal jobs were full-wage jobs only to the extent that extensive overtime was a regular component of earnings. Similarly, judging from information presented in the following chapter, the earnings of day telephonists were towards the upper end of component-wages. Some of the contrasts to be drawn between the circumstances of incumbents in full-wage and component-wage jobs are slightly subdued as a consequence of the marginal nature of the full-wage and component-wage jobs in this study. Nevertheless, differences in the domestic profile of incumbents are substantial enough to justify and illustrate the full-wage and component-wage designations. Thirdly, current relations to household financing and domestic circumstances, as well as an individual's position on recruitment, are taken as indicators of the full-wage or component-wage status of a job. For the group of people in this study, it is position at recruitment that is most telling. That this is so goes some way towards addressing the question about the causal processes involved. The pattern of contrasting domestic circumstances that exists between full-wage and component-wage workers at the point of recruitment indicates that such circumstances are part of the context in which individuals make decisions about changes in their employment status and position. Ways of improving the identification of full-wage and component-wage jobs, of differentiating between types of full-wages and of establishing minimum levels of full-wages are discussed in Chapter 4.

The characterization of the day telephonist job as a component-wage job and the night telephonist and postal jobs as full-wage jobs is justified in that a sizeable proportion of night telephonists and postal workers were maintaining dependants and households as the sole wage earner, whereas the proportion doing so in the day telephonist job was substantially less. One in every two incumbents of the full-waged jobs was providing the only wage coming in to his or her household – 56% of the women and 48% of the men. In addition, one-third of these women and over half of the men were the sole providers for households containing dependent children. In contrast, a considerably lower proportion (approximately one in four) of women and men in the component-wage job was solely responsible for the financial maintenance of a household of any sort, and apart from one case, not one of these households contained dependent children. As sole wage earners, people in the component-wage job are typically supporting themselves only, often as boarders in rented accommodation. They were not, in other words, fully responsible for the maintenance of even a one person household. The majority of component-wage earners contributed to more substantial households along with other wage earners. When information about incumbents' personal and household circumstances at the point of recruitment is considered, the relations to household maintenance of those recruited to full-wage and component-wage jobs are even more distinct.

Domestic circumstances and the distribution of people to jobs

In examining variations in the domestic circumstances of the labour force in component-wage and full-wage jobs, patterns of experience will come into sharper focus. The women and men recruited to component-wage and full-wage jobs were in different stages of family life cycles and domestic circumstances. Further, the women and men in the two types of jobs stood in a contrasting position in relation to standard employment patterns associated with the female and male labour force. Women and men in the jobs typical for their sex had a domestic profile in relation to employment that was similar to the standard pattern in the general female and male labour force. Women and men in the jobs atypical for their sex were in very particular domestic circumstances. In examining patterns of employment in relation to domestic circumstances, the age at which people were recruited to the jobs, a brief account of the variation in domestic circumstances at recruitment, and patterns in job

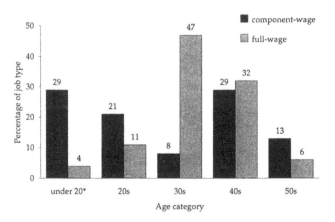

Figure 3.1 Age at recruitment to full-wage and component wage jobs: women. *The percentage recruited in the under-20 age group is based on a 5-year period rather than a 10-year period.

tenure are presented first. This is followed by a more extensive analysis of the current marital and family circumstances of the female and male labour force in component-wage and full-wage jobs.

The distribution of women's age at recruitment to component-wage and full-wage jobs is illustrated in Figure 3.1. The difference between the two types of jobs is striking. For women in the component-wage job, the distribution of recruitment age is similar in structure to the economic activity rates of the female population generally: it is bi-modal. The first peak in recruitment is in the under 20 age category: 29% of female day telephonists are recruited at this age. Recruitment was less in the 20s (21%) and dropped sharply to the lowest point in the 30s. Only 8% of female day telephonists were recruited in their 30s. Recruitment increased again in the 40s to the second peak (29%) and then declined to 13% in the 50s. The bi-modal recruitment age pattern for women in the component-wage job is in marked contrast to the recruitment age pattern for women in full-wage jobs. It is precisely in the age category when recruitment to the component-wage job dropped – the 30s – that recruitment to the full-wage jobs was at its peak: 47% of women entered full-wage jobs in their 30s. Few women were recruited to the full-wage jobs under the age of 30 and recruitment in the 40s and 50s was similar for both types of job. Black postwomen were recruited at a younger age than were white postwomen and, as we shall see later, this corresponds with some differences in their domestic circumstances. The average age of recruitment for black postwomen was 33, and of women recruited to full-wage jobs in their 30s, 68% were black. The average age of recruitment for white postwomen was 40, and of the women recruited to full-wage jobs in their 40s, 85% were white.

The high recruitment of women in the childrearing age range to full-wage jobs is coincident with differences in the family circumstances of women at the point of recruitment to the two types of jobs. Two-thirds of postwomen had dependent children when they entered their current job. This was particularly the case for the black postwomen – all but two had dependent children when recruited to the postal job. Approximately half of the white postwomen had dependent children when recruited. Both night telephonists recruited onto the night shift had dependent children when they entered their current job. Only one-quarter of day telephonist women were in a similar family position.

In addition to differences in the family circumstances of women when recruited to full-wage or component-wage jobs, marital situations were also divergent. For example, although similar proportions of women in the full-wage jobs and component-wage jobs were recruited when aged 40 or over, the marital circumstances of the women in this age group varied by job type. In the component-wage job most women were married, whereas in the postal job in particular the majority were divorced, separated or widowed.

Table 3.3 shows the number of years women had been employed in the component-wage and full-wage jobs. Coincident with the bi-modal recruitment age pattern for women in the day telephonist job, there is no relation between recruitment age and job tenure. In both the younger and older age groups, women day telephonists had been in their job for approximately five and a half years. Although the younger age groups in all jobs had a similar length of job tenure, there were differences among the older group of women. Those in full-wage jobs had been in their jobs for a longer period of time. This reflects both the greater recruitment of women in their 30s to full-wage jobs and a longer length of average job tenure generally.[16]

Thus, older women who entered full-wage jobs had, at the point of recruitment, greater financial obligations with respect to domestic responsibilities. They were typically recruited at an earlier age than older women who entered the component-wage job, and had been in their jobs a longer period of time.

The distribution of men's age at recruitment to component-wage and full-wage jobs is illustrated in Figure 3.2. The distribution of recruitment age to the component-wage job is strongly skewed towards the younger ages. Recruitment to the component-wage job is highest for men in the 20s (44%) and is at a low point of 14% in all other age categories. In the telephonist job, young men were more likely to have had previous em-

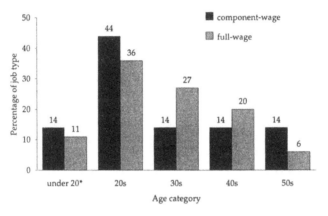

Figure 3.2 Age at recruitment to full-wage and component-wage jobs: men.
*The percentage recruited in the under-20 age group is based on a 5-year period rather than a 10-year period.

ployment experience than the young women, and their modal category of recruitment age is older. Although there was some recruitment of men aged 40 or over to the day telephonist job (28%) it was less than the recruitment of women in this age range (42%). The distribution of men's age at recruitment to the full-wage jobs is less skewed and there is a more gradual decline in recruitment of men aged 30 or over. As in the component-wage job, recruitment of men to full-wage jobs was concentrated in the 20s.

Despite the single peak in the 20s in both types of jobs, there was an important difference in the domestic responsibilities carried by men of this age when recruited to component-wage and full-wage jobs. For example, all of the men recruited to the day telephonist job in their 20s were single. Of the men who started the night telephonist job when they were in their 20s, the majority were married and, of these, most had dependent children at the point of recruitment. The situations of the younger postmen show even greater levels of domestic responsibility. Almost all who started the postal job in their 20s were married with pre-school age children. Indeed, the timing of entry into the postal job is closely related to the birth of the first child. Among the married male postal workers who have ever had children, over half entered their current job either at the birth of their first child or when their first child was of pre-school age. The man who said he came into the postal job "to get a secure job, before we went into a baby" (page 00) seems to be expressing a common experience.

82

All day telephonist men were recruited in the two years prior to the interviews so they had no established pattern of job tenure (see Table 3.3). It was likely, however, to be fairly short since, as we saw previously, most of the younger and older day telephonist men did not intend to stay in their job. It was noted above that, in the younger recruitment age groups, the postmen were in domestic circumstances with the heaviest financial obligation when recruited to their job, and here we see that they also had the longest period of job tenure among the younger age group.

For both women and men, family and marital circumstances at the point of recruitment appear to be related to both patterns of recruitment and job tenure in component-wage and full-wage jobs. The relations between current domestic circumstances and employment are presented now in more detail. Understanding the importance of domestic experiences in the distribution of men in the two types of jobs is relatively straightforward, and the following analysis begins with the key feature in this process – marital status. After considering further aspects of relations between domestic and employment experiences for men, the analysis moves on to consider the more complex structuring of the women's domestic circumstances and their relation to variations in the distribution and experience of women in the different jobs.

Men: domestic and employment relations

Table 3.4 presents the job distribution of women and men who were single, married or previously married (divorced, separated or widowed). It is evident from these data that whether or not men have ever been married is a crucial factor in their distribution between component-wage and full-wage jobs. Although just over half of single men were in a full-

Table 3.4 Marital status by job and gender.

| | Single | | Married | | Previously Married | | Totals |
	N	%	N	%	N	%	N
Men							
Day telephonist	12	48	1	2	1	17	14
Night telephonist	7	28	10	23	3	50	20
Postmen	6	24	33	75	2	33	41
Total	25	100	44	100	6	100	75
Women							
Day telephonist	9	60	12	39	3	13	24
Night telephonist	1	7	0		5	22	6
Postwomen	5	33	19	61	15	65	39
Total	15	100	31	100	23	100	69

wage job, the percentage for married men was 98%, and for previously married men, 83%. The relationship between ever married/never married and employment in a full-wage or component-wage job is, for men, a strong one,[17] and it is consistent with other research that demonstrates the positive financial return that employment bestows on married men (Joshi 1987:130, Treiman & Roos 1983:642).

Being a single man appears to coincide with greater variation in financial obligations and, indeed, the component-wage and full-wage jobs employed single men of different ages and in different household circumstances. For example, roughly two-thirds of the single men under 30 were in the component-wage job, and all but one were in households with other wage earners. In fact, the majority of young single day telephonist men were still living in their families of origin, paying something towards their room and board but by no means covering the full cost of their maintenance. This contrasts with the single men aged 30 or over: roughly two-thirds were in the full-wage jobs and were independent householders, paying commercial rents or mortgages. We may also speculate that the older single men were more likely to have financial obligations towards other family members (such as aged parents).

Two factors have been identified in the processes underlying the distribution of men to component-wage or full-wage jobs. The first, and most important, is marital status. Married men were a small minority among men in the component-wage job, whereas they were the overwhelming majority of men in full-wage jobs. Clearly, the full-wage jobs were primarily married men's jobs and the component-wage job was mainly a job for single men. The second factor involved in the distribution of men to the two types of job differentiates the single men. This factor is age. There were single men employed in full-wage jobs and most of them were in the older age group. The single men in the component-wage job were younger. Indeed, half of the men employed in the component-wage job were single and under the age of 30.

The domestic circumstances (family status and employment status of spouse) of married men in the full-wage jobs are shown in Table 3.5.[18] As we already know, a substantial percentage of married men in full-wage jobs were supporting a non-waged spouse (37%). For the most part, however, wives were in employment, typically in non-manual jobs, with just over half of employed wives in part-time jobs. If we express the average take-home pay of wives as a percentage of the average earnings of their husbands, we can get an indication of the contribution of the women's earnings to their household.[19] The average take-home pay of wives of night telephonists was 30% of husband's earnings for wives working part time and 65% for wives employed full-time. Postmen's wives took home 26% of their husband's earnings as part-time workers

Table 3.5 Domestic circumstances of married men in full-wage jobs, showing average number of overtime hours per week.

	No children		Dependent children		Children not dependent		Total	
	N	%	N	%	N	%	N	%
Employment status of spouse								
Employed full time	4	50	4	18	4	31	12	28
Employed part time	1	13	8	36	6	46	15	35
Not employed	3	38	10	45	3	23	16	37
Total	8	19	22	51	13	30	43	100
Average number of overtime hours per week								
Night telephonists	–		17.4		0.0			
Postmen	10.4		11.4		7.6			

and 62% on average per week as full-time workers. It is clear that,
although significant in many respects, women's financial contributions
to the household were limited by gendered inequalities in earnings from
full-time and particularly part-time employment. The general differences between the social capacities of women's and men's full-time
wages, in terms of relations to household financing, are outlined in more
detail in the next chapter.

In cases where there were dependent children in the family, the claims
on the full-wages of the postal and night telephonist jobs were of even
greater weight. Half of the married men in full-wage jobs had dependent
children and, for a large number of them, the youngest child was pre-
school age. Close to half of those with dependent children were also providing financial support for their spouse. Only a small minority of
married men with dependent children were sharing financial responsibilities with another full-time worker. In fact, most of this small group
were expecting their first child and their wives intended to stop paid
work for a period of time. The employment profile of wives of full-wage
husbands with dependent children was fairly representative of couples
with dependent children of the time. According to figures from the more
representative General Household Survey, 46% of employed husbands
with dependent children were supporting an unwaged spouse, while
39% had wives in part-time employment and 15% had wives employed
full time.[20] For men in the full-wage jobs, the comparable percentages
were 45%, 36% and 18%.

In the case of these more disadvantaged forms of full-wage jobs, men
with dependent children were working both unsocial and long hours.
Postmen with dependent children typically worked the shifts with the

higher bonus payments – earlies or nights. Although married postmen with no children did a large amount of overtime, married men with dependent children also did a high number of overtime hours per week. Postmen with dependent children averaged 11.4 overtime hours per week and night telephonists averaged 17.4 overtime hours per week. As others have noted, the excessive hours that men often have to work in order to maintain a household financially while children are dependent, restricts their enjoyment of and participation in domestic and family life (Moss 1980, Rimmer 1988). Time for family life is a significant issue for men with dependent children, as discussed in Chapter 6.

It is obvious from these data that men in the job atypical for their sex – the component-wage day telephonist job – were not typical of the range of domestic circumstances found among the male labour force. For the most part, they were single, half were under the age of 30, and many were still living in their families of origin. The men in jobs typical for their sex – the full-wage night telephonist and postal jobs – had domestic commitments representative of married men in the general male labour force. For close to a quarter of married men in the full-wage jobs, financial pressures were at a high point. Their wages were supporting dependent children and a dependent wife. As with the men, patterns of standard and non-standard relations to employment and domestic commitments also emerge for women.

Women: domestic and employment relations

The bi-modal pattern in age of recruitment to the component-wage job resembles the overall pattern of activity rates in the general female population, and reflects the significance of the family life cycle in structuring women's employment participation. In terms of more detailed aspects of domestic circumstances in relation to employment, the day telephonist women were again more characteristic of the general female labour force than were women in full-wage jobs. In addition, black women had a pattern of employment in relation to domestic commitments that had more in common with typical male experience than with that of white women.

Variations in both marital status and job distribution between the white and black women are considerable. None of the single women, 39% of the married women and 30% of the previously married women were black.[21] As is the case with men, having ever been married is associated with full-wage employment among the black women in the sample. In fact, as Table 3.6 shows, all the married and previously married black women were employed in full-wage jobs. Although we would by no means suggest on the basis of this information that black women have easy or general access to full-wage employment, it is very clear

Table 3.6 Marital status by job type for black and white women.

Job type	Single		Married		Previously married		Totals	
	N	%	N	%	N	%	N	%
Black women								
Component-wage	0	0	0	0	0	0	0	0
Full-wage	0	0	12	100	7	100	19	100
White women								
Component-wage	9	60	12	63	3	19	24	48
Full-wage	6	40	7	37	13	81	26	52
Total	15	100	19	100	16	100	50	100

from the literature that many black women do carry extensive domestic obligations as wage earners. Generally, Afro-Caribbean women have the highest employment activity rate of all groups of women in Britain. For example, the third PSI survey (Brown 1984:186) showed that whereas white women have an economic activity rate of 46%, with 21% in full-time employment, West Indian women have an activity rate of 74%, with 41% in full-time employment. Married West Indian women are much more likely to be in employment when their children are dependent, particularly during the pre-school years, and they are more likely to be employed full time.[22] They are, in short, full-time wage earners for dependent families to a greater extent than is the case for white women. In this respect, a point that has already been mentioned is worth repeating here. Most of the married black women who had children entered their full-wage job when their children were still dependent.

For white women in the sample there was some variability in job distribution, in that roughly half were in component-wage jobs and half in full-wage jobs. The significant difference between white women and both the black women and the men is in the distribution of married people. Whereas married black women and married men were in full-wage jobs, the majority of married white women were in the component-wage job. Among white women, a terminated marriage seems to be a key domestic feature of those in full-wage jobs.[23] Indeed, for previously married women in the full-wage jobs, the length of time in their current job coincided with the number of years since the termination of their marriage. Those whose marriage ended 10 or more years ago had been in their current job an average of 10.3 years. Those whose marriage ended less than 10 years ago had been in their current job an average of 5.9 years. Just over half of the previously married women entered their full-wage job within one or two years of the termination of their marriage.

Further details on the impact of marital breakdown on women's work histories are presented in Chapter 5.

The last point to note, as regards the marital status of white women in component-wage and full-wage jobs, concerns the distribution of single white women. As with the single men, the distribution of single women to full-wage or component-wage jobs varied by age. Most single women under 30 were employed in the component-wage job, compared with the case of older single women, who were mainly employed in the full-wage jobs. Again this variation appears to coincide with different relations to domestic circumstances for the single women. A substantial number of the younger ones were still in their families of origin, while typically older single women were supporting independent one adult households.

We have seen above that previously married white women and ever married black women were concentrated in the full-wage jobs, whereas married white women were concentrated in the component-wage job. Another contrasting experience is current family status (see Table 3.7). The majority of married black women were supporting dependent children via their full-wage earnings, and the same was true for a good proportion of previously married black and white women (43% and 31%, respectively). The contrast in current family status between the full-wage married black women and the component-wage married white women is marked: compared with 58% of the former, 17% of the latter were supporting dependent children.[24] Further, although a small number of married women in component-wage jobs were supporting dependent children, their children were older. All dependent children of the married white component-wage women were over the age of 10, whereas a substantial proportion of the dependent children of the black married full-wage women were younger than 10, and some were pre-school age.

All of the full-wage women supporting dependants worked unsocial hours, and many worked a large number of overtime hours. Several of

Table 3.7 Family status by marital status and job type for black and white women.

	Black women				White women			
	Married		Previously married		Previously married		Married	
							Component-wage	
	Full-wage		Full-wage		Full-wage			
Family status	N	%	N	%	N	%	N	%
No children	1	8	0	0	2	15	5	42
Dependent children	7	58	3	43	4	31	2	17
Children not dependent	4	33	4	57	7	54	5	42
Total	12	100	7	100	13	100	12	100

the postwomen with dependent children worked the early shift. Frequently the husbands of the married postwomen worked an opposite shift, so that one parent saw to the children in the morning and the other at night – an arrangement Young & Willmott (1973:200) dubbed "the working-class variant of the 'dual career' family". For single-parent women, none of the postal shifts was ideal, but the early shift was most popular because it provided the possibility for time off in the afternoons for shopping and the women were able to fetch their children from school. Often someone was hired (or a neighbour or relative was relied upon) for a couple of hours in the morning to get the children up, fed and off to school. Although the early shift offered the possibility of "free" afternoons for single-parent postwomen, this flexibility existed more in theory than in practice. Single-parent postwomen did the highest number of overtime hours, averaging 15.2 per week.[25] A large proportion of other full-wage women with dependent children also clocked in at least an extra day of overtime on average per week: single-parent night telephonists averaged 12.5 hours and married postwomen 7.9. Despite their lower wages and regardless of family status, component-wage women almost never worked overtime hours. In Chapter 6, we shall see that these contrasting experiences of "motherhood" between full-wage and component-wage women feature prominently in their perceptions of inequalities in opportunities for participation in family life.

Finally, it is important to indicate that the domestic circumstances of married women in component-wage and full-wage jobs are distinguished also in terms of the financial resources of husbands. The husbands of white and black postwomen were the least advantaged, with the husbands of white postwomen worst off. Both groups of husbands were concentrated in non-skilled manual work, though this is particularly the case for the husbands of white postwomen. In addition, husbands of postwomen took home roughly the same wages as their wives, although again many of the white postwomen were contributing more financially to the household than their husbands. These circumstances were far removed from those of married component-wage women, who had husbands with take-home pay 130% greater than their own. In terms of potential claims on other financial resources in the household, the married day telephonist women were better off than the married black and white postwomen.[26]

This section has introduced the distinction between full-wage and component-wage jobs, and has shown the differences in domestic relations entailed in the distinction. The general process underlying the distribution of people across the two types of employment encompasses variations in domestic circumstances and relations to household maintenance. Within this general process there is a gender-specific pattern, and within the female sample there is variation by racial group. Both the general and specific patterns identified are especially apparent at the point of recruitment, but are also evident in patterns of current marital and family circumstances.

The structuring of employment experience: an overview

It should be clear from the information presented in this chapter that, while one of the main features of the telephonist and postal jobs is their skewed sex composition, the social circumstances of the women and men employed in the jobs vary strongly in particular ways. Each job continued to be characterized by a gender-segregated labour force, but the processes underlying the distribution of women and men in the different jobs encompass a patterning of social circumstances that is more extensive than this simple characterization implies.

Employment in the telephonist and postal jobs was structured by both general social resources and relations to household maintenance. Within the overall structuring of employment opportunities and social resources, all of the jobs were poorly placed. They offered little in the way of career prospects and were not well paid. There were, however, two significant divisions between the jobs. First, because of the non-manual nature of the telephonist job, it was in the lower range of employment options for people from slightly more advantaged social backgrounds. Secondly, because of bonus payments for the unsocial hours worked in the night telephonist and postal jobs, plus the ability to boost earnings by working overtime, these two jobs were full-wage jobs, albeit marginal ones. A larger percentage of the labour force in the night telephonist and postal jobs were sole wage earners in their households, and in many cases their households included dependent children. Details of these two patterns are summarized below.

In terms of opportunities afforded by education and families of origin, the postal workers were the least advantaged. They came from non-skilled manual families of origin and low educational backgrounds. Their employment experience had been mainly in non-skilled manual jobs. Some postwomen in the black sample had seen a deterioration in their employment experience since taking up employment in Britain, and there was some evidence of the black sample having better educational resources than their white counterparts. Generally, however, both the black and the white sample of postal workers shared past and current disadvantaged circumstances. Compared with postal workers, telephonists were better placed in relation to the structuring of opportunities, but there were important differences within the telephonist labour force. Two groups of telephonists could be distinguished. One group was composed of the night telephonists and the older women on the day shift. In contrast to the postal workers, they were somewhat more advantaged with respect to occupational experience and education. The main distinguishing feature between the postal workers and this group of telephonists was the social locations of families of origin. The night telephonists and older women on the day shift were more likely to come from non-manual families of origin. The second distinctive group of telephonists was composed of the young, and older male, day telephonists. This group was the most educationally qualified of all the sample. In addition, the men attained their qualifications at higher types of schools and were from the most advantaged families of origin.

The fact that this latter group of telephonists was in a job that required no educational qualifications, offered minimal career prospects, and was badly paid appears out of line with the relative advantages they had in terms of social background. In this context, it is significant that they were precisely the people who had the least commitment to their current job. Compared with the other telephonists, the overwhelming majority of younger telephonists and older men on the day shift hoped to leave their current job, and many had already initiated action to this effect.

The social circumstances of the most advantaged group of telephonists were similar in another respect. Typically, they were single and had no extensive financial commitments with regard to the maintenance of households. Indeed, many of the younger day telephonists were still living in their families of origin. The financial obligations of the older male day telephonists were generally greater, in that most were independent householders, and a large proportion of them had applied to transfer to the telephonist job that provided a higher wage – the night shift.

The older female day telephonists had longer term intentions regarding their current employment, but they too were in domestic circumstances in which their wages contributed to the financial maintenance of households, rather than acted as the sole financial support of households. Although similarly placed with the night telephonists in relation to the structuring of opportunities, the older day telephonist women were distinguished from the night-shift workers in that they had less demanding financial commitments. They shared financial maintenance with a husband who was employed full time and earning the highest wages of all husbands of married women in the sample. Finally, they were in households that typically were not providing for dependent children and would not be doing so in the future.

Variations in relations to household maintenance structure the distribution of people to component-wage or full-wage jobs. The nature of the domestic circumstances of the women and men in the day telephonist job was crucial to their being able to sustain employment, for longer or shorter periods of time, in a job that provides a component-wage. In contrast, although the night telephonist and postal jobs may have employed people from somewhat different social backgrounds, they were aligned as jobs in which a substantial proportion of the labour force were solely responsible for the financial maintenance of a household. They were, in this sense, full-wage jobs, and many in the full-wage jobs were also providing for unwaged household members.

Underlying the distribution of men in full-wage and component-wage jobs is primarily a differentiation by marital status. Men who had ever been married were in full-wage jobs and they had relations to household maintenance that were representative of the range of circumstances in the households of the general male labour force. The distribution of single men to the two types of jobs is differentiated by age – older single men constituted a greater proportion of single men employed in full-wage jobs and younger single men predominated in the component-wage job.

Underlying the distribution of women in the full-wage and component-wage jobs is, in the first place, a differentiation between white and black women in terms of typical patterns in employment experience, and, in the second place, marital breakdown among white women. All of the ever married black women were in full-wage jobs, and a large proportion of them were supporting dependent children. Typically, black women were recruited to the full-wage jobs in their 30s, that is, at a time when many white married women had withdrawn from the labour force. There is a dramatic difference in the type of job held by married and previously married white women. For white women, it was the termination of a marriage that was related to employment in a full-wage job. Previously married white women, many of whom were lone parents, were usually recruited to full-wage jobs around their 40th birthday. Most married white women were in the component-wage job, along with younger single women. The distribution of white women's age at recruitment to the component-wage job forms a bi-modal pattern similar to the profile of employment activity in the general female population.

Instead of a stark gender distinction as the general characteristic of occupational segregation, the above patterns suggest greater complexity in the structuring of employment distributions. Gender distinctions are significant, but they are located within a more general process – a process encompassing contrasting relations to household maintenance between the (male and female) incumbents of full-wage and component-wage jobs. Overall, those who were in employment typical for their sex (the full-wage men and the component-wage women) had a standard

92

gendered pattern of employment in relation to domestic circumstances. The reverse is true for those in employment atypical for their sex. The particular nature of the domestic circumstances of men in the component-wage job, and of women in the full-wage jobs, is of major importance in explaining their position in jobs where their gender was in the minority.

Throughout the discussion of the contrasts in the domestic profiles of full-wage and component-wage workers, there is a tension between circumstances at single points in time (such as at recruitment) and the variation in circumstances across the life course. To give some indication of how an individual's current full-wage or component-wage employment sat in relation to their past domestic and employment experiences, Chapter 5 will examine the work histories of women with children. This investigation helps to confirm the sociological relevance of the distinction between full-wage and component-wage jobs, and further elucidates relationships between patterns of occupational segregation and patterns of wage inequality. Before turning to these investigations, however, it is necessary to ask whether the contrast between full-wages and component-wages has validity beyond the boundaries of the jobs in this study.

The distinction between full-wages and component-wages is an attempt to examine the adequacy of wages in terms of access to specific social capacities in the maintenance of households. The current domestic circumstances of incumbents, as well as circumstances at recruitment, have been used as indicators of the full-wage or component-wage status of jobs. Although this is an instructive exercise, and the Post Office sample has been very useful in this respect, a generalized version of the full-wage and component-wage distinction is desirable. It is possible to define this distinction in the social capacities of wages more directly, and in a manner that would facilitate a general assessment of women's and men's wages. Further, it is clear that there are significant divisions to be established within the full-wage category. These are the tasks of the following chapter.

Notes

1. This distinction was first introduced in Siltanen (1986).
2. Racial groups are not equally likely to be engaged in non-skilled manual jobs. According to the PEP report (Smith 1977), racial minority men were employed in non-skilled manual jobs to a greater extent than white men, but only Pakistani men were heavily concentrated in non-skilled manual jobs. West Indian, Indian and African Asian men were more likely to be employed in skilled manual jobs, and more so than white men. Shift work had greater

prominence among minority men, again particularly among Pakistani men. In the female labour force, approximately half of West Indian, African Asian and Indian women were in non-skilled manual jobs. This contrasts with 29% of white women. Although the concentration of racial minorities in non-skilled manual jobs was higher than for the white labour force, this concentration was not over all industries. Those most likely to be in transport and communication industries were West Indians, Indians and African Asians. As Brown (1984) demonstrates, these general differences persisted over the 1970s and into the 1980s.

3. The national origins of the men were Ghana, Jamaica, Pakistan and Uganda.

4. All day telephonists interviewed were white. Among the night telephonists interviewed, all but two were white and British born.

5. With only a few exceptions, those who immigrated to Britain came from black countries and they themselves were black. The exceptions were of Asian origin. For ease of reference, those who immigrated will be referred to as black women and men, or collectively as the black sample. Where differences in national origin within the black sample are significant, this is noted. The white people in the study will be referred to collectively as the white sample.

6. Non-skilled refers to unskilled and semi-skilled manual jobs. Occupations of fathers and mothers are the main paid occupations held by each. Percentages for mother's occupation are based on the number who were employed after marriage. For the relationship between employment in the postal and telephonist jobs and both mother's occupation and father's occupation (non-skilled manual versus higher level jobs), chi-square is significant at 0.01, and phi is 0.27 and 0.34, respectively.

   Typically in this study, chi-square is used as the test of statistical significance. In tables where any cell has an expected frequency less than 10, the issue of correction for continuity arises. In cases where an expected frequency is less than 10, and where all marginal frequencies are greater than 50, both raw and Yate's corrected chi-square are reported. In 2×2 tables where expected frequencies are less than 10, and all marginal frequencies are 50 or less, the Fisher's Exact Test is used in preference to correcting chi-square for continuity (Bradley 1968; Finney et al. 1963).

7. For the difference between postal workers and telephonists in terms of those qualified, chi-square is significant at 0.01, phi = 0.28. For both postal workers and telephonists, age was related to the possession of qualifications. Of the postal workers who were qualified, over half were under 30 years of age. In this younger group, 58% were qualified whereas only 15% of the older group had qualifications. To a very large extent the difference between the two age groups was a consequence of the younger group holding lower level qualifications (CSE) unavailable to the older group. Of the telephonists under 30, two-thirds had qualifications and the majority had O level or A level passes. Of those aged 30 or over, 41% had qualifications. Therefore, even when the different age profiles of the occupations are taken into account, the telephonists had a higher educational background.

8. For the difference in the first job held by telephonists and postal workers

(non-skilled manual versus other jobs), chi-square is significant at 0.001, phi = 0.37; and for the difference in the previous job, chi-square is significant at 0.001, phi = 0.35.

9. There is no significant difference between younger female and male telephonists in terms of the extent of parental involvement in non-skilled manual work or qualifications. For the difference in type of schooling, Fisher's exact = 0.03, phi = 0.68.

10. Comparing the extent of qualifications across the generations highlights the similarity between older male telephonists and their younger counterparts. For men, there is no significant relationship between educational qualifications and age, and phi is extremely low at 0.01. For women, however, there is a relationship: Fisher's exact = 0.03, and phi = 0.42.

11. This compares with the 15% of postwomen who entered their job from full-time domestic work. However, more postwomen were in full-time employment immediately prior to the current job.

12. There were 24 people in the black sample, with the following job distribution: 4 postmen, 18 postwomen, 1 male and 1 female night telephonist.

13. It is obviously difficult to compare qualifications across the range of ages in the 30 or over age group. Nevertheless, differences in educational attainment between black and white postmen do not appear to be due to a different age distribution in the two older age groups.

14. The discussion of father's and mother's occupation for the black postwomen is based on 16 of the 18 in this group. Information on education and employment histories of the black postwomen is based on the entire group.

15. It is difficult to know, with the information available, exactly how to locate those whose fathers owned farms, but even if we count them as non-skilled manual, fathers of the black postwomen were less likely to be non-skilled manual workers (7 out of 16) and more likely to be skilled manual workers than were fathers of the white postwomen.

16. The lower average job tenure for older postwomen compared with older female night telephonists is due mainly to the history of recruitment in the postal job. In the London Sorting Office, postwomen were hired again in 1965 following the final purge of female temporary labour, and, consequently, no postwoman in the London Sorting Office had been in her job for more than 14 years.

17. The significance level of chi-square (raw and corrected) is less than 0.001, phi = 0.53.

18. Family status refers to the presence or absence of dependent children. It has three categories: no children, dependent children and children not dependent. For the definition of a dependent child, an amalgam of the General Household Survey and census definitions is used. A dependent child is under the age of 16, or aged 16-24 and in full-time education. Only one person (a woman) was supporting a child aged over 16 years and in full-time education. Four men were expecting their first child, and they have been included among those with dependent children.

19. These comparisons will underestimate women's contributions to the net disposable income of a household, but they give a rough indication of this.

20. Percentages are derived from Table 5.8, *General Household Survey 1979* (London: HMSO, 1981). It is worth noting that in addition to the comparison drawn here, the general level of sole support among married men in the full-wage jobs in the sample was also similar to that found in the General Household Surveys. For the former, it was 37% (Table 3.5), a figure comparable to the 38% of married men in the 1979 General Household Survey who were supporting an unwaged wife.

21. The absence of single black women in the sample is puzzling. It certainly reflects the extremely white profile of the telephonist day shift, where most of the single women in the sample are employed. Systematic disadvantage in relation to hiring practices may provide part of an explanation. To the extent that the telephonist day job recruits from a somewhat more advantaged social group, black women may be excluded or under-represented. There was one black single woman working the day shift. She was included in the pilot study. She was educated well beyond the level of most of her colleagues, and hoped to move from her current job as soon as possible.

22. See Barrett & McIntosh (1985:31), Bruegel (1989), Mama (1984:26), Moss (1980:52-3) and Webb (1982:166-7). Figures in Brown (1984:187) indicate that among the 25-34 age range, 54% of white women, compared with 75% of West Indian women, were economically active. Smith (1977:65) notes that between West Indian women and the general female population "the difference in the proportion at work is at its greatest during the child-rearing years between the ages of 25 and 44". See also Phizacklea (1982) for a discussion of the strong tradition of financial maintenance by West Indian women, and of the family and labour force circumstances of a sample of West Indian women in north-west London.

23. Among white women, the association between a terminated marriage and employment in a full-wage job is a fairly substantial one. Chi-square (raw and corrected) is significant at 0.01, phi=0.40.

24. For the difference in family status between white and black married women, Fisher's exact =0.02, phi=0.44. The difference in family status between previously married white and black women is neither significant nor strong (phi=0.11).

25. This level of overtime working among previously married women with dependent children compares with that done by married men with children (11.4 per week for night telephonists and 17.4 per week for postmen).

26. Of course, there are questions to be addressed here about the differential control of and access to household resources by husbands and wives. We might speculate that although component-wage women lived in more advantaged households overall, the full-wage women may in fact have had greater control over household resources. This would fit with Pahl's findings (1989:108-9) that "wife control" of household finances is associated with low-income, working-class households, and that "wife-controlled pooling" is more common the greater the contribution of the wife's earnings to household finances.

Chapter Four

Full-wages and component-wages in the 1980s

The distinction between full-wages and component-wages is an innovation of this research. So far, we have seen that the distinction helps to identify differences in the family and household circumstances of people in jobs, and is consistent with variations in relations to household maintenance. In this chapter, we sharpen the definition of full-wages and component-wages, and propose a general basis for identifying full-wage and component-wage levels. We also examine the social adequacy of women's and men's wages over the 1980s in terms of their full-wage and component-wage capacity.

A preliminary discussion of the need to clarify the definition of full-wages and component-wages, and on the potential usefulness of determining general component-wage and full-wage levels, is in order at this point. In the previous chapter, the current domestic circumstances of women and men, and their circumstances when they were recruited to their jobs, are taken as indicators of the relations to the financial maintenance of households afforded by the wages in postal and telephonist jobs. In identifying the distinction between full-wages and component-wages, the status of the wage in a household was taken as the major criterion; in particular, whether workers were the sole wage earners in their household, or whether they were sharing financial maintenance with other household members. This gives, however, a very imprecise picture of the social capacities facilitated by different levels of wages. Four considerations are of most importance in this respect. The first concerns the types of households that a full-wage is sufficient to support.[1] People in the full-wage jobs considered in this study were in several types of households. Some were in one adult households, some were in lone parent households, and others were in married couple households with or without dependent children. Given the interest in defining full-wages as sufficient to support a household, it is necessary to distinguish types of household and to establish levels of full-wages appropriate for each type. In this chapter, we shall concentrate on two types of full-wages: those for a household of two adults and two children, and those for a one adult household.

Secondly, we have so far defined the full-wage status of a job in terms of the percentage of people who are sole earners in their household. As a general procedure, this may overestimate the full-wage status of a job because it gives no indication of the adequacy of wages in terms of standard of living. The difficulties many households face when supporting young children on one adult wage are an obvious instance of this problem. It is essential to the definition of a full-wage, therefore, that it be a wage sufficient to allow an individual to be the sole support of a particular type of household at, at least, a minimum standard of living. This means that in determining full-wage levels we shall need to compare wage levels with distributions of household income and, further, to establish some criterion for what would constitute a minimum income for different types of households. In doing so, we would need to take into account the proportion of household income that is typically supplied through wages.

Thirdly, basing the full-wage/component-wage distinction on the "sole earner" status of people in jobs may, on the other hand, underestimate the social capacities facilitated by wage levels, in that the presence or absence of multiple earners in a household is not a reliable indication of the sufficiency of any one household wage. For example, while at one time married women's labour force participation was negatively correlated with the husband's wage, this relationship is now negligible. Moreover, in Britain there is a positive correlation between a husband's and wife's wages (Rainwater et al. 1986:69). In other words, the employment status of wives is not a good indicator of the adequacy of a husband's income; however, if a woman has high earnings her husband is likely to have high earnings also. A full-wage, then, must be defined in relation to potential capacities for household financing. A salaried professional may have an employed spouse earning a high wage, but he or she is nevertheless likely to have earnings sufficient to support the household single-handedly at a minimum standard.

Fourthly, defining minimum full-wages in terms of the potential capacity for the sole support of a household also overcomes a confusion resulting from the use of the "sole earner" criterion as to whether any particular wage is a component-wage or a full-wage. In the previous chapter, the component-wage job was identified as such in terms of the percentage of incumbents sharing the financial maintenance of a household with another person. But some of our "full-wage" earners in the night telephonist and postal jobs were in this position as well. To sharpen the definition of a component-wage, we shall instead use the criterion of the potential capacity to support a household at a minimum standard, although in this case the capacity is lacking. More specifically, component-wages will now be defined as wages insufficient to support a one adult household at a minimum standard.

The potential usefulness of identifying full-wage and component-wage levels should be clear. With these levels defined, we would have an immediate indication of the social capacities of wages, and could assess the adequacy of women's and men's wages accordingly. There are a number of indicators of low pay currently in use, but these provide only a minimal idea of the range of social capacities in the financial maintenance of households facilitated by different levels of wages. Low-pay thresholds are typically defined in relation to mid-points of earnings distributions, and although they provide a statement of inequality, they do not, in themselves, give further social meaning to that inequality. In contrast, we propose to define full-wages and component-wages directly in relation to a minimum standard of household income, for households of different composition. The full-wage/component-wage distinction does provide, therefore, an immediate social context for assessments of the adequacy of wages by indicating the potential relations to the financial maintenance of households that different levels of wages represent.

Two further points must be addressed. The primary objective of the full-wage and component-wage distinction is to assess the social potential of wages in terms of household financing and household formation. Although related to minimum standards of living for different types of households, the distinction is not an indicator of whether any individual wage earner is likely to be living in poverty. It can, however, have uses in the analysis of poverty in that it would identify the social capacities of different wages coming into a household, and could also be used to assess inequalities in access to full-wages for different types of households. The ability of households to "package" their income to meet minimum household requirements would have a direct relation to the ability of household members to command full-wages or component-wages.[2] For example, women can rarely earn sufficient (i.e. full) wages to support dependent children in a lone parent household. This lack of earning potential is a major reason why female-headed households often live in poverty, primarily on state benefits (Millar 1987). Similarly, recent research examining the calculations made by unemployed men regarding their "reservation wage" (McLaughlin et al. 1989:106) reveals that the reservation wage for men in households with dependants is one sufficient to provide the family with enough to live on without relying on other sources of waged income. In other words, the reservation wage is a

99

full-wage, and inequalities in access to full-wages indicates differential access to the means of escaping the poverty trap. Equally, younger people are often on wage rates that do not allow them to support themselves as an independent adult; that is, they are likely to earn component-wages. Although they may not be living in poverty, in that they may be in their families of origin with access to other sources of financial support, the inability to support themselves as independent adults is a form of social deprivation. Although the likelihood of living in poverty cannot be directly read off the full-wage or component-wage status of any individual's earnings, the full-wage or component-wage status of earnings will be related to experiences of poverty and other forms of social inequality.

Finally, levels of full-wages and component-wages should be applied uniformly when assessing the social capacities of men's and women's earnings. Some assessments of the social adequacy of earnings do not take the same amount of earnings as the reference point for women and men. For example, where 60% of average earnings has been proposed as a low-pay threshold, this has in the past been calculated for men against men's average earnings and for women against women's average earnings, on the argument that there is a different relationship between earnings and deprivation for women and men (Townsend 1979:628). However, although women, or men, on low wages may not experience material deprivation because of the support they receive from other household members, there is the issue of how low wages contribute to forms of dependency that are inimical to the status of citizenship in contemporary society.[3] Set in this context, no distinction should be drawn between women and men as to the appropriate minimum pay. The view taken here is that, irrespective of gender and irrespective of the household in which an individual lives, wages should be sufficient, at least, to support the wage earner as an independent adult. As we shall see, many women in full-time employment are earning wages that are inadequate in this respect.

The rest of this chapter is in three main sections. The first one begins with a discussion of the considerations involved in determining minimum full-wage levels. It reviews current definitions of low pay and asks whether these are suitable for establishing levels of full-wages. This discussion is not intended as a review of contemporary debates concerning low pay and minimum wages, or of the relationship between low pay and household poverty. Its primary purpose is to indicate that the differentiation in social capacities involved in the full-wage/component-wage distinction is more elaborate than that implied by current low-pay thresholds, and that this distinction allows a more precise identification of the relations to household maintenance afforded by wages. The sec-

100

ond section describes procedures that can be used to identify the levels of component-wages and minimum full-wages. Two minimum full-wage levels are established: one for a household of two adults and two children, and one for a one person household. It must be stressed that this is a very preliminary attempt to identify full-wage and component-wage levels. Improvements in these procedures are no doubt desirable, and hopefully possible. The procedures used here, however, are fairly simple and provide an initial indication of full-wage and component-wage levels over the 1980s. The third section goes on to examine the distribution of women's and men's wages across the component-wage and full-wage categories between 1979 and 1987.

Full-wages, component-wages and definitions of low pay

It is central to the definition of full-wages that they are sufficient to cover the basic financial requirements of a household.[4] This immediately raises the question of how this definition of full-wages relates to the variety of household types, and in this respect it is useful to differentiate between types of full-wage according to types of household. In this section, we concentrate on full-wages for a household of two adults and two children because this is the closest reference point for the gross wage levels associated with low-pay thresholds. Later, we shall also identify the minimum full-wage level for a household of one adult. The minimum full-wage level for a one adult household is a significant point for, as discussed previously, it will be taken to define the dividing line between full-wages and component-wages. We shall see later that estimates of the social capacity of wages, especially those earned by women, are considerably sharpened when adequacy is judged by the more socially specific criteria of full-wages and component-wages.

Currently, a major means of assessing the social adequacy of wages is to determine a wage threshold below which people are considered to be low paid. In what is to follow, we consider whether low-pay thresholds are a suitable indicator of full-wage levels for a household of two adults and two children. Although low-pay thresholds are often defined directly in relation to mid-points in earnings distributions, they have a close relation to the earnings equivalent of benefit levels for a household of this type. Given this association, it is necessary to determine whether low-pay thresholds could be used to define minimum full-wages for a two adult, two child household.

A variety of ways of defining a low-pay threshold have been proposed by government bodies, labour organizations, lobbyists and the academic community. Here we concentrate on the low-pay thresholds as defined by the Low Pay Unit, the Trades Union Congress and the Council of Europe, and compare them with the threshold associated with the gross earnings equivalent of benefits paid to a two adult, two child household. The first three low-pay thresholds are calculated in relation to pay directly. The Low Pay Unit (LPU) favours using pay below two-thirds of the median male earnings. The Trades Union Congress (TUC) recommends as a threshold two-thirds of the mean male manual earnings. The Council of Europe (CE) has a "decency threshold" set at 68% of the mean full-time earnings. In contrast, the threshold established by the gross earnings equivalent of state benefit levels involves an explicit reference to the "minimum" needs of a household. Typically, the household is one containing one man, one woman and two children of specified ages. To determine the earnings equivalent of benefit entitlements for this type of household, the calculations take as a base point the supplementary benefit rates (SB, now income supplement) for the couple, the children and an average single payment. To this base is added child benefit and the following costs: rent, water, rates, work expenses, income tax and national insurance (Low Pay Unit 1988:8).

When wages are compared against these thresholds, a large number of workers in Britain, particularly female workers, are low paid. For example, Table 4.1 shows the percentage of women and men in full-time employment who fell below the Low Pay Unit's low-pay threshold and below the Council of Europe's decency threshold in 1987. Altogether about one-third of adult full-time employees in 1987 are low paid, and the differential between women and men is marked: close to one quarter of men and over one-half of women fell below both thresholds.[5]

These two definitions of low pay yield similar estimates of the extent of low pay in Britain because, although based on different calculations, they end up with a similar wage level as the low-pay threshold.[6] Table 4.2 shows the wage level of all four indicators of low pay in 1979 and in 1987. In fact, all of the thresholds defined directly in relation to wages (LPU, TUC and CE thresholds) are very close to each other, and more

Table 4.1 Percentage of men and women in full-time employment falling below LPU and CE low-pay thresholds, 1987.

	Below LPU threshold	Below CE threshold
Men	22.7	24.6
Women	51.9	54.2
All	32.3	34.4

Source: Low Pay Unit (1988:9,11), extracted from Tables 3 and 4. Earnings figures are for workers on "adult rates" and are exclusive of overtime.

Table 4.2 Low pay thresholds, 1979 and 1987.

	1979	1987
LPU (two-thirds median male full-time earnings)	62.60	132.27
TUC (two-thirds mean male manual full-time earnings)	62.00	123.67
CE (68% mean full-time earnings)[1]	60.90	135.25
Earnings equivalent of supplementary benefit (1 man, 1 women, 2 children)[2]	61.20	125.55

1. The 1979 figure is an estimate based the *New Earnings Survey*. 2. For 1979, one child is under 5 years and one child is between 5 and 10 years. For 1987, one child is under 11 years and one child is between 11 and 15 years. The 1979 earnings equivalent would be somewhat higher if calculated with 1987 age details.
Sources: 1979 figures – Pond (1979) and *New Earnings Survey 1979*, Tables 22 and 23 (HMSO, 1979:A37–A38); 1987 figures – Low Pay Unit (1988).

importantly for this discussion, are very close to the earnings equivalent of the benefit entitlement of a household containing one man, one woman and two children. At one time, the Low Pay Unit recommended the earnings equivalent of benefit payments as a useful benchmark for definitions of minimum wages, and its position in this respect was similar to that of the TUC. For example, in its submission to the Royal Commission on the Distribution of Income and Wealth, the Low Pay Unit argued (1978:269) that a minimum wage target that yielded take-home pay at the supplementary benefit level for a family with two children:

> will also prevent poverty amongst those families where the breadwinner is in full-time work. As the vast majority of heads of households are responsible for their families' living standards during part of their working life, the level should be such as to guarantee them an income during this period that is at least equal to the State's own minimum level. This minimum is applied to male and female workers, not only because of our belief that every one irrespective of their sex is entitled to the minimum wage, but that increasingly women are the main breadwinners of a family.

Although the Low Pay Unit argues that its threshold of two-thirds median male full-time earnings represents (1988:9) "a broadly acceptable measure of low pay tied to movements and expectations of earnings in the economy as a whole", the comparisons in Table 4.2 show its close association with the gross earnings equivalent of benefit levels for a household of two adults and two children in 1979 and 1987. The fact that

103

there was little difference between the earnings equivalent of benefits for this type of household and all of the three thresholds defined directly in relation to earnings raises the question of whether these are suitable benchmarks for defining a minimum full-wage for such a household. The following suggests that these thresholds are not appropriate for this purpose.

The insufficiency of benefit levels as an indicator of adequate living standards is a widely and strongly held view.[7] The similarity between the LPU, TUC and CE low-pay thresholds and the earnings equivalent of benefits for the type of household we are considering is a preliminary indication of the unsuitability of the former for our definition of minimum full-wages for a household of this type. Comparing the wage level of these thresholds against the income and expenditure of two adult, two child households in Britain is a further indication of their unsuitability. This information is set out in Table 4.3. We can make only very speculative types of comparisons here, since household income typically includes income from sources other than wages, but this exercise provides some picture of the position of the low-pay thresholds in relation to the income and expenditure of a two adult, two child household.

For 1979, all of the low-pay thresholds were below the lowest decile of the gross normal weekly income of households with two adults and two children. The highest threshold in 1979 (LPU) was approximately three-quarters of the lowest decile, and the lowest (the earnings equivalent of SB) was 72% of the lowest decile. In 1987, two of the low-pay thresholds were just below the lowest decile (TUC and the earnings equivalent of SB) and two were slightly above it (LPU and CE). The low-pay thresholds

Table 4.3 Income and expenditure for a household of one man, one woman and two children, 1979 and 1987.

	1979	1987
Gross normal weekly household income		
Mean	148.91	342.83
Median	138.19	284.65
Lower quartile	107.39	207.70
Lowest decile	84.57	127.67
Gross normal weekly household expenditure		
Mean	118.56	233.36
Median	101.96	203.12
Lower quartile	80.03	147.07
Lowest decile	65.16	111.67

Sources: *Family Expenditure Survey 1979*, Tables 44 and 48 (HMSO, 1980:106, 118); *Family Expenditure Survey 1987*, Tables 20 and 24 (HMSO,1989:59, 68).

look a bit more substantial in relation to the lowest decile in 1987 compared with 1979, but a large factor in this is the increase in inequality in household income over this period.[8] In 1979, the lowest decile was 61% of the median, in 1987 it was 45%. Comparisons with expenditure data are even more speculative, but it is clear that none of the low-pay thresholds would have supported this type of household at the lowest decile of expenditure in 1979 (£65.16), although the higher thresholds might just have done so in 1987 (£111.67). Again this improvement is more apparent than real. The lowest decile of expenditure was 64% of the median in 1979, and 55% in 1987. Thus the expenditure possibilities of the low-pay thresholds look relatively better in 1987 because the expenditure floor for a household of two adults and two children had dropped over the 1980s.

These comparisons probably underestimate the adequacy of low-pay thresholds in relation to the financial maintenance of a two adult, two child household because we are comparing individual earnings against total household income, and earnings are rarely the sole source of income in a household. However, even when we take this factor into account, the low-pay thresholds do not compare well. Table 4.4 shows the sources of income for different levels of household income. It indicates the percentage (and mean level) of household income provided by

Table 4.4 Sources of income at different levels of household income for a household of one man, one woman and two children, 1979 and 1987.

| Gross weekly household income | Income from wages/salaries | Percentage of household income[1] | |
		From wages and salaries	From social security
1979			
Under £80	£29.13	45	32
£80 to <£100	£66.84	73	11
£100 to <£120	£85.51	79	8
£120 to <£150	£109.65	82	7
£150 to <£200	£143.14	84	5
£200 or more	£203.76	75	3
1987			
Under £175	£47.98	41	37
£175 to <£250	£153.28	71	9
£250 to <£375	£239.18	77	6
£375 or more	£452.14	72	2

1. Percentages are calculated across rows. "Other" sources of household income have not been included in the table. They would bring the percentages to 100.
Sources: *Family Expenditure Survey 1979*, Table 47 (HMSO, 1980:117), *Family Expenditure Survey 1987*, Table 23 (HMSO, 1989:67).

wages and salaries, and the percentage provided by social security benefits.

For the lowest income households, income from wages was less than half the total household income. In other categories of household income, wages provided between 71% and 84% of the total income. If we look at the household income categories in 1979, we see that the £80 to <£100 category was the lowest in which wages provided the majority of household income. The mean level of income from wages in this category was £66.84 – a figure that is above the highest low-pay threshold for this year (£62.60). Similarly, in 1987 the lowest category of household income in which wages provided the majority of income was the £175 to <£250 category, and the mean level of income from wages in this case was £153.28. Again this is above the highest low-pay threshold for this year (£135.25). Although we would get more precise information from continuous distributions of household income, and the percentage of income from wages in relation to this, the information discussed here suggests that the wage levels of the low-pay thresholds are too low to be taken as the minimum level of full-wages for a two adult, two child household. One further piece of evidence confirms this point, and also indicates the position of the low-pay thresholds in terms of a full-wage for a one adult household.

Townsend & Gordon (1989:56) report, for various household types, subjective assessments of the weekly disposable income required to keep a household out of poverty. These data are from the survey of "Londoners' Living Standards" conducted in 1985/86. For a household containing a married couple and two children (one under age 11, one aged between 11 and 15), the subjective assessment of required income was £109.12 (not including housing costs), which is 149% of the basic level of disposable income on SB for the same period. For a household of one adult under age 60, the subjective assessment of required disposable income was £64.26 (not including housing costs), which is 218% of the disposable income from SB. If we apply these differences between the net disposable income based on subjective assessments and benefit levels for the two types of households in 1989 (that is, we take 149% of the net income after housing costs on income supplement for a two adult, two child household, and 218% of the net income after housing costs for a one adult household on income supplement), we would get the assessments of net disposable income shown in Table 4.5. In this table, all incomes exclude housing costs.[9] In 1989, the net disposable income required to keep a one adult household out of poverty would be £72.81, and for a two adult, two child household the figure is £153.54. This table also shows the net disposable income for the LPU, TUC and CE low-pay thresholds for 1989. They are all less than the assessment of income

Table 4.5 Subjective assessments of net disposable income (excluding housing costs) needed to keep households out of poverty, and calculated net disposable income (excluding housing costs) for LPU, TUC and CE low-pay thresholds, 1989

	Net income (excluding housing costs)
Assessments for a household	
With two adults and two children	£153.54
With one adult under age 60	£72.81
Calculations based on low-pay thresholds	
For two adult and two child household:	
Council of Europe	£124.39
Low Pay Unit	£123.21
Trades Union Congress	£120.83
For one adult household:	
Council of Europe	£98.19
Low Pay Unit	£94.22
Trade Union Congress	£86.50

Sources: Gross wage figures for the low pay thresholds are from *The New Review of the Low Pay Unit*, No. 1, Dec 1989/Jan 1990, p. 11. Figures for net income for the low-pay thresholds are extracted and calculated from the DSS Tax/Benefit Model Tables, Table II (single person aged 25 or over, pp.46–7, and married couple with two children aged 13 and 16, pp. 71–5), October 1989.

required to keep a two adult, two child household out of poverty, and indeed, at these levels of income, such a household would still be in receipt of some means-tested benefits. In contrast, the thresholds are closer to the assessments of the income required to keep a one adult household out of poverty, although they yield a higher net disposable income in all cases.

We might speculate, then, that the minimum full-wage for a two adult, two child household will be higher than the gross wage of the low-pay thresholds, especially when housing costs are considered, and that the minimum full-wage for a one adult household would be lower, although the inclusion of housing costs may even out some of this difference.

Levels of minimum full-wages

As a way of conceptualizing wage inequalities, distinctions between full-wages and component-wages, and between different types of full-wage, are intended as indicators of the social capacities afforded by wages. They provide explicit information as to the social responsibilities that can be assumed by wage earners at different levels of wages, in terms of maintaining households of various compositions at a minimum standard. We shall turn now to outline a simple procedure for establishing the minimum full-wage levels. At the moment this is a very preliminary attempt to define full-wage and component-wage levels. The procedure is discussed first in terms of a household of one man, one woman and two children. Following this, a minimum full-wage for a household of one adult is proposed, and from this figure the component-wage level is derived.

It has been emphasized that a key feature of minimum full-wages is that they are the major source of household income. The first step in our procedure involves establishing the typical contribution of wages to total household income, where wages are the primary source of income. A reference back to Table 4.4 reveals that when wages were the largest part of income in households with two adults and two children, they ranged from 71% to 84% of total income. We shall take 77% as the mid-point of this range and regard it as the typical contribution of wages to household incomes.[10] The next step in finding the minimum full-wage level is simply to take 77% of the median of gross household income for both years.[11] For 1979 and 1987, the appropriate gross wage levels are £106.41 and £219.18. These would be our minimum full-wages for a two adult, two child household in 1979 and 1987. They are each about 175% of the gross earnings equivalent of supplementary benefit levels for these years.

The same procedure can be used to determine the minimum full-wage for a household of one adult below retirement age. In Table 4.6, we have the income and income sources for one adult households. In this case, when wages are the primary source of household income they range from 79% to 84% of total income. Again we shall take the mid-point of this range for our typical contribution: 81%. For 1979, the minimum full-wage for one adult would be £58.37 (81% of the median household income, £72.06). For 1987, the minimum full-wage for a one adult household would be £127.12 (81% of the median household income, £156.94). The minimum full-wage levels for a one adult (not retired) household also establish the threshold for component-wages. Wage levels less than £58.37 in 1979 and less than £127.12 in 1987 would be judged not to supply sufficient resources to allow an individual to support themselves as an independent adult in a one adult household.[12]

Much needs to be done to confirm the validity of these wage levels in terms of their full-wage and component-wage status, and it is certainly possible that other procedures could produce more appropriate estimates.[13] For example, one difficulty with the current procedure is the fact that calculating minimum full-wages in relation to median household incomes builds into the minimum full-wage calculation general inequalities between households of different compositions. It would be

Table 4.6 Levels and sources of income for a one adult
household (not retired), 1979 and 1987.

Gross normal weekly household income	1979	·	1987
Mean	78.34		181.75
Median	72.06		156.94
Lower quartile	46.03		77.63
Lowest decile	25.28		37.22

	Percentage of income from	
	Wages and salaries	Social security
1979		
Under £30	9	62
£30 to <£45	38	41
£45 to <£60	67	16
£60 to <£75	83	6
£75 to <£100	84	3
£100 or more	81	2
1987		
Under £60	7	75
£60 to <£125	52	20
£125 to <£200	81	3
£200 or more	79	1

Sources: *Family Expenditure Survey 1979*, Tables 47 and 48
(HMSO, 1980:116, 118) *Family Expenditure Survey 1987*,
Tables 23 and 24 (HMSO, 1989:67–8).

very interesting to establish a minimum full-wage level for a household
of one adult and one or more children. However, in both 1979 and 1987,
the median income for households of one adult and one or more children is less than the median for one adult households, and less than half
of the median household income is supplied through wages and salaries. On both counts, therefore, the median household income of a lone
parent household is clearly inadequate for our purposes. In place of the
procedure outlined here, one could examine the continuous distribution
of household incomes and locate the point at which wages stabilize as a
contribution to household income. This point would then be the full-
wage point for that type of household.

For the moment, and with the tentative nature of our calculations in
mind, the simple procedure proposed here does provide a preliminary
indication of where the two full-wage and the component-wage benchmarks would be placed in the distribution of earnings. We turn now to
examine men's and women's wages against these benchmarks.

109

Women's and men's earnings as
full-wages and component-wages

Using data from the New Earnings Survey, we can compare women's and men's full-time earnings against the levels of component and full wages established in the preceding exercise. In the following, we do this in two ways. First, we compare the median earnings of full-time manual and non-manual workers against the full-wage level for a household of two adults and two children. We do this with earnings including and excluding overtime. Secondly, we look at the full distribution of the wages, excluding and including overtime, earned by women and men in full-time employment, and examine how this distribution falls across the full-wage and component-wage categories. It is well known that earnings distributions became more unequal over the 1980s (LPU 1988) and comparisons with full-wage and component-wage levels indicate one aspect of the social consequences of this. Similarly, the wage differentials between women and men in full-time employment place them in a different relation to full-wages and component-wages, and this comparison highlights the stark social implications of women's lower pay.

Men's median full-time earnings came close to the minimum full-wage level for a household of two adults and two children (Table 4.7). However, the median of non-manual earnings was closest to the mark.

Table 4.7 Men's median full-time earnings as a percentage of the minimum full-wage for a household of two adults and two children, 1979 and 1987.

	1979		1987	
Minimum full-wage for a household of one man, one woman and two children	£106.41		£219.18	
Male median full-time earnings[1]	£	As % of full-wage	£	As % of full-wage
Including overtime				
Non-manual	103.6	97	235.7	108
Manual	88.2	83	173.9	79
All	93.9	88	198.4	91
Excluding overtime				
Non-manual	99.2	93	225.3	103
Manual	75.7	71	150.2	69
All	82.8	78	176.4	81

1. Earnings are for full-time employees on adult rates, whose pay was not affected by absence.

Sources: *New Earnings Survey 1979*, Tables 22 and 24 (HMSO, 1979:A37, A39); *New Earnings Survey 1987*, Tables 38 and 39 (HMSO, 1987:B44-45, B46-47).

Overtime earnings nudge the median up to just below the minimum full-wage level in 1979, but in 1987 the median of non-manual earnings was over the full-wage level, including and excluding overtime earnings. Men's manual earnings compare less well against the full-wage level. Excluding overtime earnings, the median was around 70% of the minimum full-wage in both years. Including overtime earnings, the median of men's manual wages rose to 83% of the full-wage level in 1979, but to only 79% in 1987.[14] Even with the boost of overtime earnings, the median of men's manual wages was significantly below the minimum full-wage level required to support a two adult, two child household.

Over the decade, as earnings inequalities increased, differential access to minimum full-wage levels increased. Between 1979 and 1987, the earnings position of men in manual jobs deteriorated somewhat in terms of its full-wage capacity (with the median declining from 83% to 79%). At the same time, the full-wage capacity of men's non-manual earnings increased, with the median moving from 97% of the full-wage level in 1979 to 108% in 1987. The figures for men's earnings excluding overtime show the same overall pattern – a relative deterioration in the full-wage capacity of earnings for non-manual men in relation to households containing two adults and two children.

Whereas the necessity for a breadwinner's wage (or family wage) has often entered into bargaining strategies and assumptions about men's relations to wages, assumptions about appropriate levels for women's wages have typically been otherwise. As McLanahan et al. state: "Despite women's increasing responsibility for their own economic support and despite their increasing labour force participation, the pattern of earnings differentials is still one that would seem to presume the economic dependence of women on men" (1989:120). Indeed, women's full-time earnings are very inadequate in relation to minimum full-wages for a household with dependants (Table 4.8). In 1979, women's median full-time non-manual earnings (excluding overtime earnings) were 56% of the full-wage level for a two adult, two child household, and median manual earnings were about half this level, at 49%.[15] The situation improved somewhat over the decade, but only for non-manual women. Their median full-time earnings rose to 64% of the full-wage level while, for manual women, median earnings declined slightly relative to this level. In contrast to men, overtime earnings generally added only a small amount to women's gross weekly earnings. The social capacities of women's wages do not alter much when overtime earnings are considered; the median of earnings for both manual and non-manual women was still below two-thirds of the minimum full-wage level in both years.

The political issue in the social capacity of men's and women's wages is the extent of their adequacy not simply in relation to larger house-

Table 4.8 Women's median full-time earnings as a percentage of the minimum full-wage for a household of two adults and two children, 1979 and 1987.

	1979		1987	
Minimum full-wage for a household of one man, one woman and two children	£106.41		£219.18	
Women's median full-time earnings	£	As % of full-wage	£	As % of full-wage
Including overtime				
Non-manual	60.8	57	142.2	65
Manual	53.3	50	108.2	49
All	58.4	55	132.9	61
Excluding overtime				
Non-manual	60.1	56	139.2	64
Manual	51.9	49	103.9	47
All	57.4	54	129.5	59

1. Earnings are for full-time employees on adult rates, whose pay was not affected by absence.
Sources: *New Earnings Survey 1979*, Tables 23 and 24 (HMSO, 1979:A38, A39), *New Earnings Survey 1987*, Tables 38 and 39 (HMSO, 1987:B44–45, B46–47).

holds with dependants, but also in relation to one adult households. As Table 4.9 indicates, some men and many women were not earning full-time wages that were sufficient to support themselves as an independent adult.[16]

Both at the beginning and towards the end of the 1980s, the modal category of earnings for women in full-time employment was that of a component-wage: 56% were earning component-wages in 1979 and 50% in 1987.[17] Overtime earnings reduced the prevalence of component-wages for women, but not by any substantial amount. The extent of component-wages for manual and non-manual women shows some important differences, however. For non-manual women, their situation improved over the decades with the number earning component-wages falling to 43%. For manual women, their earnings position showed some deterioration over this period, with the number of women earning component-wages rising from 71% to 78%.

This information helps place the low-pay women receive in a social context. *A substantial number of women were earning full-time wages that would not have been sufficient to support themselves as an independent adult in a one adult household.* Indeed, for women in manual jobs, the social capacity of wages declined absolutely, and declined relative to women in non-manual jobs.

Table 4.9 Percentage of men and women in full-time employment earning full-wages and component-wages, 1979 and 1987.[1]

| | Full-wages | | | | Component-wage[4] | | |
| | 2 adults, 2 children[2] | | 1 adult[3] | | | | |
	Excl. OT[5]	Incl. OT	Excl. OT	Incl. OT	Excl. OT	Incl. OT	Totals
Men							
1979 All	21	42	66	50	13	8	100
Non-manual	38	54	55	40	7	6	100
Manual	8	34	74	57	17	10	100
1987 All	31	40	48	45	21	15	100
Non-manual	53	57	37	34	11	9	100
Manual	11	25	58	56	31	20	100
Women							
1979 All	4	7	41	40	56	53	100
Non-manual	5	9	46	43	50	48	100
Manual	0	1	29	32	71	67	100
1987 All	10	12	39	41	50	47	100
Non-manual	13	14	44	45	43	41	100
Manual	1	2	21	26	78	72	100

1. All earnings are for full-time employees on adult rates, whose pay was not affected by absence. 2. Figures for this column are gross weekly earnings for 1979 of £110 and over (for the minimum full-wage level of £106.41), and for 1987 of £220 and over (for the minimum full-wage level of £219.18). 3. Figures for this column are gross weekly earnings for 1979 of £60 to £109.99, and for 1987 of £130 to £219.99. The minimum full-wage levels for a one-adult household were £58.37 in 1979, and £127.12 in 1987. 4. Figures for this column are gross weekly earnings below £60 for 1979 and below £130 for 1987. 5. OT = overtime.
Sources: *New Earnings Survey 1979*, Tables 92 and 93 (HMSO, 1979:D17-19, D20); *New Earnings Survey 1987*, Tables 92 and 93 (HMSO, 1987:D33-36, D37-38).

Considering the previous information on the relation of women's median full-time earnings to the minimum full-wage for a two adult, two child household, we would not expect many women to be earning wages that would facilitate sole financial responsibility for this type of household. Women in manual jobs rarely earned wages sufficient to meet this social responsibility. For women in non-manual jobs there was an improvement over the decade in this respect, with 13% earning wages sufficient to support a two adult, two child household in 1987. Nevertheless, although non-manual women were more likely to be earning full-wages than were manual women, the typical full-wage for non-manual women was that of the one adult household full-wage.

In contrast, most men were earning full-wages, although there was a decline in their full-wage earning capacity over the decade: 87% of men earned full-wages in 1979 and 78% did so in 1987. Overtime earnings added considerably to the full-wage capacity of men's earnings, lifting the prevalence of full-wages to 92% in 1979 and 85% in 1987. Again, however, there was a marked difference between non-manual and manual men, and in this case the distinction was in terms of the type of full-wages earned. In 1979, overtime earnings boosted men's non-manual earnings so that the modal category of earnings was that of a full-wage for a two adult, two child household. By 1987, the earnings position of non-manual men had improved considerably, with the majority of men in this full-wage category even without the addition of overtime earnings. For men in manual jobs, the modal full-wage category in both years was that of a one adult household. Overtime earnings placed one-third of manual men in the higher (two adult, two child) full-wage category in 1979, but were less effective in doing so in 1987. In this year, overtime earnings brought 25% of men into this full-wage range.

In general, for men, the percentage falling within both full-wage categories declined over the decade, and this decline corresponded with a rise in the extent to which men's full-time earnings fell within the range of component-wages. During this period, the percentage of men earning component-wages increased, so that by 1987, 21% of men were earning component-wages.

Summary

At the beginning of this chapter, we saw that there is a considerable incidence of low pay in Britain among full-time workers, with roughly one-quarter of full-time men and one-half of full-time women earning wages below the 1987 LPU and CE low-pay thresholds. It was also pointed out that one limitation of these thresholds is that they do not provide an immediate sense of *what low pay means in social terms*. The thresholds give an indication of how many people fall below a certain earnings point, but there is no direct indication of the potential consequences of this for social relations and obligations. This is the potential advantage of the distinction between full-wages of various types and component-wages. They give an immediate indication of the social capacities facilitated by different wage levels, in terms of the relations to household maintenance that wage earners could assume.

The low-pay thresholds defined directly in relation to earnings (LPU, TUC and CE) yielded a gross weekly wage that was similar to the gross earnings equivalent of state benefits paid to a household containing two adults and two children. It is argued, in part because of this similarity, that the low-pay thresholds are not a suitable benchmark for the minimum full-wage level for a household of this type. It is essential to the definition of full-wages that they provide the potential capacity for wage earners to assume sole financial responsibility for households at a minimum standard of living. According to the preliminary estimates of the minimum full-wage levels for a household of two adults and two children, the appropriate gross wage levels were about 176% higher than the low-pay thresholds in 1979 and 1987. In contrast, the wage level defining the top of the component-wage range was very close to the LPU, TUC and CE low-pay thresholds. This proximity, and the more socially specific definition of component-wages, helps to contextualize the low pay received by women and men. At this level of wages, wage earners would not have the financial resources to support themselves as an independent adult in a one adult household.

A comparison between the distribution of earnings in Britain and levels of minimum full-wages and component-wages shows the substantial inequality in the social capacity of wages earned by women and men, and by manual and non-manual workers. Typically, women earn component-wages, manual men earn full-wages for a one adult household, and non-manual men earn full-wages for a two adult, two child household.

The increase in earnings inequalities over the 1980s exacerbated differential access to full-wages. Although the position of non-manual women improved, the earnings position for women in manual jobs deteriorated, with more of them in component-wage jobs than at the beginning of the decade. Similarly, whereas the position of non-manual men improved, in that by the end of the decade the majority are earning basic wages sufficient to support a two adult, two child household, the situation of men in manual jobs declined. By the end of the decade, overtime earnings pushed only one-quarter of manual men into the two adult, two child full-wage range, and without overtime earnings this portion was halved. At the other end of the spectrum, the percentage of manual men earning component-wages almost doubled over the decade, and by 1987 one-fifth were in this category even when overtime earnings are taken into account.

Improvements in the estimation of full-wage and component-wage levels may be desirable, and it would be especially useful to establish a minimum full-wage level for a household of one adult with children. However, the procedures adopted here give a convincing first approximation of the levels of wages associated with sole financial responsibility for a one adult household and for a two adult, two child household.

Whether or not any individual wage earner is living in poverty cannot be read directly from the full-wage and component-wage indicators. Nevertheless, the fact that earnings in Britain compare unfavourably with full-wage levels does underline the differential access people have to full-wages, and the necessity of women's financial contribution to the maintenance of households with dependants. Similarly, the extensive level of component-wages among women highlights the state of dependency that low wages confer on many women even when employed full time.

Notes

1. A household, as the term is used here, is composed of one family unit (in the terminology of the General Household Survey). Elsewhere in this work, I have restricted the use of "family" to refer to the presence of children (chapters 3 and 6), and so I use the term household as a broader reference for a domestic unit that is either sharing household finances, or composed of one adult.
2. The concept of "income packaging" is discussed in Rainwater et al. (1986).
3. For discussions of issues of citizenship and economic independence, see, for example, Atkinson, (1985, 1990), Hernes (1987), Jones & Wallace, (1992), and Pateman, (1989). There is some similarity between the more familiar concept of a "family wage" and a full-wage for a two adult, two child household, in that each is intended to provide for the dependants of wage earners. However, the concept of full-wages is more flexible in that it can be defined for a range of household types, including those without dependants. Also, unlike the case of the family wage, there is no gender bias in the concept of full-wages. As a concept, it implies nothing about the gender of wage earners, although *in fact* women are less likely to be full-wage earners.
4. Approaches to assessing the social adequacy of wages in terms of household needs are reviewed in Townsend (1979). Further work is required to outline fully the distinctive nature of the approach used here. At a minimum, it should be pointed out that full-wages are established for different household types, in relation to current distributions of household income, and that men's and women's wages are judged against the same criterion.
5. Figures for part-time workers show that most (about 80%) fall below the two thresholds. Because the current study is based on people in full-time employment, the discussion in this chapter focuses on women and men in full-time employment.
6. Because the Council of Europe threshold includes women's full-time wages, the similarity between the two thresholds will depend on the differential between women's and men's full-time earnings. The TUC threshold moves in relation to the LPU threshold depending on the differential between male manual and non-manual earnings, and between the median and mean earnings levels.

7. For example, McLaughlin et al. 1989, Millar & Glendinning (1987), Pond (1979), Townsend (1979), Townsend & Gordon (1989), and Wedderburn (1983).
8. The SB estimate for 1979 is for a slightly less expensive family (i.e. younger ages of children), but this would not account for much of the difference in its relation to the lowest decile over this period. The SB earnings equivalent was 44% of the median in both years.
9. Townsend & Gordon report evidence from a later survey suggesting that assessments of disposable income required to keep households out of poverty were even higher than SB levels in 1987 (1989:65). The more conservative estimates from the middle of the decade are used in the example here. On average, they found that for the 1985/6 survey subjective assessments were 61% higher than contemporary SB levels. This corresponds very closely with the estimate from their multiple deprivation analysis: in this case the average income required in addition to SB was 66%. The figures they present for the subjective assessments of disposable income exclude housing costs, and this is the practice followed here.
10. This figure may in fact underestimate the contribution of wages and salaries to household income as it does not include income from self-employment. In the Family Expenditure Survey tables, the latter is included in "other" income, which also incorporates income from investments, imputed rent, etc. Unfortunately, this category can not be disaggregated. Rainwater et al. (1986:46) report that in married couple households with children in Britain, households received 85.2% of the total family income from the husband's earnings. They report also that women with children earned 10% of the total household income, with the median contribution standing at 15% (p. 65). Unfortunately, they do not seem to report how the husband's contribution varied with the wife's contribution, in cases where both were in employment. In general, they indicate that of British families in employment who were receiving government transfers, transfers comprised 11% of the family income (p. 135), but "family" in this case does not necessarily mean there were children present.
11. The validity of using the median needs to be examined in relation to the net income resulting from this procedure and the dynamic of the "poverty trap". It seems to be the most appropriate point to use for current purposes. On a very summary inspection, using the lower quartile would not yield a wage level at which households would be substantially better off in terms of net income, compared with their situation if income came only from state benefits.
12. As suggested previously, the low-pay thresholds for both 1979 and 1987 were close to the component-wage levels. The former were just above the component-wage level for 1979, and the LPU and CE thresholds were just above the component-wage level in 1987.
13. For example, one could potentially compare the results of the procedure used here with wage levels representing the gross earnings equivalent of Townsend & Gordon's (1989) subjective assessments of necessary disposable income.
14. The wages of men in the night telephonist and postal jobs were similar to the median of male manual full-time earnings in this respect. With overtime

117

earnings they were about 84% of the minimum full-wage level. Women's earnings in these jobs were slightly lower as a percentage of this full-wage level.

15. While not directly comparable, it is interesting to set this figure against research reported in the US. McLanahan et al. note (1989:120) that in 1979 "nearly half of all working women found themselves in industries paying an average wage that was less than the minimum set by the Bureau of Labour Statistics for the support of a family of four".

16. The cut-off points for Table 4.9 are approximations of the minimum full-wage levels for the appropriate years. On the whole, they are very close approximations and give a good, though rough, indication of the distribution of earnings across these divisions. For 1979, the cut-off points are £110 (for the two adult, two child household full-wage level of £106.41) and £60 (for the one person household full-wage level of £58.37). For 1987, the cut-off points are £220 (for the two adult, two children household full-wage level of £219.18) and £130 (for the one adult household full-wage level of £127.12). In all cases, the prevalence of full-wages for a two adult, two child household will be slightly underestimated, and the prevalence of component-wages will be slightly overestimated. Against this latter possibility, we must note that the New Earnings Survey under-represents young workers (Playford & Pond 1983) and, consequently, the extent of component-wage employment may be understated.

17. The weekly pay of the component-wage job in this study fell under the minimum full-wage for a single adult household. It was 93% of the 1979 level.

Chapter Five

Occupational segregation, wage inequalities and work histories

The previous chapters present evidence that challenges aspects of current understandings of occupational segregation "by sex" as a feature of employment inequalities. It has been argued that a general distinction exists between full-wage and component-wage jobs, and that this distinction captures a significant social divide in domestic and employment relations. The identification of a minimum full-wage for a one adult household is a critical point, because it defines the boundary between those who are and those who are not working for wages that cover their own reproduction costs. Whereas the percentage of men earning component-wages appears to have increased over the 1980s, for many women component-wages continue to be a major feature of their employment experience.

It is by no means unusual to claim that most women in employment are earning poor wages. What is being proposed here is a different way of expressing this inequality – one that has a sharper political angle and more adequate sociological substance. The purpose of this chapter is to provide further evidence that, in order to move the explanation of gender inequalities in employment on, a conceptual shift is necessary. It does so by examining the limitations of the more familiar terms and understandings in the current literature as regards the relationships between employment activity, occupational segregation and wages.

There is much more fundamental disagreement in the research literature about the relation of occupational segregation with employment activity patterns and wage inequalities than is recognized, or openly acknowledged, in sociological discussions. The chapter begins with an examination of the nature and significance of this disagreement. It will be argued that a necessary aspect of any way forward is a reworking of basic analytical categories, to yield more complex and adequate distinctions. Possibilities for this reworking are indicated in the later part of the chapter, which examines relationships between the work histories of women with children and employment in full-wage/component-wage jobs.

Segregation and stratification

When the contrast between horizontal and vertical occupational segregation by sex was introduced to British research, it was suggested that the two phenomena are "logically distinct even if they often occur together" (Hakim 1979:43). Most have interpreted the joint occurrence of horizontal and vertical occupational segregation as meaning that occupations in which women are concentrated (or over-represented) are also low-status, low-paying occupations. For example, in their comments on the relationship between horizontal and vertical segregation, Crompton (1986) and Joshi (1988) reiterate a widely held view. Crompton (1986: 123) observes that horizontal segregation "is accompanied by vertical segregation – men work most commonly in higher-grade occupations and women work most commonly in lower-grade occupations". In a similar vein, Joshi (1988:12) remarks that women's jobs "are not only, on the whole, different from those held by men, they are also less likely to be near the top of occupational ladders". Although these statements contain some truth, we need to pay attention to the qualifications attached to them. It must be stressed that the relationship between the horizontal and vertical forms of occupational segregation is not one of a simple identity.

Discussions of occupational segregation by sex typically take gendered jobs, that is "women's jobs" or "men's jobs", as their general categories of analysis. In doing so, this approach rarely addresses a problem that has increased in importance over recent years: the problem of explaining in a consistent manner both the inequalities between gendered categories and the inequalities that exist within each category. The fact that stratification fault lines run through predominantly female and male jobs, as well as between them, has created difficulties in establishing the precise significance of gender-skewed job distributions in explanations of employment inequalities.

The existence of horizontal gender segregation may itself be a form of inequality in cases where occupations are not equally accessible to men and women. However, in terms of vertical segregation the important dimensions of inequality are the resources and conditions of employment. In the stratification of gendered employment, the most extensively investigated resource is pay. It may come as a surprise to some to learn that although horizontal and vertical segregation are considered to be "most commonly" linked "on the whole", the relationship between the gender-skew in occupations and pay is strongly contested. Further, while there is growing evidence of definite relationships between women's work history characteristics and disadvantage in employment, the relationship between work histories and horizontal segregation is in dispute. Disagreement exists more openly in the economics literature where an engagement with the human capital approach has focused on relationships between work histories, wages and horizontal segregation. The sociological literature has yet to take full cognizance of these disagreements. It should do so because there is a need to shift the conceptual terrain of the debate in order to examine more appropriately the processes structuring employment inequalities and the location of gendered experience within these processes. At this point, an outline of the contested nature of relationships between segregation, wages and work histories is required.

Horizontal segregation, wages and work histories

The connection of horizontal segregation to work history characteristics and wages is a matter of considerable difference of opinion. To some, the phenomenon of horizontal segregation has a pivotal role in explanations of gender inequality. It is regarded as a primary cause of wage inequalities between women and men and as a major consequence of the disadvantaged nature of the "supply" characteristics of female labour. Others discount the significance of women's work histories for the explanation of patterns of horizontal segregation, or give little credit to horizontal segregation in the explanation of the gender gap in wages. In exploring the nature of these disagreements, it will become clear that the conceptualization of the central phenomena involved leaves much to be desired.[1]

Although most people would agree that women's employment is concentrated in the more disadvantaged forms of employment, more detailed relations between the gender composition of occupations and inequalities in pay have been hard to specify. For example, Miller (1987:893) concludes his inquiry into the wage effects of gender segregation in Britain with the statement that it "makes only a minor contribution to the gender wage gap". This conclusion echoes that of Joseph, who summarizes British research into the relationship between female concentration and wage levels as "inconclusive with respect to the precise effects of female overcrowding on relative female earnings" (1983:173–5). Indeed, using data from the New Earnings Survey, Joseph could find no significant relationships between female concentration (the percentage female in an occupation) and a variety of earnings data,

121

including male and female hourly earnings and the ratio of female to male earnings. One criticism that can be levelled at this research, however, is that it uses too gross a measure of horizontal segregation. Miller's analysis is based on just six occupational groups (management, professional, other non-manual, skilled manual, semi-skilled manual and unskilled manual), and the likelihood of variation in the degree of gender segregation within each group is very high. Although Joseph's analysis is based on more detailed occupational divisions (he uses 39 occupational titles), there is still the possibility of significant variation in gender concentration within each occupational title. This possibility is acknowledged explicitly by Treiman & Roos (1983), who decide against "occupational" segregation as an explanation of differences in women's and men's earnings across nine countries. Their analysis is based on seven occupational groups, and they conclude (1983:640) that although "women may be segregated into low-paying *jobs*, differences in the distribution of women and men over the *major occupation groups* have virtually no effect on income. Sex differences in income are on average as large within each of the major occupational groups as they are for the labour force as a whole."

The significance of drawing distinctions between "occupations" and "jobs" has been identified by other researchers. As emphasized by Treiman & Hartmann (1981:24) "even within finely detailed *occupations* (e.g. lawyer, sales clerk, hairdresser), *jobs* are frequently segregated by sex".[2] Further, the sex composition of a particular "job" may vary by workplace (Martin & Roberts 1984, Witherspoon 1988), and may vary within any single workplace by employment conditions, for example by whether the job is done on a part-time or full-time basis (Robinson 1988). The cases of postal workers and telephonists aptly illustrate the point that although "occupations" may be sex-typed, the construction of an occupation in the workplace can encompass both predominantly female and predominantly male "jobs". In general terms, as we move away from socially unlocated "occupations" towards distinctions that place employment in a specific social context, gender segregation comes into sharper relief. A striking example of this is provided by the work of Bielby & Baron (1987:213). Using the index of dissimilarity, they calculate the degree of segregation for three levels of occupational and job detail within a sample of employment establishments. When segregation is calculated across seven major occupational groups, 9% of establishments are completely gender-segregated. When the calculation is across 645 detailed occupations, the percentage of completely gender segregated establishments rises to 34. When the calculation is by job titles within the organizational hierarchy of each establishment, the number of completely segregated establishments rises to 55%.

In light of this research, we must be sensitive to the fact that occupational titles refer to a range of employment situations that may be differentiated in terms of gender composition. Just as some occupations relating to an occupational group may be more female dominated than others, so some jobs relating to an occupational title may be more female dominated than others. Thus, analyses that measure horizontal segregation as the percentage female in an occupation or an occupational group, and then fail to find significant differences between horizontal segregation and wages, may simply have insufficiently detailed employment positions.

Nevertheless, having a more precise measure of gendered employment positions in the analysis of horizontal segregation and its relation to gender inequalities does not fully resolve problems in specifying the relationship between gender composition and pay. People have had difficulty establishing a very strong relationship between the sex composition of occupations and earnings, even when occupations are coded in greater detail. For conclusions based on more extensive occupational breakdowns we need to look to American research.

England et al. (1982) and Treiman & Hartmann (1981) use 499 occupational titles from the 1970 US census to regress median earnings of full-time year-round employees on occupational characteristics, including the percentage female, and a limited number of personal characteristics. Both studies make a strong claim for the impact of the sex composition of an occupation on earnings. Treiman & Hartmann assert (1981:29–31) that the "sex composition of occupations, independent of other occupational characteristics and of average personal characteristics, has a strong effect on the earnings of incumbents". Yet, the net effect of the percentage female in an occupation is not very dramatic: for every 1% increase, wages decline by US$28 per year. The impact of this variable can be compared with the net effect of completed years of education, which per year raises annual earnings by US$681. The effect of sex composition on wages is also much less than each of the net effects of years of labour force experience, the complexity of the occupation, and the motor skills required by the occupation. England et al. (1982) came up with similar results for the impact of sex composition on wages. They established that a 1% increase in the female concentration of an occupation reduces women's annual full-time earnings by US$17 and men's by US$30. They estimate that this effect, plus the fact that more women are concentrated in "female" jobs, would explain close to one-third of the gender gap in earnings for full-time, full-year workers. Although these more sophisticated analyses do show a relationship between the gender concentration, or the "percentage female" in an occupation, and wages, the effect is more muted than many might expect.

123

The general issue, of course, is that if similar jobs and similar occupations can vary in gender composition, then the reverse must also be the case: the same pattern of gender composition (i.e. the same percentage of female incumbents) is associated with a range of jobs or occupations. An indication of the employment inequalities that may be found within similar levels of gender concentration is provided by comparable worth studies. The extensive range of job worth and wages within gendered employment positions helps to explain why it has been difficult to establish stronger relationships between gender concentration and inequalities in pay. Treiman & Hartmann (1981:59–61) report results of a comparable worth study conducted for state government jobs in the State of Washington. About half the jobs selected for evaluation had at least 70% male incumbents, and half had at least 70% female incumbents. Figure 5.1 shows the range of job worth points and the average monthly salary for the evaluated jobs. It is clear from the distributions that jobs with a high concentration of male incumbents cover a wide spectrum, in terms both of job worth and salary, as do jobs with a high concentration of female incumbents. Some of this variation in "worth" and wages within mainly female and male jobs may be accounted for by gender concentrations between 70% and 100%, but this is unlikely to explain that much. Additional case studies reported by Treiman &

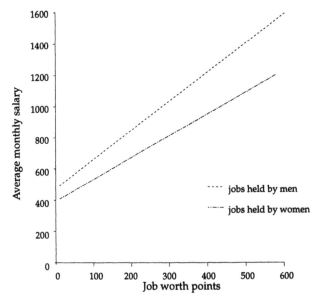

Figure 5.1 Monthly salaries by job worth points for predominantly male and female jobs (USA). Source: adapted from Treiman & Hartmann (1981:61).

124

Hartmann (1981:60) reveal considerable spread in job worth and wage levels even among completely segregated female and male jobs. What Figure 5.1 demonstrates quite dramatically is that, with only few exceptions, jobs held mainly by women are paid less than jobs held mainly by men, even though the jobs are of equivalent worth.

Figure 5.2 shows a similar pattern for British data (Stewart et al. 1985). Here the data are based on people's perceptions of earnings and "worth" for jobs that they have identified as predominantly male and predominantly female. In this case, one can read the matching of jobs on indicators of responsibility, control and amount of thinking as a control for "worth". The results are analogous to those of the American comparable worth studies. There is a similar relationship between worth and earnings for both types of sex-skewed jobs, but earnings for female jobs are at a lower level.

What the preceding collection of research indicates is that more precisely defined employment positions, and more clearly identified levels of gender concentration, reveal a stronger relationship between gender concentration and pay, but the relationship continues to be undercut by extensive inequalities between jobs with similar concentrations of male or female incumbents. To the extent that a relationship exists between horizontal segregation, or more precisely the "percentage female", and

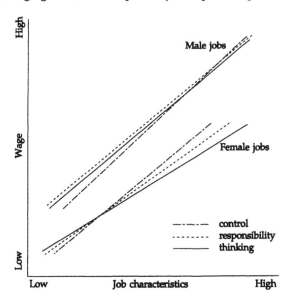

Figure 5.2   Wage by job characteristics for predominantly male and femal jobs (Britain). Source: Adapted from Stewart et al. (1985:292).

125

wages, further questions arise: what does the "percentage female" in a job signify, and how is it implicated in the process of wage determination?

One immediate possibility for answering these questions suggests itself. There is much evidence in the literature of the negative effects of standard aspects of women's work histories (such as discontinuity of employment) on occupational placement and rewards. To the extent that jobs with a high concentration of female incumbents are low status and low paying, we might expect particular patterns of work histories to be more prominent in such predominantly female jobs. However, there has yet to be a sufficiently systematic and convincing examination of the interrelation between women's work histories, patterns of segregation and wage inequalities. It is interesting to note that although the studies by Treiman & Hartmann (1981), and particularly England et al. (1982), include extensive measures of occupational characteristics, neither includes work history information. There are no variables controlling for aspects of women's work histories that are known to be significant depressors of women's employment position and earnings, such as continuity of employment and duration of employment interruptions. Could "percentage female" be a proxy for certain types of work histories or stages of work histories? Most studies have found that work history variables also explain roughly one-third of the gender gap in full-time earnings. Main (1988:118) states that work history variations explain 28% of the gender gap in full-time wages. American results, including full-time and part-time workers, put the figure between 30% and 50% (Corcoran et al. 1984:184–5).[3]

The connection between the sex composition of occupations and work history characteristics would be strongly denied by England and some of her American colleagues. In building an argument against attempts by human capital theory to extend its explanatory potential to occupational gender segregation, England (1982) and Corcoran et al. (1983) attack the possibility that women with certain types of work histories are more likely to be found in predominantly female jobs. It is unfortunate that the validity of a relationship between the sex composition of jobs and work history variations has got caught in the dispute with human capital theory. The existence of this relationship would not be support exclusively for human capital theory, or confirmation of the theory of occupational choice that the theory proposes (Polachek 1981). Connections between work history details and gender segregation are consistent with other interpretations of the dynamic of employment relations. In any case, the argument against the relationship, as set out by both authors, is not very convincing. They use extremely "broad brush" measures of work history characteristics (for example, England uses the average proportion of years women spend in employment after leaving school) and horizontal segregation (for example, Corcoran et al. aggregate the proportion female of a woman's jobs over a particular time period). Neither study attempts to take into account the hierarchical variation within levels of female concentration, or the possibility that the relationship between employment continuity and employment position may not be a linear one.[4]

Given the early stage of research into these matters, it can only be said that the cases for and against the relationship between work history patterns and horizontal segregation require further development. In large part, the difficulty in exploring this relationship for British women has been one of data. With the collection of work histories throughout the 1980s, the situation has improved since Hakim's call (1979:55) for more work on the impact of women's work profiles on inequalities in employment. Still, the limitations imposed by the nature of existing data remain a significant problem.[5] In addition, there are conceptual issues to be resolved. The existence of work history data provides the opportunity to move beyond simplistic and static notions of "women's position in the family" as a significant feature in the structuring of employment inequalities. They provide a picture of diversity in domestic and employment relations not only across women's experience at any one point in time, but also throughout an individual woman's lifetime experience. For the impact of work history patterns on gender segregation to be fully explored, the complex detail of these patterns must be preserved, until such time as it is clear that more parsimonious representations are equally effective in isolating significant variations in experience. To the extent that work history patterns are related to gender inequalities in employment, and to the extent that horizontal segregation is related to vertical segregation, we would expect *some* relationship between the dynamic of women's work histories and patterns of horizontal segregation. That the American researchers, in challenging the validity of human capital explanations, have insisted otherwise seems a remarkable case of throwing the proverbial baby out with its increasingly ineffectual bath water.

However, as the preceding discussion has emphasized, any attempt to link indicators of inequality and disadvantage with patterns of horizontal segregation must reckon with the fact that occupations dominated by women do not sit uniformly below occupations dominated by men. Within the past decade, much work has been done to identify inequalities between female-dominated employment positions and, as the stratification measures for "women's" occupations confirm, these inequalities are considerable.[6] This fact is prompting revision of conceptual approaches: for example, terms that have been used to characterize the contrast between men's and women's occupations (such as primary and secondary sector) are now used to indicate types of female-dominated occupations (Dex 1987). Further conceptual work is needed to develop explanations of variations within gendered jobs that are consistent with aggregate-level gender inequalities. It is now apparent that conventional market-based approaches are unable to provide adequate explanations, and as the search for alternatives continues, the place of wider social processes is assuming greater prominence. In this light, the importance of refining the conceptualization of work histories and employment positions in the analysis of gender inequalities has been emphasized. The degree of refinement required is indicated in the following analysis of the work histories of women who have had children, and employment in male-dominated full-wage and female-dominated component-wage jobs.

Work histories and full-wage/component-wage jobs

Data on women's work throughout their lifetimes suggest that the negotiation of parenting and employment is very variable. To extend the picture of parenting and employment relations discussed previously, work histories were compiled for women who had ever had children.[7] This analysis is limited by the specific nature of the telephonist and postal jobs and their incumbents. All workers have minimal educational resources, and all jobs are disadvantaged in terms of content and rewards. It is not possible, given other data available, to examine how the patterns established for these jobs would be modified or extended across a wider spectrum of employment circumstances. The current sample of women is distinctive in that all were in full-time employment, and this is a notable feature of the women who still have dependent children. Nevertheless, as this section will demonstrate, the patterns in work histories to be presented, and the inequalities they entail, are consistent with the results of other studies. In this respect, particular reference is made throughout to the work history patterns identified in the Women and Employment survey (WES). In addition, the work history analysis based on the telephonist and postal worker (TP) sample has something to add to the general picture of women's work histories in terms of information about variation by "race" and the impact of marital breakdown.

There is now a considerable literature on women's work histories, as well as on the costs of motherhood for women's employment experience. Although many of the details of the work histories of women who have had children are of interest in their own right, three features seem most productive in identifying relations between work histories,

128

employment distributions and earnings. These features are: (a) whether or not a woman has had a work history of continuous employment; (b) the duration of hometime (or time out of the labour force); and (b) the nature of employment experience following periods out of the labour force, particularly whether jobs are part time or full time. As we shall see, these work history features are substantially different for women in the component-wage and full-wage jobs.

Continuity and discontinuity of employment

Table 5.1 shows the four major patterns of continuity and discontinuity for female telephonists and postal workers. Women who were in employment continuously during years of childrearing comprised 20% of the women who have had children. Their current age (all were over 30 and the majority were in their 40s and 50s) indicates that they were unlikely to take any more breaks for parenting purposes. Although withdrawals for other domestic reasons, or a move to part-time employment, were possibilities, it is likely that, in terms of employment interruptions, their current work history profile was close to its final form.

Table 5.1 Continuity and discontinuity in work histories by type of job for women with children (TP sample).

Work history	Total		Component-wage		Full-wage	
	N	%	N	%	N	%
Continuous employment	8	20	0	0	8	26
Single interruption	21	53	6	66	15	48
Two or more employment interruptions	8	20	3	33	5	16
Employed after childrearing only	3	8	0	0	3	10
Total	40	100	9	100	31	100

A number of work history investigations identify continuous workers as a significant comparison for women who experience employment breaks for parenting. However, many of these investigations do not distinguish between continuous workers who are childless and continuous workers who have had children (Stewart & Greenhalgh 1984, Main 1988, Main & Elias 1987). Dex (1984) and Martin & Roberts (1984) are exceptions. As with the current study, Dex (1984) defines women with children as continuous workers if they return to employment within six months of every birth. She further distinguishes between women who are "family formation continuous" only – that is they were employed continuously during the family formation phase, but not the final work phase – and women who are "successful continuous workers" in that they have been employed continuously throughout both the family formation and final work phases.[8] From Dex's analysis, it is possible to identify a sub-group of WES that shares some of the characteristics of the TP sample of women who have had children. The WES sub-group comprises women aged 30 or over who have had children, and who returned to employment at some point after the birth of the first child.[9]

Altogether 11% of the WES sub-group were continuously employed during parenting years: 9% were successful continuous workers, and a further 2% were family formation continuous only.[10] The TP sample over-represents women who were in employment continuously in the family formation phase, but it is clear from the WES sub-group that these women are not an insignificant group in the larger female population. If we were able to calculate the same figures for those in the WES sub-group who were currently in full-time employment, the extent of continuous employment might well be greater.[11]

The family formation continuous women from both samples were likely to have employment histories dominated by full-time employment. Women in the TP sample with continuous work histories only ever worked full time, while full-time employment comprised between 68% and 77% of the years employed for each type of continuous worker in the WES sub-group (Dex 1984:77).

As Table 5.1 shows, all continuous workers in the TP sample were in the full-wage jobs, and a work history of continuous employment was a prominent pattern among women with children in full-wage jobs (26%). Women in the component-wage job were more likely to have interrupted their employment for childrearing for more than six months at a time, and they were more likely to have had two or more hometime periods. In other words, in the case of the telephonist and postal worker jobs, continuous employment is associated with employment in the higher-paying, predominantly male jobs.

There is evidence in the research literature that the relationship between employment continuity and employment circumstances is complex, and likely to be curvilinear (Martin & Roberts 1984:126, Daniels 1980). Some continuously employed women are more advantaged women pursuing career paths of various sorts. They are likely to have provisions for paid maternity leave and the resources to purchase childcare on their return to employment. The literature suggests that there are also others whose continuous employment during the family formation phase may be a response to the increased financial demands of an expanded and more disadvantaged household. Several commentators have stressed the strong financial motive operating for women who return to employment soon after childbirth (Bird & West 1987, Brannen 1987, Dex 1984, Martin & Roberts 1984). The continuously employed women with children in the TP sample, with no qualifications and employment in a semi-skilled occupation, fit quite clearly into the disadvantaged end of this curvilinear pattern. The push to resume employment quickly after the birth of children is emphasized if we recall from Chapter 3 that these women also have low-earning husbands.

Duration of hometime and subsequent employment experience

The research literature has also shown that, in addition to whether employment interruptions have occurred, patterns of inequality cohere around the duration of time out of the labour force (Main 1988, Stewart & Greenhalgh 1984). In the TP sample, durations of hometime were very different for the full-wage and component-wage women. Among all those with breaks in employment for full-time parenting, full-wage women were generally older than component-wage women at their first exit from employment, and younger at their permanent re-entry to employment. Consequently, not only were full-wage women with children more likely to be employed continuously, those with employment breaks had less time as full-time mothers, compared with component-wage women. The difference in hometime between women in the two types of jobs is dramatic, as Table 5.2 indicates. On average, full-wage women were full-time mothers for 6.3 years, compared with 12.1 years for component-wage women.[12]

Table 5.2 Length of time as full-time mothers by current job type (TP sample)[1].

| Job type | N | Years of full-time motherhood | | | | | |
		Under 3	3–5	6–8	9–11	12+	Mean
Component-wage	9	1	1	1	1	5	12.1
Full-wage	23	5	7	6	1	4	6.3

1. Discontinuous work histories only.

Several pieces of research have demonstrated the negative relationship between duration of hometime and both occupational attainment and earnings. For example, Stewart & Greenhalgh found (1984:504) that women (aged 45–54) with less than five years' hometime had a significantly more advantaged occupational position and earnings than women with longer durations of hometime. Indeed, their research suggests that the occupational attainment and earnings of women with under five years' hometime were similar to those of women who had no breaks from employment.

It is interesting to observe, in this respect, that the majority of full-wage women were full-time mothers for five years or less (Table 5.2).

Although there is a strong relationship between duration of hometime and earnings, recent research indicates that the nature of the relationship may alter over the course of a work history. Both British (Dex 1984, 1987, Joshi 1987, Main 1988) and American research (Corcoran et. al 1984, Mincer & Ofek 1982) indicate that women's earnings may to some extent recover from the negative consequences of time out of employment. However, to the extent that this recovery occurs, it is associated with full-time employment. For example, Main (1988) argues that the labour market has a short memory, in that only the most recent spell of hometime is significantly associated with downward pressure on wages. Any upward pressure on wages comes from years of full-time, and not part-time, employment experience. Similarly, Corcoran et al. (1984:189) remark that women "are often urged to choose part-time work rather than to stop work altogether to keep their 'hands in'. Our results provide little evidence that the wage consequences of these two alternatives differ.... The decision whether to work full time or part time is considerably more important than is the choice between part-time work or no work."

Undoubtedly, how women fare after their return to employment is dependent upon the mix of full-time and part-time jobs in this phase of their work history. Table 5.3 shows, for both the TP sample and the WES sample as analyzed by Martin & Roberts (1984), the mix of full-time and part-time employment in the final work phase for women returners. In the WES sample, 26% of women returned to employment via a full-time

Table 5.3 Mix of full-time and part-time employment in the final work phase for women currently in employment (WES and TP samples).

Type of employment in final work phase	WES sample			TP sample	
	N	% of sample	% of full time	N	% of full time
Currently full time					
Full time always	368	17	45	17	53
Returned full time, has worked part time	57	3	7	5	16
Returned part time	396	18	48	10	31
Total	821	38	100	32	100
Currently part time					
Part time always	1131	52			
Returned part time, has worked full time	85	4			
Returned full time	141	6			
Total	1357	62			

Source: The WES figures are adapted from Martin & Roberts (1984:135), Table 9.23. They refer to "all women who have worked since last birth", excluding those "not currently working".

job, and 74% via a part-time job. Of those currently in a full-time job, the majority (52%) had returned to a full-time job and 45% had been in only full-time jobs since returning to employment. The WES sample currently in full-time employment is the most appropriate group to compare with the TP sample, and the mixes of full-time and part-time experience in the final work phase of the two groups resemble one another. The majority of the TP sample also began their final work phase in a full-time job, although the percentage is higher (69%). In addition, the final work phase for the majority of the TP sample was composed of full-time employment only. Here again we must distinguish between the component-wage and the full-wage women (see Table 5.4), for this distinction differentiates between types of employment experience in the final work phase. Compared with component-wage women, full-wage women were almost twice as likely to return to and remain in full-time employment (33% and 61% respectively).

Table 5.4 Mix of full-time and part-time employment in the final work phase for women in component-wage and full-wage jobs (TP sample)[1].

Type of employment in final work phase	Component-wage		Full-wage	
	N	%	N	%
Currently full-time				
Full-time always	3	33	14	61
Returned full time, has worked part-time	2	22	3	13
Returned part time	4	44	6	26
Total	9	100	23	100

1. Discontinuous work histories only.

In the TP sample, continuity of employment, shorter durations of hometime if discontinuity occurred, and employment in full-time jobs on returning to the labour market are the characteristics that mark the work histories of women in the higher paying, male-dominated full-wage jobs. This pattern fits with the wage effects of discontinuity of employment and the mix of full-time and part-time employment that have been observed in other studies. Main nicely illustrates some aspects of the relationships involved by considering a woman at age 40 who has a work history of eight years in the initial work phase, followed by an eight year interruption, followed by seven years' employment in the final work phase.

If the first employment phase was full-time and the second part-time then the expected hourly earnings . . . would be £1.67. If, however, the final employment phase was all in full-time employ-

133

ment, expected hourly earnings would be £1.85. Finally, if the woman has maintained a continuous employment phase, all in full-time employment..., then the expected wage would be £2.21. (Main 1988:118)[13]

Summary

Associations observed in the general literature between characteristics of work histories and employment inequalities are consistent with the experience of women in full-wage and component-wage jobs. Combining the three features of work histories associated with advantage and disadvantage in employment (continuity, duration of hometime and full/part-time mix of employment), we get a strong picture of the work history profiles for the two groups of jobs. As Table 5.5 indicates, just under half of all women in full-wage jobs were either full-time continuous workers or workers with a shorter duration of hometime who returned to uninterrupted full-time employment. None of the component-wage women had these work history patterns. At the other extreme, two-thirds of component-wage women had more extended periods of hometime and had experience of part-time employment at some point after the birth of the first child.

Work history patterns are clearly associated, in this case, with the gender composition of the full-wage and component-wage jobs. It is worth noting that this pattern would be much less visible if the analysis was performed on the two occupational titles (telephonist and postal worker) rather than the full-wage/component-wage distinction, which aligns the

Table 5.5 Continuity, duration of hometime, and full-time/part-time employment for women (with children) in component-wage and full-wage jobs (TP sample).

Work history patterns	Component-wage		Full-wage	
	N	%	N	%
Continuous full time				
Hometime of 5 years or less employed full time only	0	0	15	48
Hometime of 6 years or over employed full time only	3	33	10	32
Hometime of 5 years or under employed full and part time				
Hometime of 6 years or over employed full and part-time	6	67	6	19
Total	9	100	31	100

male-dominated night telephonist job with the male-dominated postal job. The relationship between characteristics of work histories and gender composition of occupation would be muddied because of the work history differences between women in the two telephonist jobs.

We turn now to a brief examination of two important variations in women's work histories within the full-wage jobs: those by "race" and, for white women, those by marital history.

Work history variations by "race" and marital history

None of the larger British work history studies has identified variations by racial group, and in this sense the current study is a small contribution. Just as full-wage women, generally speaking, had more extensive employment experience, and full-time employment experience, than component-wage women, black women in full-wage jobs had work histories with these characteristics to a greater extent than white full-wage women. The number of black full-wage women with children was small ($N=14$), but their work history experience reflects patterns suggested by cross-sectional data on employment participation.

Compared with white full-wage women with children, black full-wage women with children were more likely to maintain employment throughout the family formation stage. Over one-third were employed full time continuously during their child bearing and rearing years (compared with under one-fifth for white full-wage women). A very brief period of time was taken from employment for childbearing, and these women had virtually no experience of parenting without the responsibilities of employment. If periods of hometime were part of the work histories of black full-wage women, the total duration of hometime was not extensive. The average period of hometime for black full-wage women was 5.3 years (compared with 6.7 years for white full-wage women). As indicated in Table 5.1, a small number of women entered employment only after the birth of their first child. They were all black full-wage women, and their entry into employment also corresponded with their immigration to Britain. Although their entry into employment was relatively delayed, 97% of their employment experience was in full-time jobs.[14]

As indicated previously, most of the black full-wage women were of West Indian origin. The predominance, among this group of women, of work histories characterized by either continuous full-time employment or full-time employment with a hometime break of relatively short duration is consistent with cross-sectional data on employment participation rates for Afro-Caribbean women in Britain (Bruegel 1989, Brown 1984, Barber 1985, Phizacklea 1988). All cross-sectional data have shown a high level of involvement, and full-time involvement, in employment for married Afro-Caribbean women in age groups marking the years of childbearing and childrearing. The retrospective work history data reported here are consistent with the more extended and intense employment participation of Afro-Caribbean women compared with white women (or, more specifically, component-wage white women) with parenting responsibilities.

Although the work histories of black full-wage women are dominated by full-time employment, this is not uniformly the case for white full-wage women. Table 5.6 shows a significant distinction between white and black full-wage women in terms of the mix of full-time and part-time employment experience in the final work phase. All black full-wage women began their final work phase in full-time employment and, with one exception, remained in full-time jobs. Many full-wage white women began their final work phase in a full-time job, but, as with component-wage white women, a substantial number began their final work phase in part-time jobs (43% and 44%, respectively). To explain this variation in full-time and part-time starts in the final work phase, we need to look at marital history.

Table 5.6 Mix of full-time and part-time employment in the final work phase for black and white full-wage women (TP sample).[1]

Type of employment	White Full-wage		Black Full-wage	
	N	%	N	%
In final work phase				
Full time always	6	43	8	89
Returned full time, has worked part time	2	14	1	11
Returned part time	6	43	0	0
Total	14	100	9	100

1. Discontinuous work histories only.

For the black full-wage women, there was little variation in patterns of work histories by marital status. The duration of hometime was similar for married and previously married women, and the majority of both groups had only ever been employed full time. In the case of white full-wage women, there are important contrasts to be drawn, in terms of hometime and engagement with full-time employment, between the work histories of currently married women and women who experience marital breakdown. The picture is not of a straightforward division between the two marital groups. Some married and previously married women shared the same work history characteristics, but one particular group of previously married women stood out as having distinctive work histories. We have seen already that marital breakdown was a key element in the employment of white women in full-wage jobs. The following discussion introduces a factor instrumental in shaping variations within the work histories of previously married white women: the point at which marital breakdown occurred.

The majority of white married women were likely to have returned to a part-time job following a break from employment for childrearing. The number of white married women who entered a part-time job on returning permanently to the labour force was twice as high as the number who entered a full-time job. Women who were previously married were more likely to have begun their permanent return to employment in a full-time job, although it is interesting to note that only half had done so. Although greater engagement with full-time employment is often pointed to as a distinguishing feature of previously married women's employment (Rimmer 1988), it is obvious that some have had fairly standard "female" work histories, including the conventional return to part-time employment.

The problems of gaining access to employment, and sufficiently well-paid employment, that are faced by previously married women with parenting responsibilities are well-known matters of concern (Bird & West 1987, Dale 1987, Joshi 1988, Millar 1987, Popay et al. 1983). Some work history studies have attempted to set out the consequences of marital breakdown on the shape and details of women's employment participation. In general, marital breakdown appears to coincide with a return to, or an intensification of, employment (Dex 1984), although there are variations from this pattern both within and across generations (Bird & West 1987, Yeandle 1984). Case studies have been instrumental in establishing distinctive aspects of previously married women's employment position that are not fully recognized or explored in larger surveys. Often in large-scale studies, previously married women are not identified as such. They are either grouped with single women as "non-married" or grouped with married women as "ever married" (see, for example, Joshi 1984, and Roos 1985, respectively). Although a number of authors have emphasized the significance of distinguishing the negotiation of employment and domestic life by previously married women (Popay et al. 1983, Martin & Roberts 1984), there is uncertainty in the overall picture as to how disruptive marital breakdown is for women's work history profiles. For example, Dex (1984: 39, 69) expresses surprise that marital breakdown appears to have no impact on aspects of the final work phase, when it was shown to disrupt and alter the family formation phase. For most of these studies, we do not know when marital breakdown occurred, and the current case suggests that this information may help to clarify the work history patterns for previously married women and the impact of marital breakdown on employment experience.

Among the 26 white women with children in the TP sample, half were married and half were separated, widowed or divorced. Those who were previously married divide into two groups of roughly equal size: those whose marriage ended after they reached 40 years of age, and after their permanent return to employment; and those whose marriage ended during the family formation phase, while they were in their 20s and 30s. Although there are a limited number of women involved in these comparisons, the differences in the work histories of white women, by age and work history phase at marital breakdown, are informative. Over two-thirds of currently married women had time out for parenting and began their permanent return to employment in a part-time job. Previously married women who experienced marital breakdown *after* the age of 40 had a similar experience: about three-quarters of them had time out for parenting and returned to a part-time job after their last employment interruption. This contrasts with the work histories of previously married women who experienced marital breakdown *before* they reached aged 40, during the family formation phase. Although most had time out for full-time parenting, they all returned permanently to the labour force via a full-time job and were in full-time employment throughout their entire final work phase.

The similarity between married white women and previously married white women who divorced or separated after age 40 can be seen also in the length of time spent out of the labour force in full-time motherhood. The majority of both groups had over five years as full-time mothers, and half of both groups had more than 10 years as full-time mothers. Again their experience differs substantially from those who underwent marital breakdown before the age of 40, none of whom were full-time mothers beyond five years.

This information suggests that the timing of marital breakdown is a significant factor in isolating and identifying the impact of marital breakdown on the shape and details of women's work histories. Quite simply, the earlier the breakdown occurs, the greater the divergence between the work histories of married and previously married women.

Previously married women with children often do not return to employment because of difficulties with childcare and the limited possibility of access to wages sufficient to support their household. Many have commented on the difficulties previously married women face in obtaining an adequate income. As Joshi observes (1988:26–7), "a large proportion of divorcees, particularly if they have children, do not find that the labour market offers such good opportunities to finance independence".

In the terms of the current study, previously married women with parenting responsibilities had difficulty securing a full-wage sufficient to cover the needs of themselves and their children.[15]

Research shows that, if previously married women are in employment, they are more likely to be employed full time (Martin & Roberts 1984). Considerations of re-marriage aside, full-time employment is the best chance previously married women have of keeping their households above the poverty line, of achieving financial independence and of recovering from the economic consequences of divorce (Arendell 1987, Millar 1987, Rimmer 1988). Information from postwomen and female telephonists does support the observation that when women in the family formation phase return to full-time employment after the breakdown of a marriage, they return quickly. All had very young children at this time and all, either immediately or within a very short time interval, moved into their current full-wage job. Previously married women who experienced marital breakdown after the age of 40, and after returning permanently to employment, moved into full-time from part-time employment or tried to move into higher paying full-time employment (for example, by working night shifts). Not all of the older women had dependent children at this time and a small number of these took component-wage jobs. For the majority, however, the end of their marriage was closely followed by their entry into their current full-wage job. But, the options of full-time, and certainly full-wage, employment are available to only a small minority of women who are heads of dependent families. Statistics reveal that over the 1980s this minority was reducing in size, with a substantial drop in full-time employment among previously married women and a corresponding increase in dependence on supplementary benefit and income support (Millar 1987). The prevalence of component-wages among women in full-time employment demonstrated in the previous chapter, underscores the limited access women have to full-wages sufficient to support themselves, let alone access to full-wages sufficient to support dependants.

Summary

This chapter has had a twofold aim: to confirm further the sociological validity of the full-wage/component-wage distinction by demonstrating its relationship to significant variations in women's work histories; and to raise substantial issues in the identification of general patterns of gender inequality as they are articulated in relationships between horizontal segregation, wages and work histories.

In earlier chapters, we have seen that gender configurations of a spe-

139

cific form are an important feature of the full-wage/component-wage distinction, but the latter is fully compatible with a more extensive structuring of negotiations of domestic and employment relations. The significance of this point is underlined in the material presented in this chapter, which demonstrates the close relationship between work history profiles of women who have had children and employment in full-wage and component-wage jobs. Examination of the research literature on the association between women's work histories and gender inequalities in employment positions and rewards indicates that three work history features are of most importance in the structuring of inequalities: whether or not a woman's employment history has been interrupted for full-time childrearing; the duration of time out of the labour force if interruptions have occurred; and the extent of full-time and part-time employment following a woman's return to the labour force. The study of postwomen and female telephonists shows that women in component-wage and full-wage jobs have strongly contrasting experience on all three dimensions. Women in full-wage jobs either had been employed continuously during childrearing years or had interrupted their employment for relatively short durations (typically five years or less). In both cases, their employment experience was dominated by full-time jobs. Of those who had interrupted work histories, the majority began their final work phase in a full-time job and remained in full-time employment. By contrast, none of the women in component-wage jobs had a work history of continuous employment during the years of childbearing and childrearing. All had breaks in employment for parenting purposes, and the duration of hometime was relatively extensive. The majority had been full-time mothers for 12 years or more. Typically, component-wage women experienced a mix of full-time and part-time jobs on their return to the labour force, and a substantial number began their final work phase in a part-time job.

In Chapter 3, we found that black women and previously married white women comprised a large proportion of those employed in full-wage jobs. The work history analysis in this chapter revealed interesting variations by "race" and, for white women, by marital history. Although the numbers involved in this case are very small, the patterns are perhaps suggestive of wider experience. Although full-wage women, in contrast to component-wage women, had greater continuity of employment and greater involvement in full-time jobs, the work histories of black full-wage women are especially characterized by these features. Over one-third of black full-wage women with children were continuous full-time workers throughout their work history. For those who took breaks in their employment for parenting, the breaks were short and all returned to full-time employment. These work history patterns are consistent with the picture of black (Afro-Caribbean) women's employment participation in Britain derived from cross-sectional data: greater involvement in employment, and full-time employment, during child-bearing years. A comparison of the work histories of married and previously married white women revealed the importance of determining when martial breakdown occurred. Women who experienced marital breakdown after the age of 40 had work history profiles similar to those of many married women – they had a break from employment, often of a substantial length, and they returned to part-time jobs. However, in response to marital breakdown, these women shifted to full-time jobs, and it is at this point that most shifted into their current full-wage job. Women who experienced marital breakdown before the age of 40, and typically while their children were still school age, had work histories characterized by a truncated period of hometime and a return to full-time employment. We know from other research material that, if in employment, previously married women with children are more likely to be working full time. Nevertheless, the labour force participation rate of these women is low and, as the data in the previous chapter indicated, this is connected with the fact that women's wages are typically component-wages and not sufficient to support even themselves in an independent household. The postal and night telephonist jobs offered the rare opportunity for women with little education or training to earn full-wages for a household with dependants, albeit on the basis of extensive overtime hours.

The general associations between work history features and full-wage/component-wage employment also involve a link between work history features and the gender composition of jobs. The full-wage jobs were dominated by men, and the component-wage job was female dominated. Thus, the more familiar form of women's work histories – that of employment breaks followed by returns to part-time employment – was associated with the female-dominated job, while greater employment continuity and returns to full-time employment are associated with the male-dominated jobs. Given the unavailability of comparable data, it has not been possible to attempt to trace this pattern out to a greater range of employment positions. Consequently, important questions remain to be addressed. What forms of women's work histories would be found in more advantaged female-dominated jobs? Similarly, how would the continuous employment profiles of the full-wage women compare with the work history characteristics of women in more advantaged male-dominated jobs? In particular, it seems that employment continuity may have a curvilinear relationship to the hierarchy of employment positions, with educational resources specifying aspects of this relationship. In any case, the clear relationships between types of work history, wages and the gender composition of jobs found in the current study have not been so clearly established in larger scale investigations.

Indeed, in the general research literature the significance of variations in women's work histories for segregated employment distributions is an especially contested point. Equally, the significance of segregated employment distributions for the gender gap in wages is acclaimed by some and denied by others. In reviewing this literature, it has been argued that the interrelations of work histories, wages and horizontal segregation are very finely tuned, and that frequently the operationalizing of employment positions and work histories is insufficiently detailed. Because vertical segregation, or wider patterns of employment inequality, cannot be neatly mapped onto the gender composition of occupations, there will be a limitation on the extent to which the work history variations associated with the former will be related to the latter. Nevertheless, given the case study and survey evidence of the consequences of standard patterns in women's work histories for disadvantages in employment experience, and given the fact that many female-dominated jobs are disadvantaged, we should see some relationship between work history patterns and horizontal segregation.

Until further and more adequate research is available, it would be premature to discount the influence of work history characteristics in the reproduction of gendered employment positions. Research interests that foreground processes internal to employment in the structuring of gender inequality are inclined to dismiss or limit the impact of gendered relations on domestic responsibilities. For example, Beechey (1983:43) offers as an underlying rationale of the need to locate occupational segregation in processes internal to waged work, the point that women's "position within the occupational structure cannot be simply 'read off' from an analysis of the sexual division of labour within the family". Similarly, Walby (1988:1) begins the introduction to *Gender Segregation at Work* with the claim that it "defies conventional theories of gender relations in employment since it is inexplicable in terms of women's position in the family". Against the fine distinctions used in the research discussed in this section, past attempts to examine relations between "women's position in the family" and employment inequalities appear over-simplistic. As our data and theoretical distinctions become more refined, and more appropriate to the life-course dynamic of the negotiation of parenting and employment, the explanatory potential of "family" experience may be restored. Processes internal to employment are certainly significant in the structuring of gender inequality: gendered understandings of managers, employers, trade unionists and fellow workers have their effects, as do structured aspects of employment relations that assume full-time, continuous employment patterns. Even so, many of the practices disadvantaging women that are regarded as internal to employment are premised on understandings of gendered domestic and employment relations (*pace* Curran 1988).

This is not to suggest that "supply" characteristics of women's labour are sufficient to explain patterns of gender segregation and wage inequalities, or that such explanations must be founded on "market" processes. Comparable worth investigations confirm other findings (Craig et al. 1982, Stewart et al. 1985) that the wage differentials between female-dominated and male-dominated jobs do not reflect the characteristics of labour or labour power. These investigations seriously challenge conventional market-based explanations of employment inequalities and suggest the operation of wider social processes in employment allocation and wage determination.

At this point, the analysis moves on to consider variations in women's and men's understandings of domestic and employment relations. We shall see in Chapter 6 that not only do variations in work histories cohere around the distinction between full-wage and component-wage jobs, they are also closely tied to differences in understandings of employment and parenting experience.

Notes

1. Generally in the literature, horizontal segregation is understood to mean the concentration (or share) of women in occupations. I use such terms as they appear in the original discussions, although elsewhere (Siltanen et al. 1992) we have argued for the need to distinguish between the concepts of concentration and segregation. According to our definitions, the female share of an occupation is a measure of concentration, not segregation. Further, the term "horizontal" segregation is something of a misnomer as the data pattern it refers to includes a vertical dimension.
2. Emphasis added. Treiman & Hartmann define jobs as "specific positions within establishments or the economic activities of specific individuals. They entail particular duties and responsibilities and involve the performance of particular tasks in particular settings" (1981:24). As they note, data are typically more available for occupations than for jobs.
3. Main reports that work history variations would explain roughly two-thirds of the gender gap for part-time workers (1988:118). This is similar to the general result reported by Zabalza and Arrufat (1985).
4. For example, England (1982:368) finds no statistically significant relationship between the percentage female in detailed US Census occupational categories (organized in groupings of 9.9 percentage points) and the average proportion of years a woman spends in employment after completing school. This finding is corroborated by Corcoran et al. (1983:300), who use longitudinal data

from the Panel Study of Income Dynamics. They aggregate the sex-typing (proportion female) of a woman's jobs over a particular time period and correlate this with indicators of intermittent employment participation (number of spells out of the labour force and total hometime) during the same time period. They (1983:302) "confirm England's finding of no relationship between discontinuity of work and sex-typing of concurrent occupation". Work histories are not fully operationalized in either study, although this is especially the case for England's work. The aggregation of horizontal segregation that is the basis of Corcoran et al.'s investigation is very dubious, especially since it is highly likely that the experience of horizontal segregation varies over an individual's work history (as Corcoran's later work demonstrates, Corcoran et al. 1984). Analysis of this sort has yet to be performed on British data, although some preliminary indications of lifetime patterns in segregation are available (Scott & Burchell, forthcoming).

5. The detailed coding of occupation and work history variables in the recently available Social Change and Economic Life Initiative data will go some way to resolving this issue.

6. See Dale et al. (1987), Murgatroyd (1984), Prandy (1986), Roberts & Barker (1989).

7. Complete information on work histories is available for 40 of the 45 women who ever had children. It would be equally interesting to investigate variation within the male labour force in terms of the relations between types of employment and work histories. The current study did not collect work history information for men that was as detailed as required for this purpose.

8. Dex (1984) distinguishes five types of work history patterns for women who return to employment at some point after childbirth. "Family formation continuous" and "successful continuous" women are a subset of the "works after every birth" and the "returns after every birth" patterns (1984:74-5). The terminology used in the current study differs somewhat from that used by Dex. In the current case, a work history refers to sequences of paid and unpaid work; employment history refers to sequences of paid work. I have used Dex's terms for the "family formation phase" and the "final work phase". The family formation phase (Dex 1984:14) begins with the first pregnancy, and the final work phase (1984:60) begins at the return to employment after the birth of the last child.

9. For purposes of work history comparisons with the TP sample, it would be preferable if the WES sub-group were currently in full-time employment also. Dex (1984:80) does report that of women aged 30 or over who were in employment, 50% were working full time.

10. The figures for continuous workers are derived from Dex (1984:74-5) who reports for women aged 30 or over a total of 258 successful continuous workers (with children) and 64 family formation continuous only. Their representation within the work history profiles of women aged 30 or over has been calculated using the figures from Table 16, "Family formation pattern frequencies by age (10 year groups)" (1984:37). The figure taken as a base for the calculation of percentages is all women aged 30 or over who experienced some employment after the birth of the first child ($N=2742$). Dex also gives equivalent figures for women aged 40 or over. In this group there are 76 fam-

ily formation continuous only and 10 successful (with children), representing 5% of the relevant portions of this age group.

11. These observations are also consistent with Yeandle's study (1984:75), although the extent of continuous employment is not directly comparable owing to the greater age range in Yeandle's sample. Approximately 9% of the women interviewed were employed continuously during the family formation phase. All were married and most were involved in full-time employment while their children were of pre-school age. For a more general population including women without children, Main & Elias (1987:98) report that for a range of 20th century cohorts, no less than 10% of women have been continuous workers into their 30s and 40s.

12. The duration of hometime for component-wage women is comparable to results in Stewart & Greenhalgh (1984). They report an average of between 11 and 12 years' hometime for older women (with interrupted work histories) employed full time in their final work phase. Comparing the work histories in the TP sample across generations of women with children shows some differences. The predominant work history pattern among the older generation is of one fairly long employment interruption, while the younger generation of women are more likely to have two interruptions, each of shorter duration. This difference between the younger and older married women in the number and duration of interruptions experienced, corresponds with evidence that there has been an increase in the number of women returning to employment before the birth of their second child (Martin & Roberts 1984: 128).

13. This woman also has school leaving credentials and has always worked for the same employer.

14. A work history pattern of a delayed start has also been noted as more characteristic of black American women (Corcoran & Duncan 1979, Mincer & Polachek 1980). Stewart & Greenhalgh (1984) find a total of approximately 6% delayed starts in the overall range of work histories identified with the National Training Survey (their analysis does not isolate women with children, however). In Dex's analysis of WES (1984:36), 2% of women with children had a work history pattern involving no employment before the birth of the first child. Ethnic breakdowns are not reported in either of the latter two studies.

15. See also Rainwater et al. (1986:107 ff.) for a discussion of sources of household financing for lone parent women in Britain, Sweden and the US.

145

Chapter Six

Understandings of relations to employment

One argument that has run consistently through this work is that with more complex, detailed and dynamic presentations of family and domestic experience, the significance of the latter for explanations of employment patterns and positions can be more appropriately identified. This point is germane also for explanations of understandings of employment. An influential criticism of earlier treatments of women's attitudes to and perceptions of paid work was that they assumed the salience of family experience for women, and interpreted women's relations to employment through a permanent filter of family obligations and commitments. The use of gender differentiated models of explanations of work experience has been argued to ignore variations in women's and men's relations to employment, and to give less attention to how both domestic and employment experiences structure perceptions of employment for women and men (Feldberg & Glenn 1984). As summarized by Purcell (1988:158), the role of gender stereotypes and ideologies in explanations of the experience of employment have "more often been assumed rather than investigated".

Over the past decade, studies of gender inequality have begun to deconstruct women's experience, emphasizing difference and complexity both in terms of "race" and class, and in terms of life-course patterns (for example, Allatt et al. 1987, Barrett & McIntosh 1985, Ramazanoglu 1989). In the context of employment, much effort has been directed at acknowledging and elaborating differences among women at any one time, and over time, in the negotiation of paid work and its relation to wider aspects of personal life. Although many investigations into women's employment experiences now highlight the importance of diversity, the significance of this diversity for women's understandings of employment, and the extent to which these are differentiated from men's, is less

146

developed. From the perspective of the full-wage and component-wage jobs in this study, and the patterns of lifetime negotiations of domestic and employment relations they embody, it is possible to explore in some detail the connections between variations in parenting and employment experience and understandings. This is the purpose of the current chapter.

The chapter is divided into two main section. The first begins by examining the extent to which women and men give priority to family life and employment when assessing important aspects of their social experience. It then explores perceptions of inequality in family life and employment, and looks at the extent to which these perceptions are gendered. Conceptions of salient aspects of social life, and of relative advantage and disadvantage, are tied to immediate and lifetime employment and family experience, as well as people's relations to typical gender patterns in these areas. In the second section, this analysis is extended to examine understandings of claims on employment. It assesses the meaning of gender, marital status and household circumstances in people's perceptions of who should have priority in the allocation of employment. Women's and men's priorities in the allocation of employment are identified and then located in variations in the negotiation of parenting and employment relations. We shall see that there are significant variations in understandings of women's and men's relations to employment, and that these variations are tied to perceptions of household requirements and to differences in the salience of gendered experience in domestic and waged work.

In the interview questionnaire, special questions were designed to investigate the presence of gender differences in perceptions of employment and their location in wider social experiences. The analysis focuses on identifying the conditions within which gendered perceptions are and are not present, and on identifying conditions underlying variations in women's and men's perceptions. Where possible, qualitative information from the interviews is used to help interpret responses, and support the general framework of the analysis. The data from the postal and telephonist sample are not robust enough to pursue all of the considerations involved in establishing and interpreting understandings of social experience. Despite this limitation, the following analysis does offer interesting insights into the complex structuring of women's and men's understandings of employment and inequality.

147

Understandings of family and employment –
diversity and gender divisions

The last job I had was a good job. It had lots of prospects. I was happy there, but I saw this job and the wages were a bit more.

A good job is when you're not doing a dead-end sort of job.

This is a good job for me , it's a secure job.

A secure job, and a job you can do on your own without any supervisors hassling you.

Good pay, not too boring and where you're not pushed about.

These statements were made by married women with dependent children.[1] The identification of good jobs as ones with prospects, good pay, security and autonomy is not typically associated with the employment priorities of married women with dependent children. Indeed, these statements jar dramatically with the conventional portrait of married women's understandings of, and relations to, waged work. The benchmark of this portrait is the family filter: the assumption that, contrary to men, women's experiences of employment are filtered through, and even overshadowed by, their family experience.[2] In contrast to this view, recent research has begun to demonstrate that women's attachment to family experience is not as exclusive, or as static, as the conventional portrait indicates. Dex, for example, concludes her investigation into women's attitudes to employment with the statement that there are (1988:148) "considerable variations between women, not just by age and life-cycle, but according to their experience, education and prospects . . . We should not be tempted to think that childbirth is the only, or even the major effect on women's attitudes towards gender roles or employment."

There is an accumulation of evidence indicating that women's conceptions of their employment experience is highly variable and attuned to significant differences in both immediate and lifetime patterns of domestic and employment circumstances. One strong challenge to the notion that "women" are "family-centred" and place less value on their employment developed throughout the 1980s in case studies of women's unemployment. Certainly, some of the women studied did revert to their domestic roles full time with little difficulty. For many women, however, the loss of their job was a personal and family crisis, and several studies have outlined how the nature of that crisis, and the responses to it, varied by life-course, household and other circumstances (Coyle 1984, Martin & Roberts 1984, Wajcman 1983, Wood 1981). There is also now good survey evidence showing the importance of life-course stage, generation and the particularities of domestic and employment relations for diversity in women's perceptions of their domestic and employment experience (Dex 1988, Martin & Roberts 1984, Witherspoon 1988).

Information on the variability in women's attachment to family life, and its significance in structuring relations to and understandings of employment, is an important addition to the substantial body of work establishing that men's employment patterns and perceptions vary over the life-course with their marital and family circumstances (for example, Backett 1982, Beynon & Blackburn 1972, Blackburn & Mann 1979, Goldthorpe et al. 1968, Rimmer & Popay 1982). There is still, nevertheless, a residual expectation in the research literature that a gender difference in the salience of family and employment experience will manifest itself, as the following quote indicates:

If there is such a thing as "alienation at work" then, clearly, it is not counterbalanced by a wholesale retreat into the home as an alternative or compensatory source of meaning or fulfilment . . . Somewhat surprisingly, perhaps, there is no significant sex effect in the patterning of these responses. (Marshall et al. 1988:213)

Of course, the forces sustaining gender divisions between and within domestic and waged work are an important aspect of current social circumstances and of current understandings. The argument is not that gendered experience is insignificant for understandings of family and employment. Rather, the implication of the demonstrations of diversity in the extent to which relations of parenting and employment are gendered, both across social conditions and over the life-course, is that gendered understandings need to be particularized and located in the circumstances of their production. Although this suggests a more specific relation between gendered experience and gendered understandings, we must be sensitive to the fact that past and anticipated future experiences are implicated in the structuring of understandings, as many investigations have demonstrated.

Earlier chapters established that the distribution of women and men to component-wage and full-wage jobs involves a lifetime patterning of relations of employment and domestic responsibilities. The distinction between component-wage and full-wage jobs has been drawn in terms of obligations of household maintenance, and processes underlying the distribution of people to the two types of jobs include variations in the negotiation of family circumstances. These variations will now be explored in relation to understandings of employment and parenting experiences. The analysis begins with a direct examination of the extent to which women and men in full-time employment give priority to family life, and the conditions within which such a priority occurs. This analysis provides further evidence against the notion that parenting is a primary and continuous source of identity and importance for women resulting in a "family-centred" understanding of their relations to employment. We shall see that the identification of family life as an important feature of social experience has a strong family life-cycle dimension, and is neither a general nor an exclusive aspect of women's conceptions. This is followed by an attempt to clarify perceptions of social relations as experienced by women and men who have had children. Here the analysis focuses on perceptions of inequality and disadvantage in family and employment experience.

The salience of family and employment experience

Information about the importance of different aspects of social life is based on a series of questions that initially established the rank order of three out of five items: enjoyable work, a good social life, lots of time for family life, to be respected, and a really good wage. People were asked to choose what they considered to be the most important item of the five, and were then asked to make a second and a third choice.[3] Following the selection of important social experiences, a number of questions asked people if they could identify (and if they could, to outline the circumstances of) someone in a more advantaged position with respect to the items ranked first and second. For the same two items, people were also asked to identify and describe the circumstance of someone in a less advantaged position than themselves. Everyone was asked to make a relative comparison on wages and, instead of making a relative assessment of respect, respondents were asked what they meant by "to be respected". The precise form of the questions used is reproduced in Appendix III.

The social experience identified as most important is shown in Table 6.1. Although slight differences between women and men are present in these data, they were remarkably similar in the identification of the most important aspect of their social experience: 35% of women and men gave first priority to family life, roughly one-third nominate work and one-fifth respect.[4] Although men were as family oriented as women, according to these responses, the striking aspect of this situation is that for both genders the priority of family life was similarly patterned in relation to immediate family circumstances.

Table 6.1 Most important aspect of social experience by gender.

	Work	Family	Respect	Wages	Social	Other	Total
Women							
N	17	20	14	3	2	2	58
%	29	35	24	5	3	3	100
Men							
N	22	23	12	3	2	4	66
%	33	35	18	5	3	6	100

Table 6.2 Family priority by family status and gender.

	No children		Dependent children		Children not dependent		Total	
	N	%	N	%	N	%	N	%
Women								
Family	5	22	9	60	6	30	20	35
Other	18	78	6	40	14	70	38	66
Total	23	100	15	100	20	100	58	100
Men								
Family	4	13	13	65	6	40	23	35
Other	27	87	7	35	9	60	43	65
Total	31	100	20	100	15	100	66	100

In Table 6.2 the extent to which family life was given priority is indicated for people in different family circumstances. Family life was selected as the first priority by the majority of women and men with dependent children (60% and 65%, respectively), whereas the majority of those who had no children, or whose children were no longer dependent, selected other aspects of social experience as their first priority. Among all those who did not have dependent children, only 24% selected family life as the most important aspect of their social experience.[5] For women and men in this latter group, enjoyable work was the most frequent first selection.

From these data, it would appear that the priority of family experience is related to family life-cycle stages, and that for women and men in full-time employment, time for family life has especial significance when they have dependent children.[6] It must be stressed that the family item in the ranking exercise is quite specific: it refers to *time* for family life. There is some evidence to suggest that time for family life has the strongest priority within circumstances of relative disadvantage in terms of actual hours available for family activities. Among those with dependent children, women in component-wage jobs were less likely to give priority to family experience (50%) than women in full-wage jobs (67%) or men in full-wage jobs (65%). As indicated in Chapter 3, women with dependent children did no overtime in the component-wage job. By contrast, women and men in full-wage jobs who were supporting dependent children averaged 8-17 hours overtime per week, and it would seem they placed a higher priority on the relatively fewer hours they had to spend with their families. This is a pattern that is repeated in different ways throughout the following analysis.

In order to address a persistent view concerning different conceptions of significant experience held by women and men in employment, the data have been discussed in terms of the one aspect of social experience selected as most important. We might expect that conceptions of experience are rarely structured in such a hierarchical and exclusive fashion. Although certain aspects of experience may be especially salient at particular times, this does not necessarily imply that other aspects of social life are, at the same time, unimportant. Patterns in all the selections made by each respondent suggest that the issue of an opposition between family and employment as central aspects of life experience is a false one for many of these people.

To examine the full pattern of respondents' selections, the three items chosen as most important have been grouped into three categories of responses: selections including time for family life and some aspect of employment (either enjoyable work or really good wages); selections including an aspect of employment, but not family life; and, finally, selections including time for family life, but no aspect of employment.[7] A substantial majority (65%) of people selected both family life and employment as important aspects of their social experience. A minority of the selections included either employment or family life, but not both. The most frequent selections made by people who discriminated between family and employment were those that included employment and excluded the family (31%). Only rarely was family life considered important to the exclusion of employment (4%).

Again, we find that the total selections made by respondents were related to their current family circumstances (Table 6.3). Although men and women with dependent children gave top priority to family life, employment was also high in their selection of priorities. The overwhelming majority of both gender groups made selections including both family and employment items (90% of the men and 87% of the women). Ever-married women and men with no children or with children not dependent were correspondingly more likely to discriminate between family and employment in their selections of important social experiences, and to give greater priority to employment. Although the majority of all four groups made selections that included both family

152

Table 6.3 Total selections (grouped) by family status, marital status and gender.[1]

	No children			Dependent children[1]		Children not dependent[1]		Total	
	Single		Ever-married						
	N	%	N	%	N	%	N	%	N	%
Men										
Selections include:										
Family and employment	7	32	5	56	18	90	11	73	41	62
Employment, not family	15	68	4	44	1	5	4	27	24	36
Family, not employment	0	0	0	0	1	5	0	0	1	2
Total	22	100	9	100	20	100	15	100	66	100
Women										
Selections include:										
Family and employment	9	64	5	56	13	87	12	60	39	67
Employment, not family	5	36	4	44	0	0	6	30	15	26
Family, not employment	0	0	0	0	2	13	2	10	4	7
Total	14	100	9	100	15	100	20	100	58	100

1. All those who had ever had children were either currently or previously married.

and employment, a substantial number made selections that included employment and excluded the family (34% of the total in the four groups).

The only indication of a gender difference in the responses of men and women who had had children is that women were slightly more likely to make selections that included the family and excluded employment. The numbers here are very small, but it is worth pointing out that the women who did give family life priority, to the exclusion of employment, were not component-wage women who had made the greatest accommodations to family care in terms of interrupted work histories and returns to part-time employment. Rather, the four women who made this type of selection were all black full-wage women. As we have seen from the previous chapter, black full-wage women spent the least time as full-time mothers, and their employment while their children were dependent was dominated by full-time jobs. We shall see later that women who have had children, and little time as full-time mothers, felt a keen sense of inequality with regard to their family experience.

The one truly notable gender difference in the total selections of important life experiences is to be found among single people with no children. Roughly two-thirds of the single women made selections that included both family and employment, whereas a similar proportion of the single men made selections that included employment and excluded the family. It is not clear what underlies this difference: the pattern appears to hold within the younger and older age groups, and within both the full-wage and component-wage jobs. Perhaps it reflects the fact that single women of all ages typically have greater domestic responsibilities and caring obligations in relation to their family of origin than do single men (Emler & Abrams 1991, Finch 1989:27,102). It may also indicate that, compared with younger men, younger women give greater salience to anticipated future parenting experience.[8]

Having established the main patterns in the selection of important life experiences, we turn now to a discussion of perceptions of relative advantage and disadvantage in family and employment circumstances.

Conceptions of inequalities

As outlined earlier, after selecting the three most important aspects of their social experience, people were asked first if they knew of anyone who was in a more advantaged position than themselves, and then if they knew of anyone in a less advantaged position than themselves. If the response to either question was positive, they were asked to identify the circumstances of relative advantage and disadvantage. They were asked to make these comparisons for the aspects of experience they ranked first and second, and everyone was asked to make these comparisons for wages. "To be respected" was an aspect of experience not amenable to this type of comparison, and those who placed respect as first or second priority were asked what "to be respected" meant to them. These responses will be discussed later. The present analysis of assessments of relative advantage and disadvantage concentrates on perceptions of inequality in the items highlighted in the preceding discussion: time for family life, enjoyable work and good wages. We discuss where people positioned themselves in terms of relative advantage and disadvantage, as well as the gender and circumstances of those identified in more or less advantaged positions. Since the interpretation of the salience of time for family life is somewhat ambiguous for people without children, only the responses of women and men who had had children are analyzed. This means that at times distinctions are drawn on the basis of quite small numbers but, in this case, the consistency of the data pattern helps to confirm the interpretation.

In examining perceptions of inequality, it became clear that perceptions were not simply a matter of immediate family or employment circumstances. Women who had had children were employed in both the component-wage and full-wage jobs, and perceptions of inequality appeared to be associated with the lifetime negotiations of parenting and employment that distinguished women's work histories in the two types of job. Consequently, Table 6.4 organizes responses by job type, and shows for the three items of importance whether or not women and men could identify someone who was more advantaged than themselves and someone who was less advantaged than themselves.

Table 6.4 Can people identify someone in a more advantaged position, and someone in a less advantaged position (by gender and job type)?

	Time for family life		Enjoyable work		Really good wage	
	More	Less	More	Less	More	Less
Women						
Component-wage						
% yes	67	83	80	80	62	62
Base *N*	6	6	5	5	8	8
Full-wage						
% yes	89	44	63	63	62	62
Base *N*	18	18	11	11	16	16
Men						
Full-wage						
% yes	63	54	63	86	80	67
Base *N*	24	24	15	15	30	30

There are a number of ways to approach these comparisons, and the main strategy adopted here is to look at the extent to which more advantaged and less advantaged persons were identified within each item. If more advantaged people are identified to a greater extent than less advantaged people, this is interpreted negatively in the sense that people see themselves as relatively more disadvantaged. Similarly, if less advantaged people are identified to a greater extent than more advantaged people, this is interpreted positively in the sense that people see themselves as relatively more advantaged.

In terms of perceptions of inequality, the data indicate that time for family life has a particular salience for the component-wage and full-wage women. Although their identifications of greater and lesser advantage are equally balanced on the items of enjoyable work and really good wages, their perceptions of relative position in time for family life are marked by imbalance. Women who had work histories that included periods of time in full-time motherhood, and in many cases rather extended periods of time, saw themselves as relatively advantaged in time for family life. Component-wage women were less likely to identify people with more advantaged experience, and more likely to identify people with less advantaged experience (67% and 83%, respectively). In contrast, women who were in employment continuously while their children were dependent, or who had their time as full-time mothers restricted or curtailed in some way, saw themselves as relatively disadvantaged in their participation in family life. Full-wage women were more likely to identify someone with more advantaged family experience than to identify someone less advantaged (89% and 44%, respectively).[9] Consistent with aspects of the preceding analysis and work history information, black full-wage women felt the most disadvantaged of the full-wage women – 92% identified someone with more advantaged family experience than themselves, and a much smaller percentage (33%) identified someone less advantaged.

Compared with the component-wage and full-wage women, full-wage men did have perceptions of imbalance with respect to their employment. Although they perceived their time for family life to be somewhat relatively disadvantaged, they had a greater perception of disadvantage in wages: 80% identified people with higher wages, compared with 67% who identified people with lower wages. However, in terms of enjoyable work, the full-wage men saw themselves as relatively advantaged, with a larger portion of them identifying people with less enjoyable work.

In examining the social aspects of the identifications made to persons in more and less advantages circumstances, it is very clear that these perceptions were bounded by gender divisions in family life and employment. Women's and men's relations to both were structured in such a way as to make comparable experiences atypical. It is perhaps not surprising, then, to find that cross-gender comparisons were rarely made. Generally, women compared their own experiences with those of other women, and men compared their experiences with those of other men. Significantly, the group who made cross-gender comparisons were those with the least conventional family and employment relations – the full-wage women.

Cross-gender comparisons made by the three groups are shown in Table 6.5. Of the total 192 identifications made to people with more or less advantaged circumstances, only 17 were made across the gender divide. Those with more conventional experience of gender divisions in the negotiation of family and employment – the full-wage men and the component-wage women – were least likely to make cross-gender comparisons. It is worth noting that the few cross-gender comparisons they did make were all to persons in less advantaged situations. Two component-wage women cited men as being less advantaged in time for family life, and three full-wage men referred to the more disadvantaged work

Table 6.5 Cross-gender comparisons, by gender and job type.

	Family life		Enjoyable work		Good wage		Total cross-gender comparisons
	More	Less	More	Less	More	Less	
Women							
Component-wage	0	2	0	0	0	0	2
Full-wage	1	2	1	2	5	1	12
Men							
Full-wage	0	0	0	2	0	1	3

and wages of women. It is also interesting that their cross-gender comparisons were on those dimensions where they perceived their experience to be either particularly advantaged (component-wage women in time for family life, and full-wage men in enjoyable work) or disadvantaged (wages for full-wage men).

The majority of cross-gender comparisons were made by the full-wage women, and they occurred on all three items.[10] The full-wage women were the only group to compare their circumstances unfavourably with the opposite gender, and they did so particularly on wages. Indeed, the earnings position of full-wage women was distant enough from that of other women to create some difficulty for them in making assessments of relative advantage and disadvantage in earnings. This is illustrated by the following two quotations. When one full-wage women was asked if she knew of anyone with higher wages than herself, she replied:

> Not a woman no, because we get the men's wages don't we?
> (Postwoman, 103)

Another full-wage woman made a similar comment when asked if she knew of someone earning less than herself. To this she replied:

> My daughter-in-laws, they work part time. But, remember we get the men's wages you see, so it's a bit awkward there, to judge other women at work. We're based on a man's wages here.
> (Postwoman, 102).

When full-wage women did compare their wages position to that of other women, they saw themselves as relatively advantaged. Of the comparisons they made to women's wages, 59% were to women with lower wages.

Although we cannot make too much of these cross-gender patterns, given the small numbers, they do suggest that perceptions of inequality are structured by gendered experience in family life and employment, and by people's perceptions of their own relations to standard gender divisions. One might think that full-wage men would be more like full-wage women in the identification of more advantaged family experience in that both groups could have potentially used standard patterns of women's experience as a reference point. In fact, no full-wage men compared their family experience with that of women. They perceived only minimal possibilities for variation from their own circumstances – more or less time for family life was identified as available to men who worked either more or less overtime, or who worked shifts with more or less unsocial hours. Although full-wage women also considered overtime and shift work as aspects of variations in time for family life, they more typically referred to specific features in other women's parenting and employment experience as circumstances of advantage. Greater consumption of family life was identified as a possibility for women who were either employed part time or able to spend time as full-time mothers. The only woman to see a man as more advantaged in family experience than herself was a black full-wage woman.

Similarly, wage comparisons appear to be structured by gendered relations to wages and the relative disadvantage of women's earnings compared with men's. Only one full-wage man compared his wages (favourably) with a woman's. Full-wage men were certainly earning much more than very many women, and the absence of cross-gender comparisons on this item is interesting. It is, perhaps, an indication that although women's wages were typically lower than their own wages, the men's assessments of their personal location in the wages hierarchy, given their obligations in relation to household maintenance, were bounded by the range of full-wages sufficient to support a household containing dependants.[11] Chapter 4 demonstrated how few women earn within this range. The greater cross-gender references on wage comparisons made by full-wage women, compared with component-wage women, would be consistent with this interpretation. Full-wage women were more likely to have extensive obligations in the financing of their households and, consequently, may have been more likely to see their relation to wages as closer to the men's.

Before leaving this analysis of significant life experiences, we shall consider the item of respect, for it reveals further the importance of identifying relations to experience in the interpretation of understandings. Recall from Table 6.1 that there was only a slight tendency for women to choose respect as the most important aspect. There is, however, a substantial difference in how the women and men explained their concern with this item, with women much more likely to locate the issue of respect within the workplace.

Respect within the workplace

In nominating respect as the most important aspect of social experience, the majority of the women defined respect in terms of relations within the workplace. In elaborating on what they meant by "to be respected", three-quarters of the women, compared with one-third of the men placed the issue of respect in the context of waged work. Respect within workplace relations was of special significance to women day telephonists and postwomen.[12]

For the day telephonist women, respect was an issue related to the exercise of authority in their workplace. All of the women for whom this was a concern were in the older group of female day telephonists, and they objected to being supervised in a fashion they regarded as inappropriate in light of their maturity, past experience and job performance. As two women expressed it:

> The type of supervision . . . having to ask permission for everything you do really, that should be stopped. We're grown people, we're not children. I don't think we should have to ask all the time for permission to do this, permission to do that, it sometimes gets up my nose. You know, when I was at shop work, I was left to myself to make my decisions, whereas I feel here you haven't got the freedom to do that.   (Day telephonist, female, 020)

> We have so many young ones here that they tend to forget we're not all straight from school. The petty rules and regulations, always being watched – it's not good, it gets you down sometimes. I mean a supervisor should know who is working hard and who isn't. You need discipline, I'm not saying you don't. But they should respect the fact that you're here to do your job.
> (Day telephonist, female, 005)

We saw in Chapter 3 that, compared with all other day telephonists, the older women had the greatest intention of staying in their current job. The nature of supervision was a general problem on the day shift and almost everyone had some objection to it. Nevertheless, it seems likely that the existence of close and critical supervision would be of particular concern for those who intended to stay in the job for any length of time.

For the older postwomen, respect in the workplace was defined as a matter of reasonable behaviour towards people or how people treated you. Many of the women referred directly to the behaviour of their male

159

workmates, especially the language they used in carrying out their job. As the women themselves said:

> It's people treat you properly. I mean outside it's all right, you get treated properly. But it's in here and their language and things like that. We all swear and curse but a lot of them just don't think. They know you're hearing them sort of thing and – their language, it gets you down sometimes. (Postwoman, 182)

> When I say disrespect I mean swearing at people or doing any-thing that would offend them. I always think in here the women don't demand enough respect, because the type of jokes and horseplay, I think men should do that among themselves – the boys that is. A lot of women carry on as though they were men. Even so the men should have more respect than that. It was a rude awakening to me when I came in here. It shocked me more than anything, you know, because every second word they use it's — and I thought I couldn't stand much of that. (Postwoman, 127)

> It's sort of hard to say but I would like to feel that I'm not looked down upon. I mean, say here, they hold a bit of respect because I'm not a person to swear. A lot of people respect the fact that you don't swear and they don't swear in front of you. But you always get the certain amount who got no respect for anybody so they do it purposely, knowing that you don't do it. (Postwoman, 173)

The formal aspects of employment conditions may have been the same for postwomen and postmen, but the informal aspects, like the style of working relations, were experienced differently. The language many postmen used in the normal course of carrying out activities of the postal job was a language that often included derogatory references to women that many postwomen (and a number of postmen) found unnec-essary and offensive. That the medium of typical interaction in the postal job was objected to by most postwomen was generally recog-nized. It was not as widely acknowledged as a legitimate grievance. A male union representative in the London Sorting Office reveals the understanding of the problem that had more widespread acceptance:

> The majority of the girls on the floor, they ignore it. Some ignore it and some of them come back with better than you give them. But you know the lads don't like that too much. It's quite strange you know that little bit of Victorian attitude again. It's all right for men to do that sort of thing but they don't like women doing it. But it

depends on the attitude of the woman and the way she comes back as to how they respect her. And let's face it you know, whatever you talk about equality, the average bloke likes to respect a woman. The average bloke. You got others that have got no respect for women. But the majority of blokes they don't like women using a lot of language. Quite a few women that came in, some left over it cause they couldn't stand the pace. Blokes knew that they were around and the language got worse and worse and worse – especially where a woman has said "Can't you stop swearing?" or "Do you have to do that?". They left themselves wide open, instead of ignoring it, like they were just part of the team. But you have to lay it down to the women that they come in here to do a man's job and they got to take what comes with it.

Maintaining this particular form of interaction in the postal job appeared to be, for some men, a last stand at "getting rid of the women" by marginalizing their relation to the daily routine of the job. To many of the women it was a condition of their job experience that required continual negotiation and caused considerable discomfort.[13]

Summary

This section has examined the extent to which women and men in full-time jobs prioritized family life and employment in their understandings of important social experiences. In terms of the importance of time for family life, we saw that women and men were similar in the extent to which this item had priority. Bearing in mind the cross-sectional nature of the data, responses for both gender groups suggest a life-cycle dimension to the salience of family experience. Women and men with dependent children prioritized time for family life, and this was especially the case for full-wage women and men. In meeting their obligations to household financing, full-wage women and men with dependent children worked overtime regularly, and it seems they gave special priority to the relatively fewer hours they had for family activities.

We saw also, however, that women and men with dependent children did not consider family life important to the exclusion of the significance of employment. When we look at the full complement of their selections of important social experiences, women and men with dependent children ranked both family and employment items highly. For women, it appears as if work history variations were associated with the exclusive priority of family life, but the pattern here is against the traditional assumptions of "family-centredness". The few women who included

161

time for family life and no aspects of employment in their selections of important experiences were black full-wage women; that is, those women who had the most continuous pattern of full-time employment while their children were dependent.

Employment had priority, to the exclusion of family life, for women and men who were on either side of the family life cycle from those with dependent children. Although the majority of these groups of ever-married women and men included both family and employment in their selections, a substantial minority included only employment items. Again, there was little difference in the extent to which ever-married women and men prioritized employment when they had no children, or when their children were no longer dependent.

The one notable gender difference that appeared in this analysis was between single, childless women and men. The men were more likely to include only employment items in their selection, whereas the women included both family and employment items. We could only speculate as to the reasons for this difference, suggesting that it perhaps reflected either the greater domestic obligations that fall to single women compared with single men, or the greater salience of expected future family and parenting activities for younger women.

There were few differences in the priorities of women and men who had had children, but their different relations to gendered experiences of parenting and employment relations entered into their perceptions of relative advantage and disadvantage in these areas of life. Standard gender divisions in parenting and employment were shown to play a major part in conceptions of possible alternatives to current experience and of inequality.

Family life did have a special significance for women in the sense that it was in this experience that they perceived their own position to be either particularly advantaged (in the case of component-wage women) or disadvantaged (in the case of full-wage women). Employment items had a significance for full-wage men in the sense that they saw themselves as relatively advantaged in the enjoyment of their work and disadvantaged in wages.

A good example of when and how gendered experience structures conceptions of inequality is the extent to which people compared their experiences across the gender divide. Women and men whose negotiations of parenting and employment were characterized by conventional gender experience rarely used the other gender as a reference group for assessing their own family and employment circumstances. Full-wage men made comparisons with men, and component-wage women made comparisons with women. It was argued that the virtual absence of cross-gender comparisons among these two groups indicates that relations to experience, particularly to gendered experience, underlay perceptions of inequality. This is striking in the case of family life, where no full-wage men compared their experiences with women's, and in the case of enjoyable work and wages, where no component-wage women compared their experiences to men's. The importance of relations to gendered experience in the structuring of perceptions of inequality is underlined by the fact that the group most likely to make assessments of advantage and disadvantage across the gender divide were those women with the least experience of conventional gender divisions in relations to family life and employment: the full-wage women. They compared themselves with men on all family and employment items, but did so most often when assessing their own position in the wages hierarchy. Their extensive obligations in the financing of households placed the full-wage women in a relation to wages that was similar to that of many men and, when they compared themselves with men, full-wage women saw themselves as relatively disadvantaged.

The case of respect is one where, although women and men were not strongly differentiated in terms of giving this item priority, there were differences in how respect was socially located. Women placed the issue of respect in the context of the workplace. Older day telephonist women had the greatest commitment to their current job, and felt that the style of supervisory relations in their job did not sufficiently acknowledge their maturity and responsibility. Postwomen were especially concerned about relations with their male workmates, and considered aspects of the culture of their workplace to be disrespectful and inappropriate.

We continue the examination of understandings of relations to employment by looking at people's perceptions of appropriate criteria in the allocation of employment.

Priorities in the allocation of employment

This section explores understandings of relations to employment from a different angle by examining perceptions of claims on employment. It is often suggested that assumptions about gender divisions in breadwinning and childrearing place men at an advantage in terms of claims on employment, and that even though married couple households are supported by two wages more often than not, men continue to be advantaged by a gender ideology that privileges their access to waged work (for example, Coyle 1982:25, Hunt 1980:15, Beechey & Perkins 1987: 148–9). The following analysis addresses some aspects of this issue. It assesses the importance of gender, marital status and household circumstances in people's ideas about relative entitlements to a wage.

The information presented is taken from a series of questions constructed to elicit understandings of women's and men's relations to employment, and to identify how these relations are contextualized. Respondents were asked to assume that there was a vacant job for which six people were applying. They were told that it was a job each of the six was capable and qualified to do. The six applicants were three women and three men in situations that varied by marital status, and for married people by whether or not their spouse was in employment. The six applicants were a single man; a married man whose wife is working; a married woman whose husband is not working; a married man whose wife is not working; a single woman; and a married woman whose husband is working.

People were asked who they thought should be offered the job first. After the first selection was made, they were asked who they thought should be offered the job second. They were then asked why they made their particular first and second choices.[14] To begin, we look at whether or not people made a gender distinction in selecting the appropriate applicant for the job, and the circumstances associated with this. Then, the selections of pairs of job applicants are combined to form three main types of selections: "male", "traditional need" and "female". Variations in the types of selection made will be analyzed subsequently.

Claims on employment: gender as a criterion

The extent to which gender is considered an appropriate criterion for differentiating claims on employment can be discerned by examining responses to the request for the person respondents thought should have first priority in the allocation of the vacant job. These responses are shown in Table 6.6.[15]

Table 6.6 First choice of job applicant by gender.

	Married, spouse not working		Single		Married, spouse working		No gender distinction	Total
	Man	Woman	Man	Woman	Man	Woman		
Women								
N	22	5	4	3	1	1	10	46
%	48	11	9	7	2	2	22	100
Men								
N	31	5	5	0	3	0	2	46
%	67	11	11	0	7	0	4	100
Total								
N	53	10	9	3	4	1	12	92
%	58	11	10	3	4	1	13	100

On the whole, people seldom raised objections to making distinctions by gender in the allocation of employment: 87% selected either a man or a woman as their preferred candidate, and in the majority of cases it was a man who got the job. Some, however, objected to having to select between a man and a woman for the job, and refused to do so. The majority of those who refused to make such a gender distinction were women: 22% of the women declared gender to be an inappropriate factor in decisions regarding preferred candidates for jobs.[16]

What is characteristic of the women and men whose conceptions of claims on employment did not include a differentiation by gender? Their circumstances can be quite easily identified, and they relate primarily to family status and relations to employment. There were two men who refused to make a selection by gender, and they were in a situation where their immediate employment circumstances and relations to household financing meant they were closer to women's experience and at a fair distance from gendered negotiations of parenting and breadwinning responsibilities. The two men were young, single, childless and in the component-wage job. Given their minority position in a female-dominated job, they had experienced competition with women for "women's jobs" most directly, and were perhaps sensitive to gendered assumptions that could work against them in the selection of appropriate job incumbents. For example, one of them said:

> I feel that a woman usually finds a job fairly easily. I mean you can always temp as a typist if worse comes to worse. It's not a great job, but you'll live in it. Whereas a man, I'd say it's far more difficult. The scope is rather restricted because clerical jobs are usually a woman's preserve. The man is expected to be skilled, but what happens if he is unskilled? (Day telephonist, male, 042)

For women, the circumstances locating gendered and non-gendered selections were related also to family status, and divided into two main groups (Table 6.7). The women most likely to make a gender distinction in the selection of job candidates were women with dependent children and younger women with no children.[17] All but one of the women who refused to make a gender distinction were at a greater distance from the immediate, or future, salience of parenting. They were women whose children were no longer dependent and older women with no children. Although the majority of the women in this group (64% in total) chose between a man and a woman in selecting their preferred job candidate, just over one-third refused to regard the gender of a job applicant as a significant factor when judging claims on employment.[18] Some were prepared to choose the situation of a married person supporting a non-

Table 6.7 Circumstances in which women do and do not distinguish by gender.

Distinction by gender	Group 1 Under 30, no children	Group 2 Dependent children	Over 30, no children	Children not dependent
Yes				
N	8	12	7	9
%	100	92	70	60
No				
N	0	1	3	6
Total				
N	8	13	10	15

waged spouse, but would not choose between the woman and man in this situation:

> You'd have to have the one breadwinner in the family, whether it's a man or a woman.   (Postwoman, 127)

There is a small sub-group of women who reject gender distinctions more often than make them, and who also objected to marital status as a criterion in the allocation of jobs. They were women who on all accounts had been, and had become, the most distanced from gender divisions in parenting and relations to employment. They were no longer married, their children were no longer dependent, and their experience of full-time motherhood had been relatively short.[19] They were all full-wage women and strongly supportive of women's needs for, and entitlements to, employment, both on individual grounds and in terms of household financing.

> They're all entitled to the job. Myself, I don't think it should matter whether a man's married or single, or whether a woman's married or single, whether they get a job or not because everybody's got to work. I mean married women have to work now. The majority of the married men in here, unless they've got very young children, their wives probably do something or other. I mean even if they've got young children, they probably go out and do something. Not all, but I would say the majority of them, because they have to make ends meet.   (Postwoman, 182)

> I was always under the impression that when you went for a job, you just gave your name. Whether you were married or single or your husband was working, I don't think that matters. It should be

up to the woman. If she wants to go out to work, all right, she
wants to go out to work.   (Postwoman, 101)

Claims on employment: interpreting gender-specific selections

Although the pattern outlined above is interesting, it is still the case that
the majority of most groups within the female and male sample make a
selection from the job candidates that involves a distinction by gender,
with a general preference for men. To interpret the gender-specific selections, we must note that all of the female and male applicants were further described in terms of marital status and the employment status of
spouses. Referring back to Table 6.6 we can see that there is also a differentiation in gender-specific selections according to these situations.
Whereas four of the six job applicants are married, over three-quarters of
applicants given first claim on the vacant job are married. In choosing
between the two married applicants, those with a non-employed spouse
were selected more often than those with an employed spouse, by an
order of more than 10 times. Thus, while a man was given preference to
a woman in all three circumstances, the most significant preference was
for a married man supporting an unwaged spouse.

The fact that married men were not given priority irrespective of the
employment status of their wives is an important clue to the criteria
being used in determining claims on employment. Single men are
selected as the first person to be offered the job more than married men
with an employed wife, and the same holds for their female equivalents.
This suggests that people were using the ratio between wage earners
and numbers of household members as a criterion for allocating the job.

A fuller picture of the priorities in claims on employment, and the
relative significance of gender, marital status and the employment status
of spouses, is provided by an examination of both job candidates
selected. The most frequently chosen pairs of job applicants are listed in
Table 6.8. Here were have some confirmation of the point that a good
proportion of the women and men appear to be using the ratio of wage
earners to household members as their criterion for selection. Approximately half of the respondents (47% of the women and 53% of the men)
selected pairs that included both married persons supporting a spouse.[20]
In selecting applicants in households with the greatest number of people
and the least number of active wage earners, need was often the explicit
criterion used. For people to choose between the man and the woman in
these circumstances, many said they would require further information
about the circumstances of the household and individuals within it.

Table 6.8 Most frequently chosen pairs of job applicants by gender.

First choice	Second choice	Women N	Women %	Men N	Men %	Total N	Total %
MMWNW	MWHNW	13	36	21	48	33	41
MMWNW	SM	6	17	5	11	11	14
MWHNW	MMWNW	4	11	2	5	6	8
MMWNW	MMWW	1	3	4	9	5	6
SM	SW	2	6	3	7	5	6
MMWNW	SM	1	3	2	5	3	4
MMWW	MMWNW	1	3	2	5	3	4
SM	MMWNW	2	6	0	0	2	3
Total[1]		30	83	39	89	68	85
Total gender distinctions		36	100	44	100	80	100

Key:
MMWNW – married man wife not working   SM – single man
MWHNW – married woman husband not working   SW – single woman
MMWW – married man wife working
1. Five men selected other pairs, as did four women. Two women made no second choice.

Well it's a toss up between the woman whose husband ain't working and the man whose wife ain't working.

[Could you choose between them, or not?]

I could if there were other things I knew, like have they got any children and if there was a reason why the husband ain't working, if he was invalid or something. I'd probably give it to the woman because the husband would have to be ailing if he ain't working. They'd probably need it more.   (Postman, 217)

Taking the man on is usual isn't it, to say the least. I don't think I'd want to work for a firm that was doing that. I think either a married man whose wife is not working or a married woman whose husband is not working.

[Could you choose between them?]

Well, I'd want to know if the woman's husband was incapacitated for instance, unable to work. If so, she would be more worthy of the job. If I thought about it a bit more, I'd probably think a married man would get more if he wasn't working. I might take that into account, how much they'd get if they weren't working.
                                    (Day telephonist, female, 020)

Although reasons varied for preferring the married man to the married woman, when each was supporting a non-waged spouse, the needs of the household that included a wife not in paid work were frequently understood to be greater than the needs of households with a husband not in paid work. Because a wife was not in employment, it was assumed that the household also included dependent children.

> Well, it doesn't say here whether they have a family or not, but I'm assuming there would be a family. (Night telephonist, female, 090)

> I put the man whose wife is not working first, well, for family reasons. I mean he's got to support children probably. (Postman, 140)

> If there's children and so forth, it's essential that the man in that situation is earning.　　　　　(Night telephonist, male, 058)

Further, as already indicated by a previous quotation (page 168), the financial needs of the married woman with a husband not employed were in some cases perceived to be less because men without a job typically have greater access to sources of income other than wages, especially state benefits. Similarly, some balanced what the married woman would be likely to earn, compared with what would be coming into the household via the man's unemployment benefits.[21]

> The married man whose wife is not working comes first, cause there's no breadwinner in that situation. The married woman whose husband is not working comes second – but they'd probably be better off on his dole money.　　　　　(Postman, 203)

> Well a married man obviously has got to keep his wife. If she's not working, she's probably got children, so he'd need the job first.

> [How does the situation of the married man whose wife's not working compare with the situation of the married woman whose husband's not working?]

> Well if the husband's not working they must be getting money from somewhere, either social security or sick pay, but the married man whose wife's not working, she's not getting anything.
> 　　　　　(Postwoman, 221)

> Well, it depends on why that husband is not working. I mean if he's sick, she's got to go out and earn a living, but then they'd get benefits.　　　　　(Day telephonist, female, 015)

Calculations about support from the state and gender differences in earnings also entered into both preferences for the married man with an non-employed spouse over his female equivalent, and for married people with an unwaged spouse over a single person:

> Well the single woman gets help from the government, like the single man, so I take the married man – he's got his family to look after, and he'd get more wages than the woman. (Postwoman, 104)

Whereas the married person supporting a dependent spouse, with the man selected first, was the most common response for both women and men, the frequency of other gender-specific responses had a different ordering for the two groups. The second most popular gender-specific selections made by women were of two men – a married man whose wife is not working first, and a single man second, and their next popular choice was again married people supporting a dependent spouse, but with priority to women in this situation. For the men, both the second and third most popular pairs selected were of two men (respectively, a married man supporting an unwaged spouse, followed by a single man, and a married man supporting an unwaged spouse, followed by a married man with a waged spouse).

In light of the preceding, three groupings of gender-specific responses suggest themselves: those that give priority to men ("male"); those that give priority to people who are supporting unwaged household members, and that also give priority to the man in this situation ("traditional need"); and finally those that give priority to women ("female"). Responses grouped into these three categories are shown in Table 6.9. Included in the "male" responses are pairs of two men, and other selections that give first priority to a single man or a married man.[22] The "traditional need" response includes the married man spouse not working

Table 6.9 Types of gender-specific selections by gender.

	Male	Traditional need	Female	Total
Women				
N	14	13	9	36
%	39	36	25	100
Men				
N	18	21	5	44
%	41	48	11	100
Total				
N	32	34	14	80
%	40	43	18	100

as the first selection, and the married woman spouse not working as the second selection. The "female" responses include those who selected both households with an unwaged spouse, but give priority to a woman in this situation (the MWHNW–MMWNW pair). The "female" responses also include those who chose two women or made other selections that gave priority to a single woman or to a married woman with an employed spouse.[23] Women and men were similar in the extent to which they made "male" selections – about 40% of each group did so. As the previous data suggested, women were more likely to make "female" selections than were men, who gave greatest priority to the "traditional need" selection. The question to be pursued, then, is what accounts for this differentiation within and between the women and men. The discussion of this question will begin with an analysis of the men's responses, and follow on by examining the women's responses. The detail about women's lifetime negotiations of parenting and employment is sufficiently robust to allow a very clear location of preferences. The specific relationship between experience and understanding established earlier in the chapter will be seen to hold also for circumstances that differentiate between those who make different types of gender-specific selections. To anticipate the general pattern, more extensive and immediate experience of gendered divisions in relations of parenting and employment corresponds with a more traditional conception of women's and men's claims on employment.

Claims on employment: men's gender-specific selections

For men, the main division in selections was between "male" and "traditional need". In Table 6.10, gender-specific selections are presented for two groups of men. The first group is composed of men who were under the age of 40 and had no children, and men with dependent children.[24]

Table 6.10 Men's gender-specific selections by family status and age

		Male	Traditional need	Female	Total
Group 1					
Dependent children		7	5	1	13
Under 40, no children		9	6	0	15
Total	N	16	11	1	28
	%	57	39	4	100
Group 2					
Children not dependent		2	7	1	10
Over 40, no children		0	3	3	6
Total	N	2	10	4	16
	%	13	63	25	100

This group was closest to either immediate or possible future experiences of parenting and its associated gendered divisions between male breadwinning and female childrearing. Indeed, for the men with dependent children, this situation describes their immediate circumstances, as the majority of them also had a dependent spouse. All but two of the "male" selections were made by this group of men, and these selections constituted over half (57%) of their responses.

> The married man whose wife's not working if he's got a family, he's the sole supporter of them, and he's got a responsibility. The single man next cause the single man has got no one else to back him up, he's out on his own.

> [How would the situation of the married man whose wife's not working compare to the case of the married woman whose husband is not working?]

> You've got the same situation really, if she's got a family. I didn't take much notice of that one to be honest.   (Postman 198)

> [Can you tell me why you put the married man whose wife is not working above the married man whose wife is working?]

> Yeah, a married man whose wife is not working, I think he'd be more loyal to the company because he'd be dependent on that company for his bread and butter. He's got a wife, she's solely dependent on him as the breadwinner, and it doesn't say family but, I presume that he most probably has a family and I think these are the people who appreciate the job more than the man who, as I say, his wife is working, he can afford to be a little bit independent if his wife is earning a good wage. I mean most probably, most men are like me, they wouldn't like to have to rely on their wife, but there's always that there in the back of your mind.

> [How about the married man whose wife is not working compared to the married woman whose husband is not working?]

> Well, there again, you've got it down on the card but I look at it from another point. It's not for her to be the breadwinner, her husband should be working.   (Postman, 138)

A fair number of these men also made "traditional need" selections. It is not clear, from the information available on the men's family and household circumstances, what differentiates those in group 1 who made this selection, although there is some indication that men sharing household financing with a wife employed full-time were more likely to make "traditional need" selections.[25] The following quotes are from two young married men, with no children and a wife in full-time employment.

> The married people need a wage coming in, probably both need to work, but I think the man should go out and get a job really. It's up to the man isn't it. Let's face it, when you're married and you have children, it's up to the man to support everybody. (Postman, 160)

> Obviously, it's the fact that I'm married and I know what lack of money can do if both are out of work. Well, if my wife didn't work we wouldn't be able to get along. No way we could have got married if we both weren't working. (Postman, 163)

A "traditional need" orientation is most characteristic of the second group of men. They were aged 40 or over with no children, or men whose children were not dependent. By the time children are independent, many wives have returned to employment, and the time of greatest pressure on men's wages is past. For the group of childless men over 40, they were at a point when experience of gender divisions in relation to parenting and employment was less likely to occur. Of men in these two circumstances, only 13% made "male" selections. Although the first priority of most was still the married man supporting a spouse, they at least consistently acknowledged the employment needs of women. The majority made "traditional need" selections, and all but one of the "female" selections also came from this group of men. In total, 88% of the second group made selections in which male priority in the allocation of employment was either conditional on particular household circumstances or, in the case of "female" selections, not present.[26]

> In the case of the man whose wife is not working, like my case where the wife stayed at home to look after the children, the man is the support. In the other case, well it's obvious that if a husband is not working, it must be for some reason that he can't work, and she would have to be the support.   (Night telephonist, male, 070)

> What I'm trying to do is put an income, at least one income, into the family. The married man whose wife's not working, well he's got a family and you must give it to where the family is. A single person can fend for themselves, but when you've got kiddies ...

173

The married woman needs it too, but if they got a family he
should be the breadwinner.   (Postman, 214)

The majority of "female" selections made by this group of men were
ones that gave priority to the married woman supporting an unwaged
spouse, but again this was also conditional and usually depended on the
husband being unable to work.

I'd pick the married woman whose husband is not working, but
only if it's through illness. She'd be really hard up against it.
                                                  (Day telephonist, male, 043)

That woman would have a lot on her plate because the husband
would be crippled and dependent on her.   (Postman, 152)

Variations in responses within the two groups of men could perhaps
be clarified with further information concerning details of the men's
relations to gender divisions in parenting and employment. In particular, details concerning the work histories of their spouses would provide
a more complex picture in which to locate the men's priorities regarding
marital status, spouse's employment status and gender as criteria differentiating claims on employment.[27]

Claims on employment: women's gender-specific selections

We have seen how women's proximity and overall relation to gender
divisions in relations to parenting and employment combine to differentiate circumstances in which claims on employment are and are not distinguished by gender. Similar sorts of variations in circumstances
correspond with variations in women's gender-specific understandings
of claims on employment, and here too the significance of work history
features is highlighted for women who had ever had children. Women's
gender-specific selections of job applicants are presented in Table 6.11,
and are organized by whether or not the women had had children; the
current age and marital status of childless women; and job type and the
length of time as full-time mothers for women who had had children.
    Among women who had ever had children, those who had been full-
time mothers for longer periods of time (six years or over) gave greatest
priority to men's claims on employment. There were eleven women with
work histories including longer periods in full-time motherhood, in both
the full-wage and component-wage jobs, and eight of them made "male"
selections. By contrast, there were ten full-wage women who had shorter
periods as full-time mothers, or who had worked continuously while

174

Table 6.11 Women's gender-specific selections by job type and length of time as full-time mothers (for women who had ever had children) and by marital status and age (for women with no children).

	Male	Traditional need	Female	Total
Ever had children				
Component-wage:				
Full-time mother, 6+ years	4	1	0	5
Full-wage:				
Full-time mother, 6+ years	4	1	1	6
Full-time mother, 5 years or less	1	1	4	6
Continuous employment	0	4	0	4
Total	9	7	5	21
Never had children				
Ever married	3	3	0	6
Single:				
Under 30	1	2	1	4
Over 30	1	1	3	5
Total	5	6	4	15

their children were dependent, and only one of them made "male" selections in the allocation of employment.[28]

In fact, most of the women who had been full-time mothers for over six years had very extended periods of time out of the labour force, being supported by a male wage. Three had been full-time mothers for over 20 years, and an additional four had been full-time mothers for over 10 years. Most of these women selected two men, giving first priority to the married man with a wife not working, and usually putting the single man second.

> Well I'm not a woman's libber and I think the man should get preference. I think if there's work, only enough work, a man with a family should come first. I've had to go to work, 'cause my husband's wages were very poor. And there's times when I earned more money than my husband, but he never knew, I never told him. And I still say, a woman should be at home with her children if possible, and the man should be the breadwinner
>
> (Postwoman, 222)

> He's married, and maybe he's got a family. He needs it more than the woman does really. And the single man's got to keep himself.

[What about the married woman whose husband's not working?]

I think it's the man's place. He is the breadwinner more or less isn't he. I would never have come to work if I didn't have to, but my husband had to go on less money and that's why I started work. But he was still the man, the breadwinner.

(Day telephonist, female, 007)

The married man whose wife is not working, he's in need of the job more than the single man.

[How does the situation of the married woman with a husband not working compare to that of the married man whose wife's not working?]

Again if she's the breadwinner, and you know we are now equal, but I probably feel the single man before that woman whose husband's not working. There must be something outstanding to choose that woman rather than the single man, it would have to be something extra.

(Day telephonist, female, 021)

In terms of priorities in the allocation of waged work, the "male" selections made by these women reflect the extent of their experience of a traditional gender division between parenting and employment. Most of these women were older and in the final phase of their work histories. They valued their current employment experience (for example, two of the women quoted above selected enjoyable work as most important to them, and one put it second), and they saw their greater experience of employment as married women as an improvement over the more limited opportunities available to their mother's generation.

Well, there wasn't no work was there, years ago. I mean when I got married you had to be a widow so you could get a job office cleaning. My mother's friend went office cleaning and she only had that because her husband was blind then. You couldn't get a job. They were for widows.

(Postwoman, 222)

Women were more restricted then, weren't they. They were just there to bring up a family. Now it's a choice whether you want to work or not.

(Day telephonist, female, 007)

You know a woman's able to make her own mind up now. I find my mother still says to me, "Oh, I could never have done that when I was your age." And I can say, "I can do that." I can make up my own mind, I can go out to work, you know, make my own mind up.

(Day telephonist, female, 021)

However, their experience of being supported by a male wage for extended periods of time does coincide with a perception of men's greater claims on employment.

In contrast, women who had been employed continuously while their children were dependent made "traditional need" selections. These are women whose experience of the negotiation of parenting and employment had been most constrained by the financial needs of households, and who had the least direct experience of a gendered division between male wage-earning and female childrearing. They emphasized either the greater needs in the household of the married man or the importance of all incomes in households with dependent children.

> A married man has got a lot of responsibilities and he's got his rent to pay, he's got his wife to keep, food to buy. I'm assuming they've got children and he'd need it more than the married woman. She might have a husband in bad health and can't work, then she'd have the responsibility. (Postwoman, 172)

> Both of them probably must work to manage, both the husband and the wife, but I think a husband should support the family if he can, so I put him first. (Postwoman 128)

We saw previously that full-wage women with least time as full-time mothers saw their relations to time for family life as relatively disadvantaged. It could be reasonably argued, then, that whereas the general priority given to the employment needs of both married persons supporting dependants reflects the financial pressures in their own circumstances, the specific priority given to the married man is the identification of an option in the negotiation of childrearing and employment that they considered to be more typical, and perhaps more desirable, compared with their own.[29] Indeed, the salience of this issue was immediate for all but one of these women as their children were still dependent.

> Normally a man is the breadwinner. Well, he was. And I think a married man whose wife is not working has got more right to have a job than a married woman whose husband is not working, in that respect. Because the man has always been the breadwinner by rights. I know you get this life with the man and the woman working, but normally the man is the breadwinner. (Postwoman, 171)

> The man has responsibilities, to look after the children and pay the bills. The woman wants to help her husband with the bills and

177

things, and go out to work, but I think a man should go out to work, not a woman.

[What about people in your situation?]

Well, it's difficult, it's tricky. I wouldn't be able to live on his money. You just have to try and cope.   (Postwoman, 111)

Understandably, given their experience of financial obligations and responsibilities, these women were particularly concerned with good wages. When selecting an aspect of social experience that was most important to them, they selected good wages more than any other group of women.

Among women who had ever had children, those most likely to promote women's claims on employment had been full-time mothers for under five years. The majority of this group make "female" selections. They did not have the extensive experience of dependence on a male wage as did women whose work histories included longer periods as full-time mothers. On the other hand, given that they had spent some time as full-time mothers, they were also less likely to feel disadvantaged in their relations to family life. They were, in other words, not bound by either the extended experience of or the lack of opportunity for full-time motherhood. Some were still supporting dependent children, and some were now separated or divorced, but these factors did not distinguish them from the women who made "traditional need" selections. Two of the women who made "female" selections chose the married woman whose husband is not working as their first choice, one selected a single woman first and one woman was the only person to choose a woman whose husband is working as her first choice. She was very detailed in her calculations (and forthright in her support for women workers!):

I put the married woman whose husband is working at the top, and then the married man whose wife is working.

[Can you say why you'd put them first and second?]

Well, with a married woman whose husband is not working, she'd be more or less working for nothing wouldn't she? If he's unemployed, he's only going to get unemployment money for himself, he won't be able to claim for her. So she's got no incentive to work really. She'd go to work and lose her allowance from the labour exchange. And with the married man whose wife is not working,

178

well he's not working either so he can claim if he's not working, can't he? He can claim for him and for her. That's why I give it to those with the husband and wife in work, they've both got incentive to work. The woman first, and the man next.

[Why would you give it to the woman first?]

Well, myself, I think women are better workers. (Postwoman, 103)

Considering the responses of women with no children, there is again a fairly straightforward pattern of distance from immediate, or future, gendered relations to parenting and employment correlating with less traditional conceptions. The women who had been most independent and were likely to remain so – the childless single women over the age of 30 – promoted women's claims on employment to a greater extent than did childless married women and childless single women under the age of 30. Typically, they selected themselves as the preferred job candidate; that is, they selected the single woman.

Naturally, I'd say a single woman, wouldn't I. The single woman hasn't got anyone to look to. If the state said no benefits, she'd be out in the cold. A single bloke can go anywhere, can travel abroad to work, like work on an oil field or something, but a single woman can't do that. (Postwoman, 225)

Summary

Contrary to the notion that there is a general understanding that privileges men's claim on employment, it has been possible to identify variations in people's perceptions of appropriate criteria in differentiating entitlements to employment. This analysis has highlighted the variation in the operation of gender as well as marital status and perceptions of household need in understandings of who should have priority in the allocation of jobs. In a variety of ways, the analysis demonstrates that relations to traditional gendered experience in the negotiation of family and financing responsibilities coincided with perceptions of claims on employment, and that, in general, distance from traditional gendered divisions was associated with less traditional views about men's greater claim to a wage. Although women's and men's understandings were similarly patterned in this respect, there was some difference between them in the substance of their less traditional views.

Most people did differentiate by gender in selecting the candidate who should have the first claim on the available job. However, a fair proportion of women refused to do so. Given their perception that "taking the man on is usual", their own objection to the significance of the gender of applicants in the allocation of jobs must be to some extent a claim for their own employment needs. These women were, and had been, at some distance from traditional divisions between childrearing and breadwinning: their time as full-time mothers was relatively short, their children were no longer dependent, and they were no longer married.

In selections of the person who should have the first opportunity of employment, men were chosen more often than women, married people more often than single people, and married people supporting an unwaged spouse more often than married people with a spouse in employment. The majority of people gave the job first to the married man whose wife is not working. It is the case that the priority given to married men was not irrespective of their household position. The fact that single men were chosen as the preferred job candidate more often than were married men with an employed wife is an important clue to the relative meaning of gender, marital status and household circumstances in people's perceptions of claims on employment. When a woman was chosen as the preferred job candidate, she too was more likely to be supporting an unemployed husband, and the single woman was also chosen more often than the married woman with an employed husband. These selections indicate that many people were using household need, or the ratio of wage earners to household members, as a criterion in allocating waged work.

Indeed, selections were often explicitly justified in terms of needs, as well as access to household income from sources other than employment, and the differential earning power of women and men. According to these considerations, the married man with a wife not in employment was frequently designated as the person most in need of the job. Since his wife was not waged, it was assumed that he also had a family to support. His counterpart – the married woman supporting an unwaged husband – was thought to be less financially pressed, as husbands not in employment are more likely to have access to incomes other than a wage, either from employers in terms of sick pay, or from the state in terms of benefits. Finally, gender inequality in wages also entered into decision-making. Men's higher wages were referred to in justifying the selection of the unemployed married man, over the unemployed married woman, because the couple would benefit more from his higher earnings.

In looking at both job applicants selected for the job, it is clear that calculations of household need were a significant criterion in perceptions of claims on employment. The majority of both women and men selected both married persons supporting an unwaged spouse as their preferred job candidates. Typically, the man in this situation was given priority. Although some of them account for this preference in terms outlined above, it is also the case that a number gave preference to men because of their perceived responsibilities as breadwinners. Many indicated that for the woman to have priority over the man, there would need to be exceptional circumstances. In addition to this "traditional need" selection, the pairs of applicants chosen can be divided into those that in other ways gave priority to men ("male") and those that gave priority to women ("female").

Generally, men gave first priority in the allocation of jobs to men, but there is a difference between them according to whether or not they acknowledged women's claims on employment in situations of greater household need. Those men who were furthest away from gendered patterns of childrearing and breadwinning were most likely to include women in their selections of candidates; typically they chose both married persons supporting a spouse. Some also made "female" selections, giving priority to the married woman supporting a husband. Men who were closest to typical gender divisions in family care and financing, in terms of either immediate or likely future experience, were more likely to make "male" selections. It was suggested that these men were particularly aware of the financial responsibilities carried by men supporting households with dependants, and for a number of them this described their current situation. They had dependent children and a dependent spouse. However, a minority of men close to gendered divisions in parenting and employment also made "traditional need" selections. There is not enough detail about men's lifetime experiences clearly to locate the circumstances of this group, but there is an indication that they had more experience of sharing the financial maintenance of households with their wives.

For women, the salience of gender in claims on employment was also patterned in relation to gendered patterns of parenting and household financing, but the greater detail available on women's lifetime experiences shows the significance of this for perceptions of women's and men's relative claims. Those who gave the greatest priority to men by making "male" selections were women who had extended experience of being fully supported by a male wage. In contrast to this group, women who had the least experience of gendered divisions in the financial support of dependent children – the full-wage women with continuous work histories – were more likely to include women in their selections and give priority to both married people supporting a dependent spouse.

181

The strongest claim for women's entitlement to employment, in the form of "female" selections, came primarily from women, and it was most characteristic of two groups. The first group had never been married and they did not have, and were unlikely ever to have, children. Among women who had had children, those who made "female" selections were women whose relations to gender divisions had two main characteristics – they had less extensive experience of a gender division in the negotiation of employment and parenting, but they had had some opportunity to care for their children on a full-time basis.

The patterns in understandings of relations to employment, in both sections of this chapter, are in line with the growing body of evidence suggesting that although gendered relations to parenting are a significant aspect of women's and men's understandings of relations to employment, these understandings are complex and variable. Diversity in experience, within and across the genders, is tied to diversity in understandings, and for both women and men there seems to be a strong pattern of variation in understandings across the life-course. For women, significant features in their work histories, particularly the length of time they have spent as full-time mothers, continue to structure perceptions. However, this does not appear to happen in the relatively straightforward manner suggested by arguments that married women are "family-centred" in their understanding of priorities and inequalities in employment.

Notes

1. Interview references are, starting from the top, Postwoman 117, Day telephonist 014, Postwoman 194, Postwoman 109, Postwoman 124.
2. This conventional presentation of women's relations to paid work can be found in more orthodox analyses of employment, as well as in some feminist accounts, as the following three examples illustrate.

> What members of these groups [married women with young children, juveniles, semi-retired persons, peasant workers] have in common is that their commitment to the work they have taken on tends to be strictly limited and, in turn, their expectations of what they will be able to derive from it: typically, they have other sources of identity and satisfaction, and also perhaps of economic support.
> (Goldthorpe 1985:143)

> Men, too, are centred on their families and discuss them at work. But they relate to them differently: their family is part of their concern as father and breadwinner. With women it is the immediate, intimate and daily concern with the actual process of family care which penetrates and alters their consciousness of work. Work is overshadowed by the family.
> (Pollert 1981:113)

Already it is apparent that what has sometimes been seen as women's failure to identify their paid occupations as central life interests (in which they are unlike many men) may have unforeseen effects. If a large majority within the British labour force must face either long or intermittent periods of unemployment in the coming decades, such an attitude to employment may well mean that women are better fitted than men to cope with the changing social conditions. (Yeandle 1984:128)

3. The ranking exercise is a modified version of a question used by Blackburn & Mann (1979:313). An example of a more extended series of questions concerning the centrality of employment and family life is in Marshall et al. (1988). Respondents were also invited to add items to the list of five if they felt there was something missing. Only four men and two women made additions. These included religious devotion, good health and freedom of choice.

4. As the totals in Table 6.1 indicate, 20 responses to this question are missing. In these cases, time constraints on the interviews meant the question was not asked.

5. Chi-square for the difference in family priority between the two groups (with dependent children compared with those with no children and children not dependent) is significant at 0.001, phi=0.37. The "no children" group included those single and married. There was no difference between single and married women with no children in the selection of family life as first priority. The modal category for both groups was "enjoyable work". For men with no children, married men were more likely than single men to select family as the first priority, but for both "enjoyable work" was the modal category. That family experience is an important feature for married men in employment has, of course, been noted in other research. For example, Wajcman (1983:16) reports data from Blackburn & Mann's study (1979) indicating that in their sample of unqualified manual men "almost 90% of married respondents rated a 'good family life at home' above enjoyment in their working life".

6. Dex (1988) has also established the significance of life-cycle effects in the identification of variations in women's conceptions of employment. As she emphasizes (1988: 114-15), there are "important heterogeneities within women's attitudes so that stereotypes and overgeneralisation should be avoided at all cost. Young childless women could be differentiated from each other as well as from older women and from women with children." Blackburn & Mann (1979:227) also highlight the significance of the family situation and life-cycle position in men's orientations to employment. As they note (1979:228), "Workpeople, autonomy, intrinsic job quality, worthwhileness and type of work/industry are all orientations related to the absence of dependants". For men with dependent children, hours of work, security and wages were among their priorities as regards employment itself.

7. This grouping assumes that the item "a really good wage" refers mainly to employment and not to family experience. There could be room for reinterpretation here as good wages may be regarded by some as a key aspect of

their family responsibilities. Unfortunately, there is no way to sort this out with the current data. The three groupings do not each have an equal probability of selection. If the selection process was random, combinations of family with either work or wages would occur in 50% of the total selections (on the assumption that each of the five items has an equal probability of selection). Employment only selections would be made by 40%, and family only selections by 10%.

8. Although not able to offer a gender comparison, Martin & Roberts (1984:184) found that although young, single, childless women held more non-traditional attitudes toward gender divisions in parenting and employment than did older generations of women, a substantial number viewed their adult life in terms of returning to employment after an interruption for childrearing.

9. The connection of perceptions of disadvantage with types of work histories is confirmed by examining time in full-time motherhood directly. Of the 10 full-wage women (56%) who said they could not identify anyone with less advantaged experience in time for family life, 3 had work histories of continuous employment, 4 were full-time mothers for 5 years or less, and 3 were full-time mothers for 7 years. Altogether, 9 full-wage women were either continuous workers or full-time mothers for five years or less, and only two of them identified a more disadvantaged person.

10. Of all the gender-specific comparisons made by the three groups in Table 6.4, one-quarter of those made by full-wage women were to a man, compared with 11% for component-wage women. Of all the gender-specific comparisons made by full-wage men, 4% were to a woman. Some comparisons were made to general types of circumstance, without a gender specification.

11. It could also be argued that the general absence of cross-gender comparisons on wages reflects the strength of occupational gender segregation in structuring perceptions of comparable groups. People in male-dominated jobs may not compare their wages with those people in female-dominated jobs, and vice versa. However, the interpretation focusing on relations to wages that is offered here is supported by the fact that childless men in full-wage jobs were more likely to refer to women's lower wages as instances of less advantage – approximately one-quarter of them did so. In general, the significance of relations to employment experience in assessments of relative advantage is consistent with other research. Crosby (1982:67) concluded that "job attitudes do not seem to be linked in a simple or direct way to objective conditions of the job". In particular, she found that "family status" (defined in her case as single, married, or parents) had a profound impact on dissatisfactions and perceptions of deprivation. She argues that (1982:66) "more predictive of job attitudes than either sex or job level is family status. Both the degree of satisfaction and the degree of felt deprivation vary as a function of family status, even when age and salary level are controlled." In a slightly different context, Stewart et al. (1980) show that the understandings of employment among male clerks (such as views on the need for trade unions) vary according to relations to their current job – specifically, in relation to expectations regarding promotion and the lack of success in achieving it.

184

12. Of the 24 women who selected respect as their most important item, 22 elaborated on what this meant to them, and of these 17 referred to issues within the workplace. Out of the 7 women day telephonists who elaborated on the meaning of respect, 6 made a reference to waged work, and 5 of these included specific, and negative, references to relations with supervisors. Of the 13 postwomen who elaborated on what they meant by "to be respected", 10 referred to relations within the workplace and 8 made a specific, again negative, reference to relations with their workmates. In contrast, men were less likely to locate the issue of respect within the workplace (only 6 of the 18 who selected this item did so), and their interpretations of respect tended to be more in relation to the substance of their job, such as "doing my job properly". A small number also referred to aspects of social relations in the workplace, and these tended to have a positive connotation: "being asked for my advice" and "being called by your proper name by persons in authority".

13. That such conditions of employment constitute indirect discrimination against women has been well argued elsewhere (MacKinnon 1979, Sedley & Benn 1982).

14. If their second choice was not the gender reverse of their first choice, they were also asked how the situation of their first choice would be different from the gender reverse of their first choice. So for example, if their first choice was a married man whose wife was not working and their second choice was a single man, they were asked the reasons for their first and second choices and in addition were asked how the situation of a married woman whose husband is not working would be different from the situation of a married man with a wife not working.

15. This analysis is based on 92 respondents. Again, time constraints on the interviews meant that in some cases this series of questions was omitted.

16. The strength of the refusal to make a distinction on the basis on gender is underlined by the fact that options presented to respondents did not suggest this response and the interviewer usually prompted for a distinction.

17. The young, single, childless component-wage women were somewhat different from their male counterparts in this respect.

18. For the difference between the two groups: Fisher's exact $= 0.01$, phi $= 0.41$.

19. Length of time as full-time mothers was related to whether or not a gender distinction was made, but this appeared to be specified by current family status. There was no relationship among women with dependent children (although the one woman with dependent children who refused to make a gender distinction was a full-time mother five years or less). Among women with children not dependent, those with shorter experiences of full-time motherhood were more likely to reject gender distinctions.

20. Two sorts of selections make up these totals: the MMWMW–MWHNW pair; and the MWHNW–MMWMW pair. The proportion of women choosing such households would be slightly higher if selections that distinguished by marital status (married person supporting a spouse) but not by gender were taken into account ($N=3$).

21. Not all respondents worked through their answers in these ways. The design of the question would therefore be improved, and ambiguity in responses

185

reduced, by introducing variation in other household needs (i.e. dependent children) and sources of household income more explicitly.

22. Altogether, 13 men chose two men, 4 gave priority to a single man (three with the single woman as a second choice) and 1 gave priority to a married man with an employed spouse (with a single woman as the second choice). Altogether, 10 women chose two men, 2 gave first priority to the single man, and 1 to the married man spouse not working (all with the single woman second). Included in this category is also one woman who chose the married man whose wife is not working and made no second choice. She thought that in the case of the married woman with a husband not working, the husband should be applying for the job: "the man is more important and the wife's got things to do at home, he should go out to work first" (Postwoman, 195).

23. In addition to those who gave priority to the non-traditional need selection (MWHNW-MMWMW), one man and one woman selected two women. Selections of pairs that gave priority to women included the following: two women gave priority to married women (one with and one without an unwaged spouse) and two gave priority to single women, including the one woman who did not make a second choice; two men gave priority to married women with an unwaged spouse (with the single man as second choice).

24. Whereas being under or over 30 was the most discriminating division for women without children, the most productive division for childless men was over or under 40. This difference is consistent with the ages after which women and men in manual and low-level non-manual jobs are less likely to become parents.

25. That a more complex picture of current and lifetime domestic experience could be important in understanding variations in men's conceptions of women's and men's claims on employment is indicated by variations in the selections made by married men who were supporting dependent children with or without financial assistance from women. A slightly smaller proportion of men who were supporting dependent children with assistance from a female wage made "male" selections compared with those who were the sole financial support. In addition, the one man with dependent children who made a "female" selection, by giving first priority to the married women with a husband not working, had an employed spouse.

26. The difference between the two groups of men in terms of whether they made "male" selections or not is significant at 0.001, phi=0.45. There is no pattern here by job type, except to the extent that job type is related to family status. Most of the component-wage men were under 40 and had no children, and they comprised 6 of the 15 men in this situation in group 1. Their responses, however, were identical to those of their full-wage counterparts.

27. In general terms, a similar relation between distance from gendered experience and less gendered conceptions, as is found here, is also reported in Livingstone & Luxton's study of male steelworkers in Canada (1989:264): "Those male steelworkers who were more ambivalent about asserting the validity of the male breadwinner norm, and those who, despite massive lay-offs at Stelco, expressed support for women's equal rights to scarce jobs, tended to be men who had direct experiences of women's employment.

Either their wives had significant employment experiences or they themselves worked with women."

28. For the "male" versus other selections, the relationship with greater and less time as full-time mothers is significant and strong, Fisher's exact $=0.001$, phi$=0.57$.

29. Dex (1984:84) found an analogous situation among the continuously employed women in WES. She discovered that "approximately 40% of continuously working women with children felt women with young children ought not to work, and yet they had done so themselves". Dex suggests that they are "expressing some notion of an ideal state of affairs with which the reality of their own life – with its multifaceted considerations, is not in full accord".

Chapter Seven

Conclusions

This research addresses a number of issues in the study of women's and men's relations to and experiences of employment. Particular attention has been paid to the social processes linking employment distributions, wages and domestic responsibilities, and to the location of gendered experience within these processes. The case study of "occupational segregation by sex" that forms the core of the research has proved to be a useful vantage point for the assessment of the salience and substance of variations within and between women's and men's experiences of domestic and employment relations. It has prompted a reconsideration of the nature of occupational distributions; of the place of gendered experience in understandings in parenting and employment relations; and of the relationships between "gendered" occupational segregation, work history patterns and wage inequalities. In this concluding chapter, the main points of interest suggested by this research are reviewed.

Throughout, the interrogation of the salience of gender in processes structuring employment has been of central concern. Many contemporary discussions of the explanatory status of gender argue for a research practice that does not assume the relevance of gender, reiterate warnings about reproducing gender stereotypes in theoretical statements, and recommend caution in the generalization of gender-relevant findings. Such comments are well directed at the sociology of employment, for it is an area of sociological work that has suffered from gender-differentiated forms of explanation and the reliance on gender-differentiated attributes as explanation. The family-centred woman who appreciates the carpet flooring and the company of her co-workers, and has little interest in good wages, promotion and workplace politics, is a sociological product well past her shelf life! The growing evidence of significant diversity in women's relations to and experiences of employment stands against the over-simplistic presentations of "women" as waged workers, and the over-drawn contrasts between women's and men's interests in jobs and wages. This evidence also forces a confrontation with the use of gender categories per se.

There is tension in the research literature on women's and men's employment between the use of gender categories in statements of significant differences in experience and the identification of the need to deconstruct gender categories in order to highlight the diversities in experience they mask. This tension is acute in the study of work where, on the one hand, contrasts between domestic and waged work, and between forms of waged work, are fairly routinely examined "by gender" and where, on the other hand, variations within gender categories – for example, by "race", generation and command of social resources – are argued to be substantial features in the structuring of experience and opportunities. This tension is apparent also in theoretical arguments about the single, dual or multiple "systems" structuring the stratification of social resources and life chances. To resolve this tension it is necessary to abandon the use of gender categories as general terms of analysis, and to formulate explanations of social processes that locate and specify gendered experience. With the meaning and scope of gendered experience more precisely identified, we should be able to develop explanations that can integrate accounts of aggregate gender differences with those of variations in women's and men's experience.

This research has taken steps towards this type of formulation in its concern with "occupational segregation by sex". Although this phenomenon appears to affirm the general validity of gender categories in the dynamic of employment, the research presented strongly questions the use of unspecified gendered categories and processes in the identification and explanation of segregated employment distributions. There are variations within patterns of "horizontal" gender segregation, and problematic aspects in the relationship between "horizontal" and "vertical" gender segregation, that explanations of employment must be able to address. It is a conclusion of this research that, in the absence of further social specification and location of the salience of gender, explanations of employment allocation and rewards that focus on "gendered jobs" and "gendered workers" will not accomplish this task.

Although the trend in occupational gender segregation requires clarification for recent decades in Britain (Siltanen 1990, Blackburn et al. 1993), there is no doubt that employment continues to be characterized by a high level of differentiation between women and men. A central issue is whether this pattern is appropriately regarded as a consequence of the general operation of processes that highlight the *gender identity* of jobs and job incumbents. The strength of the aggregate pattern in the gender composition of jobs has encouraged forms of explanation that focus on "women's jobs" and "men's jobs" and that highlight processes resulting in the gender-appropriate allocation of people to jobs. However, case studies of occupational gender segregation, including this study, reveal the inadequacy of this approach. The problem is that the distinction between "women's jobs" and "men's jobs" is difficult to sustain in terms of both the labour content of jobs and the gender of job incumbents.

Research conducted at the level of the workplace has shown that there *is not* a consistent relationship between the substance of job tasks and the gender composition of jobs: a particular job may be exclusively male in one workplace and exclusively female in another. In more general terms, arguments promoting the policy advantages of comparable worth strategies for the eradication of wage inequalities between female and male workers rest on the demonstration of the similarity between "women's jobs" and "men's jobs" in terms of labour content. The history and form of gender inequality in the postal and telephonist jobs are instructive in this respect.

The history of discrimination by sex in both the telephonist and postal jobs is not easily explained in terms of the substance of the labour performed. The "men's job" on the night telephonist shift involves performing the same tasks with the same technology as the "women's job" on the day shift. Attempts to use the manual nature of the postal job as a means of evading the requirements of the 1975 Sex Discrimination Act were unsuccessful and, although the lifting and carrying of mail required strength, assessments of gendered capacities in this regard were built into work requirements, rather than used as a means of excluding women from the job. The Post Office management was in fact eager to expand the employment of women in the postal job and to extend the employment of women to cover night telephonist duties. Although resistance to the expansion of women's employment in the postal job was often expressed in gendered terms – it was described as a "job proper to men" – the major concern was the deteriorating wage position of the job. Resistance to the expansion of women's employment in the telephonist job came, in part, from women themselves. The attempt to recruit women to a job that routinely required employment during unsocial hours was unsuccessful, and female telephonists already in post objected to what they saw as a deterioration in their working conditions. Thus, the formal distinctions by gender that existed in the postal and telephonist jobs prior to 1975 were more directly a result of conflict over wages and hours of work. The "gendering" of the labour performed was less significant than the "gendering" of employment conditions and rewards.

190

Of equal significance is the difficulty of sustaining a distinction between gendered jobs in the face of the mixed composition of job incumbents. In other words, explanations focusing on the validity of this division have difficulty accounting for the presence of women in "men's jobs" and of men in "women's jobs". If the gender saturation of work tasks and technology is a main force structuring employment, how are we to account for the presence of "gender-inappropriate" job incumbents? This is a problem both in cases of female-dominated occupations that include exclusively male jobs (or vice versa), and in cases of jobs that have a skewed gender composition. One consequence of the emphasis on gender distinctions in studies of occupational segregation is an underdeveloped picture of the relationships between the material and social circumstances of jobs and the more general circumstances of the women and men employed within them. Again, the details of the postal and telephonist jobs illustrate the force of this point.

Although in terms of numerical dominance the postal job and the night telephonist job were "men's jobs" and the day telephonist job was a "woman's job", the social circumstances of job incumbents were not encompassed by a gender distinction in any straightforward way. Two related factors underline this observation. The first is that although male day telephonists, female night telephonists and postwomen were in a minority position in their jobs in terms of their gender, they shared other significant social characteristics with those whose gender was the majority. The second is that important features in the social circumstances of women and men in the predominantly female day telephonist job were substantially different from those of the women and men in the predominantly male night telephonist and postal jobs. These instances of similarity across gender categories within jobs, and of difference within gender categories across jobs, indicate the limitations in identifying and explaining the employment patterns involved in unspecified gendered terms.

The clarification of processes producing occupational gender segregation is a prerequisite to finding the answer to another question explored in some detail in this study: the relationship between segregation and stratification. Although it is certainly the case that jobs in which women are concentrated tend to be lower status, lower paying jobs, there is not an identity between "horizontal" and "vertical" forms of segregation. There is considerable stratification within "women's jobs" and "men's jobs" and this reality continually undercuts attempts to explain gender inequalities in employment status and rewards in terms of the gender composition of jobs. As with explanations of employment distributions themselves, the challenge is to develop explanations that provide an account of inequalities in the range of both "women's jobs" and "men's jobs" that is consistent with observed aggregate inequalities between jobs dominated by women and men.

The research in this monograph indicates the direction we need to travel in order to begin to identify the general processes of employment and wage distribution that are consistent with gendered patterns. In the telephonist and postal jobs, there was a gendered dynamic in the distribution of women and men, related to the more general relation of employment circumstances to work histories, domestic circumstances and life-course phases. This gendered pattern does not describe the life situations of all the women, or all the men, involved. It does describe the life-course and immediate social circumstances of women and men in jobs dominated by their own gender. Distance from this gendered pattern is associated with employment in a job dominated by the opposite gender.

For example, in the telephonist and postal jobs there is a very clear relationship between types of women's work history patterns, the gender composition of jobs and the wage level of jobs. Women in the lower paying, female-dominated job had the standard features of work histories associated with disadvantaged employment. They had taken breaks from employment for childrearing and many had been out of the labour force for substantial lengths of time. Typically, on returning to employment, these women returned initially to a part-time job, moving into their full-time job when their children were in their teens. Women in the higher paying, male-dominated jobs had an entirely different pattern of work history. Many of these women were black and had a work history profile that was consistent with British cross-sectional data on the employment activity of Afro-Caribbean women. They had been in full-time employment continuously over their childbearing and childrearing years. In addition, a large number of white women in these jobs were, or had been, lone parents. In a variety of ways their work history profile was a truncated version of the profile for white women in the female-dominated job. They either entered full-time work after a relatively short time as full-time mothers, or returned to employment for a relatively short period of part-time work, shifting into full-time work on their separation or divorce. Most returned to employment as the sole wage earner in their household and with responsibility for supporting dependent children.

Analyses using more aggregated data have not been able to establish such clear relationships between work histories, the gender composition of jobs and the wage level of jobs. Indeed, there are strong disagreements in the literature about whether such relationships exist. In this context, the case study material is very illuminating, for it reveals complexities and subtleties that have not yet been acknowledged by or incorporated into more general analyses. These complexities need to be explored across employment circumstances that are more diverse than those studied here. In doing so, it will be important to investigate how the relationship between work history variations and employment circumstances is articulated within the range of jobs dominated by one gender, as well as between male- and female-dominated jobs.

One aspect of variation within and between gendered jobs that has been introduced and developed in this monograph is the distinction between full-wage and component-wage jobs. Although each job in the study was dominated by one gender or the other, the processes underlying the distribution of women and men in the different jobs encompassed a patterning in social circumstances that was more extensive than this simple characterization implies.

Employment in the telephonist and postal jobs was structured, for men and women, by both general social resources and life-course patterns in domestic and employment relations. To capture the social division between jobs in terms of their capacity to sustain particular forms and levels of household support, the distinction between full-wages and component-wages has been proposed. Component-wage jobs are those that do not pay wages sufficient to allow an individual to support himself/herself as an independent adult. In the component-wage job in this study, women and men were typically sharing the financial maintenance of their household with other wage earners, and rarely did the households include dependants. Single people were usually still living in their families of origin. In contrast, full-wage jobs pay wages that allow individuals to be the sole wage earner in households, and different full-wage levels can be identified for different types of households. The full-wage jobs in this study were only marginally able to support a household that included dependants, and required large amounts of routine overtime in order to do so. Roughly half of women and men in the jobs were the sole wage earners in their households, while a smaller proportion were also supporting dependent household members.

In more general terms, it has been argued that development of the full-wage/component-wage distinction will provide a means of assessing the social adequacy of wages and tracing the social implications of changes in earnings distributions. It provides a useful social context for discussions of the gender gap in wages, and the basis for further exploration of women's and men's relations to the financial maintenance of households. It has been demonstrated that component-wages are a chronic feature of women's employment experience. Even when in full-time employment, many women are routinely earning wages that are not sufficient to support themselves as an independent adult in our society. Increasing inequalities in wages over the 1980s have meant that more men are now earning component-wages. However, men typically earn wages that are at least sufficient to support a one adult household. They do not routinely earn wages sufficient to support a household with dependants, and this capacity has deteriorated for manual men over the decade.

Establishing a link between the social obligations of wage earners and the social capacities afforded by differing wage levels allows for a direct examination of household and employment relations and the location of gendered experience within this. The distinction between full-wage and component-wage jobs was shown to correspond with differences in women's work histories, and differences for both women and men in their experience of the gendered negotiation of household and employment relations. This combination of circumstances was also tied very closely to the salience of gender in understandings of family and employment experience and of entitlement to a wage. These understandings were complex and variable, but appeared to have a strong link to stages of the life-course and the extent of gendered experience. In making assessments of inequality and disadvantage, perceptions of past, current and likely future experience were all significant, as were people's relations to conventional gendered patterns. Although longitudinal data would be needed to explore these issues fully, there was within the cross-sectional data reported here a consistent pattern of variation in the salience of gender associated with variation in distance from gendered experience in family and employment relations.

The ability to demonstrate such consistent patterns in experience and understandings – patterns that capture differences and similarities between women and men in employment – is convincing testimony to the advantages to be gained by identifying general processes that can locate variation in the salience of gendered experience.

Appendix I

The sample

	Number employed[1]	Number selected[2]	Number contacted	Number refused	Number interviewed
Postal job					
Early shift:					
Women	53	30	27	9	18
Men	643	30	27	7	20
Late/night shift:					
Women	69	35	27	6	21
Men	618	35	26	5	21
Total	1383	130	107	27	80
Telephonist job					
Night shift:					
Women	10	10	8	2	6
Men	34	30	22	2	20
Day shift:					
Women	126	30	26	2	24
Men	16	16	14	0	14
Total	186	86	70	6	64
Total	1569	216	177	33	144

1. Respondents who did not work a permanent shift are included in the sample information under the shift they were working when their interview was conducted. In total, there were 256 who did not work a permanent shift (composed mainly of those in their first year of employment), and they have not been included in the shift breakdown of the number employed. 2. Further details about the sampling process can be found in Siltanen (1985).

Appendix II

List of interview quotations

Job, sex and interview number	Page	Job, sex and interview number	Page
Day telephonist, female		128	177
002	59	131	33, 48
005	159	171	177
007	176, 176	172	37, 38, 177
014	148	173	160
015	169	182	160, 166
020	159, 168	194	148
021	176, 176	195	31, 186
Day telephonist, male		221	169
042	165	222	37, 38, 175, 176
043	174	225	179
Night telephonist, female		Postmen	
090	169	138	172
Night telephonist, male		140	169
058	169	141	33, 38
070	173	152	174
080	58	153	45
Postwomen		159	33
101	39, 45, 167	160	173
102	40, 45, 157	163	173
103	31, 157, 179	198	172
104	170	202	47
109	31, 48, 148	203	169
111	178	214	174
117	148	217	168
124	148	226	37
126	33, 38, 45	Union Official, female	53, 58
127	45, 160, 166	Union Official, male	40, 160

Appendix III

Interview schedule

The following is excerpted from the full interview schedule. Only those questions pertaining to the data discussed in the manuscript are presented. The interview schedule formed the skeletal structure of the interviews and certain parts were extended by further questioning when this seemed appropriate.

First of all, I would like to thank you for agreeing to this interview. I'll be asking you a number of different sorts of questions. There will be questions about you and your job; and there will also be questions about your opinion on a number of topics. There are no right or wrong answers to the opinion types of questions so when we come to one please feel free to express your views. All of your answers are, of course, completely confidential.

We'll begin with some questions about schools you've been to and jobs you've done in the past.

1. Which school did you last attend on a full-time basis?

2. What type of school was that?

3. How old were you when you left this school?

4. While at school, did you receive any formal qualifications?
   IF YES: What qualifications did you get?

5. Have you had any further educational or training courses since leaving school?
   IF YES: What kind of course was it?
   Did you get any qualifications? What kind?

Now I'd like to ask you about your past working experience.

6. Have you worked anywhere besides the Post Office?
   IF YES: I'd like to ask you about the jobs you've had before coming into your Post Office job. Let's start with the first job you had after leaving school. What sort of job was it?

197

[The following information was recorded in sequence for each paid job and period outside employment prior to the first Post Office job.]
(a) details of job description
(b) in what type of industry
(c) employed for how long
(d) employed full time or part time
(e) reason for leaving
(f) after this job, what did you do?
IF RESPONDENT DID NOT IMMEDIATELY ENTER ANOTHER PAID JOB
(g) how long was it before you started your next paid job?
IF RESPONDENT LEFT EMPLOYMENT FOR CHILDREARING
(h) how old was your youngest when you began your next paid job?
(i) what were your reasons for getting a job at this time?

7. How old were you when you came to work for the Post Office?

8. What was the first job you had with the Post Office?
   [If not current job, details as in question 6 recorded for all jobs held within the Post Office.]

9. About the job you have now, how long have you been on the (day etc.) shift?

10. Have you ever worked the other shift(s)?
    IF YES: When was that? For how long? Why did you change shifts?
    IF NO: Have you ever considered working the other shift(s)?
    IF YES: What do you like about the other shift(s) compared with the one you do now?
    Have you applied to transfer?
    IF NO: What do you like about your current shift?

11. Do you work any overtime at all?
    IF YES: How many hours overtime did you do last week?
    How many hours overtime do you usually work per week?

12. Taking your qualifications and/or training into account, is there any other Post Office job that you would like to do?
    IF YES: What sort of job would that be?
    What do you find attractive about this job?
    Have you put in an application for this job?

13. Have you ever thought of leaving your present job to work outside the Post Office?
    IF YES: What type of job would you be thinking of?
    What do you find attractive about this job?
    Have you applied for this type of job recently?

14. Do you expect to be doing your current job a year from now?
    IF NO: What do you expect to be doing?

I would like to continue with some questions about other aspects of your life.

15. In what year were you born?

16. Are you married?
    IF SINGLE: Do you live on your own (with parents, friends)?
    IF MARRIED:
    (a) Do you have any children?
        IF YES: How many?
        Age of youngest child?
        Age of oldest child?
        IF CHILDREN UNDER 5: Who looks after the younger one while you're at work?
    (b) Is your wife/husband working?
        IF YES: Do they work full time or part time?
        What kind of work does she/he do?
        What is their weekly take-home pay?

17. What job did your father do for most of his life?
    Is that the job he has now?

18. What about your mother, what job did she do for most of her life? Is that her job now?

19. There is a different kind of question now. I'm going to give you a card that has on it a list of things that people usually think are important in life. I'd like to know which of these things are important to you. (Respondent handed a card showing a list of items in the following order.)
    > enjoyable work
    > good social life
    > lots of time for family life
    > to be respected
    > really good wage
    (a) To begin, which of the things listed is the most important to you? What would come second? What would come third? Is there something in your life that you feel is important that isn't on this list?
        IF YES: What would that be?
        Where would you place it among the things you've already mentioned, would it come before any of these?
    (b) Thinking about the thing you put in first place (enjoyable work etc. as appropriate), can you thing of anyone who has (less enjoyable work etc.) than you do?
        PROBE FOR INDIVIDUAL: Could you think of a particular person? I don't want any names, just an idea of who they might be. [For each comparison, the sex of the individual, their relation to the respondent and their general circumstances were recorded.]
        How about someone who has (more enjoyable work etc.) than you do?
        Could you think of a particular person?

(c) How about the second thing you mentioned. Can you think of anybody who has (not as good, less etc. of rank 2) than you do? Can you think of a particular person?
Can you think of anybody who has (better, more etc. of rank 2) than you do? Could you think of a particular person?

(d) IF WAGES WERE NOT RANKED FIRST OR SECOND:
Can you think of anybody who gets lower wages than you do?
Could you think of a particular person?
Can you think of anybody who gets higher wages than you do?
Could you think of a particular person?

20. IF FEMALE: Do you think you have had more opportunity and choice about what to do in your life than your mother had, or has it been about the same or less?
IF MALE: Do you think you have had more opportunity and choice about what to do in your life than your father had, or has it been about the same or less?

21. We all get frustrated at times with the work that we do, can you think of any particular time when you have been bothered by what has happened at work?
IF YES: What happened? What bothered you about this incident? What did you do about it?

22. I'm going to ask you a different sort of question again. This time I'm going to give you card that lists a number of people in different marital situations. Let's suppose that they have been sent along from the employment exchange and they are all applying for a vacant job. They all have the same job experience and qualifications.
I'd like to know who you think should be offered the job first. [Card handed to respondent at this point, with choices listed as below.]

            a single man
            a married man whose wife is working
            a married woman whose husband is not working
            a married man whose wife is not working
            a single woman
            a married woman whose husband is working

(a) Can you tell me who you think should have the first opportunity to take the vacant job?

(b) Who do you think should be offered the job second?

(c) Can you tell me why you think (rank 1) should have the first opportunity for the vacant job?
Why should they be offered the job before (rank 2)?
How would the situation of (rank 1) be different from the situation of the (the gender reverse of rank 1)?
That's the last question relating to the people on the card. I'd like to go back and talk about your job again.

23. How many times in an average day would you come into contact with your supervisor?
    Is the supervising of your job pretty standard or does it depend a lot on who is doing the supervising?
    What type of person was the best supervisor you've had?
    What type of person was the worst supervisor you've had?

24. If you had to hire someone to replace you on your job, what personal qualities and skills do you think they should have?

25. There are more (POST AND NIGHT TELS men than women) (DAY TELS women than men) who do the same job as you, why do you think this is so?
    We're coming close to the end now. To finish, I would like to ask you some more general types of questions.

26. The law saying women and men must have equal opportunities in employment has been in effect now for a number of years, do you think it has brought about some good changes?
    Has it brought problems with it?
    Has it affected you personally in any way?
    Has it brought about any changes in your job?
    IF TELECOM: Men and women can now work either the day or night shifts, what do you think of this change?
    Has it brought any problems with it?
    IF POSTAL: Postwomen can now get their seniority recognized, what do you think of this change?
    Has it brought any problems with it?
    ALL: Do you know of any cases of sex discrimination in the Post Office?

27. Are you a member of the Union of Post Office Workers?
    Have you ever been a union representative?
    Do you think your union represents all sectors of its membership equally well?

Well, that's the end of the interview. I'd like to thank you very much for answering all these questions. Have you any questions you'd like to ask about the interview?

Bibliography

Original sources

Post Office Central Headquarters

1. Files

CH/BE/2 Part 1, Employment of Women (begins 16.12.71).
Part 2, Employment of Women (begins 19.9.73).
CH/BE/4, Employment of Women – "Equal Opportunities for Men and Women" Action on the Consultative Document.
CH/BE/5, Complaint by Birmingham Postwomen Under IRA 1971 to National Industrial Relations Court.
CH/BE/13, Employment of Women – Postwomen (dated 20.2.74).
CH/BE/26, White Paper "Equality for Women".
CH/BE/37, Employment of Women – Sex Discrimination Bill (21.3.75).
CH/BE/57, Employment of Women – Sex Discrimination Act 1975 (Effects on Post Office Recruitment and Employment).

2. Circulars and memoranda

CHQ.89/55, Employment of Postwomen (1955).
CHQ. 110/55, Employment of Part-time Postmen and Postwomen (1955).
CHQ. 14/78, Sex Discrimination Act 1975 (1978).
CHQ. 32/78, Post Office Policy on Equality of Opportunity (1978).
Post Office Circular (6/2/57), DF 658 (Supplement) Equal Pay – Telephone and Telegraph Grades (1957).
A&PRD 184/65, Employment of Full-time Postwomen, and Part-time Postmen and Postwomen (1965).
PO (73)224, Post Office Board: Employment of Women in the Post Office (October 1973).
PON 25, Note for the Post Office Review Committee – Organisation and Grading Structure in the Telecommunications Business (October 1976).
SBRD/M, Post Office Manpower 1971–79.

3. Printed

Post Office Report and Accounts, London: HMSO, 1965–69.
Head Postmasters' Manual B January 1968.
The Employment of Women in the Civil Service, London: HMSO, 1971.
Personnel Manual, Section P (Postal) May 1976.

Telecommunications Headquarters

1. Files

TH/DC/1 (Parts 1 and 2), Equality for Women – Employment and Related Matters.

TH/DC/4, Equal Opportunities – Transfers to Full-time Duties, and Carriage of Seniority (begins 9.11.76).

TH/DC/9, Instructions on Equal Opportunities – Day and Night Telephone Operation and Supervisory Staff.

TH/DC/10, Equal Opportunities – Joint Statement.

TH/DC/14, Steel, Mrs. L. – Implications for Telecommunications (begins 24.11.77).

TH/FZ/34, Discrimination – Sex Discrimination, Mrs. A. M. Morrison, Belfast (begins 22.6.77).

2. Printed

The Situation of Women in the European PTT Autumn 1976.

The Industrial Tribunals (Scotland) Case No. S/664/77, held Aberdeen May 1977.

UPW/UCW Research Department, UCW House

Brief notes on the UPW (mimeo, n.d.).

Package Agreement, Volume 1, January 1957.

UPW *Handbook*, November 1954.

UPW *Handbook, Supplement to Volume 1*, January 1961, Telephone Operating Force: Revised Hours and Duty Arrangements.

Reply to TUC Questionnaire "Women Working and New Industrial Techniques", 14.8.61.

Union History and Development – Points Re: Women, September 1975.

Hain, P. & N. Stagg, *Equal Pay Report*, October 1976.

Branch Officials Bulletin, 1970-80.

The Post 1953-80, including General Secretary's Annual Report and the UPW Annual Conference Agenda.

UPW *Annual Conference Agenda Pads* 1970–80.

UPW *Annual Conference Chronicle* 1970–80.

Official Publications

Family Expenditure Survey 1979. London: HMSO, 1980.

Family Expenditure Survey 1987. London: HMSO, 1989.

General Household Survey 1979. London: HMSO, 1987.

New Earnings Survey 1979. London: HMSO, 1979.

New Earnings Survey 1987. London: HMSO, 1987.

Tax/Benefit Model Tables as at October 1989, Department of Social Services (ASD4A).

Secondary Sources

Acker, J. 1988. Class, gender and the relations of distribution. *Signs* 13.

Allatt, P., T. Keil, A. Bryman, B. Bytheway (eds) 1987. *Women and the life cycle.*

Basingstoke: Macmillan.

Arendell, T. J. 1987. Women and the economics of divorce in the contemporary United States. *Signs* 13.

Atkins, S. 1986. The Sex Discrimination Act of 1975: the end of a decade. *Feminist Review* 24.

Atkinson, A. 1975. *The economics of inequality.* Oxford: Clarendon Press

Atkinson, A. 1981. Unemployment benefits and incentives, in *The economics of unemployment in Great Britain,* J. Creedy (ed.). London: Butterworth

Atkinson, A. 1985. *How should we measure poverty? Some conceptual issues.* London School of Economics, ESRC Programme on Taxation, Incentives and the Distribution of Income, Discussion Paper No 82.

Atkinson, A. 1990. *A national minimum? A history of ambiguity in the determination of benefit scales in Britain.* Discussion Paper, Welfare State Programme, WSP/47, March.

Backett, K. 1982. *Mothers and fathers.* London: Macmillan.

Barber, A. 1985. Ethnic origin and economic status. *Employment Gazette* (December).

Barrett, M. 1980. *Women's oppression today.* London: New Left Review Editions.

Barrett, M. & M. McIntosh 1985. Ethnocentrism and socialist-feminist theory. *Feminist Review* 20.

Barron, R. & G. Norris 1976. Sexual divisions and the dual labour market. in *Dependence and exploitation in work and marriage,* D. Barker & S. Allen (eds). London: Longman.

Beechey, V. 1977. Some notes on female wage labour in capitalist production. *Capital and Class* 3.

Beechey, V. 1978. Women and production: a critical analysis of some sociological theories of women's work, in *Feminism and Materialism,* A. Kuhn & A. Wolpe (eds). London: Routledge & Kegan Paul.

Beechey, V. 1983. What's so special about women's employment? A review of some recent studies of women's paid work. *Feminist Review* 15.

Beechey, V. 1986. Women's employment in contemporary Britain, in *Women in Britain today,* V. Beechey & E. Whitelegg (eds). Milton Keynes: Open University Press.

Beechey, V. & T. Perkins 1987. *A matter of hours.* Cambridge: Polity Press.

Benston, M. 1982. The political economy of women's liberation, in *The woman question,* M. Evans (ed.). London: Fontana.

Beynon, H. & R. M. Blackburn 1972. *Perceptions of work.* Cambridge: Cambridge University Press.

Bielby, W. & J. N. Baron 1986. Men and women at work: sex segregation and statistical discrimination. *American Journal of Sociology* 19.

Bielby, W. & J. N. Baron 1987. Undoing discrimination: job integration and comparable worth, in *Ingredients for women's employment policy,* C. Bose & G. Spitz (eds). New York: State University of New York Press.

Bird, E. & J. West 1987. Interrupted lives: a study of women returners, in *Women and the life cycle,* P. Allatt et al. (eds). London: Macmillan.

Blackburn, R. M. & M. Mann 1979. *The working class in the labour market.* London: Macmillan.

Blackburn, R. M., J. Jarman, J. Siltanen 1993. The analysis of occupational gender segregation over time and place: Considerations of measurement and some new evidence. *Work, Employment and Society* 7.

Bland, L., C. Brunsdon, D. Hobson, J. Winship 1978. Women "inside and outside" the relations of production, in *Women take issue*, Women's Studies Group (Centre for Contemporary Cultural Studies). London: Hutchinson.

Bose, C. & G. Spitze 1987. *Ingredients for women's employment policy*. New York: State University of New York Press.

Boston, S. 1980. *Women workers and the trade unions*. London: Davis-Poynter.

Bradley, J. 1968. *Distribution-free statistical tests*. New Jersey: Prentice-Hall.

Brannen, J. 1987. The resumption of employment after childbirth: a turning point within a lifecourse perspective, in *Women and the life cycle*, P. Allatt et al. (eds). London: Macmillan.

Brannen, J. 1989. Childbirth and occupational mobility. *Work, Employment and Society* 3.

Braverman, H. 1974. *Labor and monopoly capital: the degredation of work in the twentieth century*. New York: Monthly Review Press.

Brown, C. 1984. *Black and white Britain. The third PSI survey*. London: Heinemann.

Brown, P. & L. J. Jordanova 1981. Oppressive dichotomies: the nature/culture debate, in *Women in society*, Cambridge Women's Studies Group. London: Virago Press.

Brown, R. 1976. Women as employees: some comments on research in industrial sociology, in *Dependence and exploitation in work and marriage*, D. Barker & S. Allen (eds). London: Longman.

Bruegel, I. 1979. Women as a reserve army of labour: a note on recent British experience. *Feminist Review* 3.

Bruegel, I. 1989. Sex and "race" in the labour market. *Feminist Review* 17.

Clinton, A. 1984. *Post office workers – a trade union and social history*. London: Allen & Unwin.

Cockburn, C. 1983. *Brothers – male dominance and technological change*. London: Pluto Press.

Cockburn, C. 1986. The relations of technology – what implications for theories of sex and class? In *Gender and stratification*, R. Crompton & M. Mann (eds). Cambridge: Polity Press.

Cockburn, C. 1988. The gendering of jobs: workplace relations and the reproduction of sex segregation, in *Gender segregation at work*, S. Walby (ed.). Milton Keynes: Open University Press.

Cohn, S. 1985. *The process of occupational sex-typing*. Philadelphia, Pa.: Temple University Press.

Connell, R. W. 1987. *Gender and power*. Cambridge: Polity Press.

Coote, A. & P. Kellner 1980. What employers do and say, in *Hear this, brother*, A. Coote & P. Kellner (eds). London: New Statesman Report 1.

Corcoran, M. 1979. Work experience, labor force withdrawals and women's wages: empirical results using the 1976 panel of income dynamics, in *Women in the labor market*, C. B. Lloyd et al. (eds). New York: Columbia University Press.

Corcoran, M. & G. J. Duncan 1979. Work history, labour force attachment, and earnings differences between the races and the sexes. *Journal of Human Resources* 14.

Corcoran, M., G. J. Duncan, M. Ponza 1983. Work experience and wage growth of women workers. In *Five thousand American families – patterns of economic progress, analyses of the first thirteen years of the panel study of income dynamics, Vol. 10*, G. J. Duncan & J. N. Morgan (eds). Ann Arbor, Mich.: University of Michigan.

Corcoran, M., G. J. Duncan, M. Ponza 1984. Work experience, job segregation and wages, in *Sex segregation in the workplace – trends, explanations, remedies*, B. Reskin (ed.). Washington DC: National Academy Press.

Coulson, M., B. Magas, H. Wainwright 1975. The housewife and her labour under capitalism – a critique. *New Left Review* 89.

Coussins, J. 1979. *The shift work swindle*. London: National Council for Civil Liberties.

Coward, R. 1981. Socialism, feminism and socialist feminism, in *No turning back*, Feminist Anthology Collective. London: The Women's Press.

Coyle, A. 1982. Sex and skill in the organisation of the clothing industry, in *Work, women and the labour market*, J. West (ed.). London: Routledge & Kegan Paul.

Coyle, A. 1984. *Redundant women*. London: The Women's Press.

Coyle, A. & J. Skinner (eds) 1988. *Women and work – positive action for change*. London: Macmillan.

Craig, C., J. Rubery, R. Tarling, F. Wilkinson 1982. *Labour market structure, industrial organisation and low pay*. Cambridge: Cambridge University Press.

Crompton, R. 1986. Women and the "service class", in *Gender and stratification*, R. Crompton & M. Mann (eds). Cambridge: Polity Press.

Crompton, R. & G. Jones 1984. *White-collar proletariat*. London: Macmillan.

Crompton, R. & K. Sanderson 1986. Credentials and careers: some implications of the increase in professional qualifications among women. *Sociology* 20.

Crompton, R. & K. Sanderson 1990. *Gendered jobs and social change*. Cambridge: Polity Press.

Crompton, R., G. Jones, S. Reid 1982. Contemporary clerical work: a case study of local government, in *Work, women and the labour market*, J. West (ed.). London: Routledge & Kegan Paul.

Crosby, F. J. 1982. *Relative deprivation and working women*. Oxford: Oxford University Press.

Cunnison, S. 1966. *Wages and work allocation*. London: Tavistock.

Curran, M. 1988. Gender and recruitment: people and places in the labour market. *Work, Employment and Society* 2.

Dale, A. 1987. The effect of lifecycle on three dimensions of stratification, in *Rethinking the life cycle*, A. Bryman et al. (eds). London: Macmillan.

Dale, A., G. N. Gilbert, S. Arber 1985. Integrating women into class theory. *Sociology* 19.

Daniel, W. W. 1980. *Maternity rights: the experience of women*. London: Policy Studies Institute.

Daunton, M. J. 1985. *The Royal Mail – the Post Office since 1840*. London: The Athlone Press.

Delamont, S. 1980. *The sociology of women*. London: Allen & Unwin.

Delphy, C. 1981. Women in stratification studies. In *Doing feminist research*, H. Roberts (ed.). London: Routledge & Kegan Paul.

Dex, S. 1984. *Women's work histories: an analysis of the Women and Employment Survey*. Department of Employment Research Paper No. 46.

Dex, S. 1985. *The sexual division of work*. Brighton: Harvester Press.

Dex, S. 1988. *Women's attitudes towards work*. London: Macmillan.

Dex, S. 1987. *Women's occupational mobility*. London: Macmillan.

Dex, S. & S. M. Perry 1984. Women's employment changes in the 1970s. *Employment Gazette* 92.

Dex, S. & L. B. Shaw 1986. *British and American women at work*. London: Macmillan.

Dunnel, K. 1979. *Family formation*. London: HMSO.

Edholm, F., O. Harris, K. Young 1977. Conceptualising women. *Critique of Anthropology* 3.

Edwards, R. 1979. *Contested terrain*. London: Heinemann.

Eichler, M. 1980. *The double standard. A feminist critique of feminist social science*. London: Croom Helm.

Eichler, M. 1988. *Non-sexist research methods*. Boston: Allen & Unwin.

Eisenstein, H. 1984. *Contemporary feminist thought*. London: Unwin.

Eisenstein, Z. 1979. Developing a theory of capitalist patriarchy and socialist feminism, in *Capitalist patriarchy and the case for socialist feminism*, Z. Eisenstein (ed.). New York: Monthly Review Press.

Elias, P. 1988. Family formation, occupational mobility and part-time work, in *Women and paid work*, A. Hunt (ed.). London: Macmillan.

Ellis, V. 1981. *The role of trade unions in the promotion of equal opportunities*. EOC/SSRC Joint Panel on Equal Opportunities.

Emler, N. & D. Abrams 1991. The sexual distribution of benefits and burdens in the household: adolescent experience and expectations. 16-19 Initiative Occasional Paper No. 7.

England, P. 1982. The failure of human capital theory to explain occupational sex segregation. *Journal of Human Resources* 17, 3.

England, P. 1984. Wage appreciation and depreciation: a test of neoclassical economic explanations of occupational sex segregation. *Social Forces* 62.

England, P. & G. Farkas 1986. *Households, employment and gender*. New York: Aldine de Grutyer.

England, P., M. Chassie, L. McCormack 1982. Skill demands and earnings in female and male occupations. *Sociology and Social Research* 66.

EOC, 1985. *Occupational segregation by sex*. Research Bulletin No. 9.

Evans, M. & C. Ungerson (eds) 1983. *Sexual divisions: patterns and processes*. London: Tavistock Publications.

Feldberg, R. & E. Glenn 1984. Male and female: job versus gender models in the sociology of work, in *Women and the public sphere*, J. Siltanen & M. Stanworth (eds). London: Hutchinson.

Ferree, M. 1976. Working class jobs: housework and paid work as sources of satisfaction. *Social Problems* 23.

Finch, J. 1989. *Family obligations and social change*. Cambridge: Polity Press.

Finney, D. J. et al. 1963. *Tables for testing significance in a 2x2 contingency table*. Cambridge: Cambridge University Press.

Freeman, C. 1982. The "understanding" employer, in *Work, women and the labour market*, J. West (ed.). London: Routledge & Kegan Paul.

Gardiner, J. 1976. Women and unemployment. *Red Rag* 10.

Garnsey, E. 1978. Women's work and theories of clas stratification. *Sociology* 12.

Glenn, E. & R. Feldberg 1977. Degraded and de-skilled: the proletarianisation of clerical work. *Social Problems* 25.

Goldthorpe, J. 1983. Women and class analysis: in defence of the conventional view. *Sociology* 17.

Goldthorpe, J. 1985. The end of convergence: corporatist and dualist tendencies in modern western societies, in *New approaches to economic life*, B. Roberts et al. Manchester: University of Manchester Press.

Goldthorpe, J., D. Lockwood, F. Bechhofer, J. Platt 1968. *The affluent worker: industrial attitudes and behaviour*. Cambridge: Cambridge University Press.

Grint, K. 1988. Women and equality: the acquisition of equal pay in the Post Office,

1870-1961. *Sociology* **22**.

Griffiths, D. & E. Saraga 1979. Sex differences in cognitive abilities: a sterile field of enquiry? In *Sex-role stereotyping*, O. Hartnett, G. Boden, M. Fuller (eds). London: Tavistock.

Gowler, D. & K. Legge 1982. Dual-worker families, in *Families in Britain*, R. Rapoport, M. Fogarty, R. Rapoport (eds). London: Routledge & Kegan Paul.

Hakim, C. 1978. Sexual divisions within the labour force: occupational segmentation. *Employment Gazette* (November).

Hakim, C. 1979. *Occupational segregation*. Research Paper No. 9, Department of Employment. London: HMSO.

Hakim, C. 1981. Job segregation: trends in the 1970s. *Employment Gazette* (December).

Hamill, L. 1978. *Wives as sole and joint breadwinners*. Government Economic Service Working Paper No. 13. London: HMSO.

Hartmann, H. 1979. Capitalism, patriarchy, and job segregation by sex, in *Capitalist patriarchy and the case for socialist feminism*, Z. Eisenstein (ed.). New York: Monthly Review Press.

Hartmann, H. 1981. The unhappy marriage of Marxism and feminism: towards a more progressive union, in *Women and revolution*, L. Sargent (ed.). London: Pluto Press.

Hartnett, O. 1978. Sex-role stereotyping at work, in *The sex role system*, J. Chetwynd & O. Hartnett (eds). London: Routledge & Kegan Paul.

Hernes, H. M. 1987. *The welfare state and woman power*. Oxford: Oxford University Press.

Holmwood, J. M. & A. Stewart 1983. The role of contradictions in modern theories of social stratification. *Sociology* **17**.

Hoskyns, C. 1985. Women's equality and the European Community. *Feminist Review* **20**.

Humphries, J. 1977. Class struggle and the persistence of the working class family. *Cambridge Journal of Economics* **1**.

Humphries, J. 1983. The "emancipation" of women in the 1970s and 1980s: from the latent to the floating reserve army of labour. *Capital and Class* **20**.

Hunt, A. 1968. *A survey of women's employment*. London: HMSO.

Hunt, A. 1975. *Management attitudes and practices towards women at work*. London: HMSO.

Hunt, A. (ed.) 1988. *Women and paid work*. London: Macmillan.

Hunt, P. 1980. *Gender and class consciousness*. London: Macmillan.

Hurstfield, J. 1978. *The part-time trap*. London: Low Pay Unit Pamphlet No. 9.

Industrial Relations Legal Review (IRLR) 1977. Employment Appeal Tribunal L. B. Steel (appellant) v. (1) The Union of Post Office Workers and (2) The General Post Office.

Industrial Relations Review and Report (IRR&R) 1978. Equal Opportunities in the Post Office: The Policy and the Problems, No. 186.

Jephcott, P., N. Seear, J. Smith 1962. *Married women working*. London: Allen & Unwin.

Jones, G. & C. Wallace 1992. *Youth, family and citizenship*. Milton Keynes: Open University Press.

Joseph, G. 1983. *Women at work*. Oxford: Philip Allan.

Joshi, H. 1981. Secondary workers in the employment cycle. *Economica* **48**.

Joshi, H. 1984. *Women's participation in paid work: further analysis of the Women and*

Employment Survey. Department of Employment Research Paper No. 45.

Joshi, H. 1987. The cost of caring, in *Women and poverty in Britain*, C. Glendinning & J. Millar (eds). Brighton: Wheatsheaf.

Joshi, H. 1988. Changing roles of women in the British labour market and the family. Paper presented to the British Association (Section F).

Jowell, R. & S. Witherspoon 1985. *British Social Attitudes, the fifth report*. Aldershot: Gower.

Kanter, R. 1977. *Men and women of the corporation*. New York: Basic Books.

Kidd, T. 1982. Social security and the family, in *Sex differences in Britain*, I. Reid & E. Wormald (eds). London: Grant McIntyre.

Klein, V. 1965. *Britain's married women workers*. London: Routledge & Kegan Paul.

Land, H. 1976. Women: supporters or supported? In *Sexual divisions and society: process and change*, D. Barker & S. Allen (eds). London: Tavistock.

Land, H. 1981. *Parity begins at home*. EOC/SSRC Joint Panel on Equal Opportunities.

Langer, E. 1970. The women of the telephone company. *New York Review of Books* 14.

Layard R. et al. 1978. *The causes of poverty*. Royal Commission on the Distribution of Income and Wealth, Background Paper No. 5. London: HMSO.

Livingston, D. W. & M. Luxton 1989. Gender consciousness at work: modification of the male breadwinner norm among steelworkers and their spouses. *Canadian Review of Sociology and Anthropology* 26.

Loether, H. J. & D. G. McTavish 1974. *Descriptive statistics for sociologists*. Boston: Allyn & Bacon.

Lonsdale, S. 1987. Patterns of paid work, in *Women and poverty in Britain*, C. Glendinning & J. Millar (eds). Brighton: Wheatsheaf.

Low Pay Unit. 1988. *The poor decade*. London: Low Pay Unit.

Lupton, T. 1963. *On the shop floor*. London: Pergamon Press.

MacCormack, C. & M. Strathern 1980. *Nature, culture and gender*. Cambridge: Cambridge University Press.

McIntosh, A. 1980. Women at work: a survey of employers. *Employment Gazette* (November).

MacKinnon, C. 1979. *Sexual harassment of working women*. New Haven, Conn.: Yale University Press.

MacKinnon, C. A. 1982. Feminism, Marxism, method, and the state: an agenda for theory. *Signs* 7.

McLanahan, S. S., A. Sorensen, D. Watson 1989. Sex differences in poverty 1950-1980. *Signs* 15.

McLaughlin, E., J. Millar, K. Cooke 1989. *Work and welfare benefits*. Aldershot: Avebury.

McNally, F. 1979. *Women for hire*. London: Macmillan.

McNay, M. & C. Pond 1980. *Low pay and family poverty*. London: Study Commission on the Family.

Main, B. 1988. The lifetime attachment of women to the labour market, in *Women and paid work*, A. Hunt (ed.). London: Macmillan.

Main, B. & P. Elias 1987. Women returning to paid employment. *International Review of Applied Economics* 1.

Mama, A. 1984. Black women, the economic crisis and the British state. *Feminist Review* 17.

Marshall, G. et al. 1988. *Social class in modern Britain*. London, Unwin Hyman.

210

Martin, J. & C. Roberts 1984. *Women and work: a life-time perspective*. London: HMSO.
Martin, R. & C. Wallace 1984. *Working women in recession*. Oxford: Oxford University Press.
Mathieu, N-C. 1978a. Man-culture and woman-nature? *Women's Studies International Quarterly* 1.
Mathieu, N-C. 1978b. *Ignored by some, denied by others*. London: Women's Research and Resources Centre.
Middleton, C. 1974. Sexual inequality and stratification theory, in *The social analysis of class structure*, F. Parkin (ed.). London: Tavistock Publications.
Milkman, R. 1976. Women's work and the economic crisis: some lessons from the great depression. *Review of Radical Political Economics* 8.
Milkman, R. 1980. Organising the sexual division of labor: historical perspectives on "women's work" and the American labor movement. *Socialist Review* 10.
Millar, J. 1987. Lone mothers, in *Women and poverty in Britain*, C. Glendinning & J. Millar (eds). Brighton: Wheatsheaf.
Millar, J. & C. Glendinning 1987. Invisible women, invisible poverty, in *Women and poverty in Britain*, C. Glendinning & J. Millar (eds). Brighton: Wheatsheaf.
Miller, J., C. Schooler, M. Kohn, K. Miller 1979. Women and work: the psychological effects of occupational conditions. *American Journal of Sociology* 85.
Miller, P. W. 1987. The wage effect of the occupational segregation of women in Britain. *Economic Journal* 97.
Mincer, J. & H. Ofek 1982. Interrupted work careers: depreciation and restoration of human capital. *Journal of Human Resources* 17.
Mincer, J. & S. Polachek 1980. Family investments in human capital: earnings of women. In *The economics of women and work*, A. Amsden (ed.). Middlesex: Penguin.
Minford, P. 1985. *Unemployment: cause and cure*. London: Martin Robertson.
Moran, M. 1974. *The Union of Post Office Workers*. London: Macmillan.
Morgan, D. 1986. Gender, in *Key variables in sociological research*, B. Burgess (ed.). London: Routledge & Kegan Paul.
Moser, C. & G. Kalton 1971. *Survey methods in social investigation*. London: Heinemann.
Moss, P. 1980. Parents at work. In *Work and the family*, P. Moss & N. Fonda (eds). London: Temple Smith.
Murgatroyd, L. 1982. Gender and occupational stratification. *Sociological Review* 30.
Murgatroyd, L. 1984. Women, men and the social grading of occupations. *British Journal of Sociology* 35.
Myrdal, A. & V. Klein 1956. *Women's two roles*. London: Routledge & Kegan Paul.
Nichols, T. & P. Armstrong 1976. *Workers divided*. London: Fontana.
Oakley, A. 1981. *Subject women*. New York: Pantheon Books.
Ortner, S. & H. Whitehead (eds) 1981. *Sexual meanings*. Cambridge: Cambridge University Press.
Pahl, J. 1989. *Money and marriage*. Basingstoke: Macmillan.
Pateman, C. 1989. The patriarchal welfare state, in *The disorder of women*, C. Pateman. Cambridge: Polity Press.
Perkins, T. 1983. A new form of employment: a case study of women's part-time work in coventry, in *Sexual divisions*, M. Evans & C. Ungerson (eds). London: Tavistock.
Philips, A. & B. Taylor 1980. Sex and skill: notes toward a feminist economics. *Feminist Review* 6.

211

Phizacklea, A. 1982. Migrant women and wage labour: the case of West Indian women in Britain, in *Work, women and the labour market*, J. West (ed.). London: Routledge & Kegan Paul.

Phizacklea, A. 1988. Gender, racism and occupational segregation, in *Gender segregation at work*, S. Walby (ed.). Milton Keynes: Open University Press.

Playford, C. & C. Pond 1983. The right to be unequal: inequality in incomes, in *The wealth report – 2*, F. Field (ed.). London: Routledge & Kegan Paul.

Polachek, S. 1979. Occupational segregation among women: theory, evidence and prognosis, in *Women and the labour market*, C. B. Lloyd, E. S. Andrews, C. L. Gilroy (eds). New York: Columbia University Press.

Polachek, S. 1981. Occupational self-selection: a human capital approach to sex differences in occupational structure. *Review of Economics and Statistics* 63.

Pollert, A. 1981. *Girls, wives, and factory lives*. London: Macmillan.

Pond, C. 1979. *Low pay in the '80s*. Low Pay Unit Bulletin No. 30.

Popay, J., L. Rimmer, C. Rossiter 1983. *One parent families: parents, children and public policy*. Study Commission on the Family, Occasional Paper No. 12.

Porter, M. 1979. Experience and consciousness: women at home, men at work. Unpublished PhD thesis, University of Bristol.

Porter, M. 1982. Standing on the edge: working class housewives and the world of work, in *Work, women and the labour market*, J. West (ed.). London: Routledge & Kegan Paul.

Prandy, K. 1986. Similarities of life-style and occupations of women, in *Gender and stratification*, R. Crompton & M. Mann (eds). Cambridge: Polity Press.

Purcell, K. 1979. Militancy and acquiescence amongst women workers, in *Fit work for women*, S. Burman (ed.). London: Croom Helm.

Purcell, K. 1988. Gender and the experience of employment, in *Employment*, D. Gallie (ed.). Oxford: Basil Blackwell.

Rainwater, L., M. Rein, J. Swartz, J. 1986. *Income packaging in the welfare state – a comparative study of family income*. Oxford: Clarendon Press.

Ramazanoglu, C. 1989. *Feminism and the contradictions of oppression*. London: Routledge.

Rapoport, R. & R. Rapoport 1976. *Dual-career families re-examined*. London: Martin Robertson.

Reid, I. 1981. *Social class differences in Britain*, 2nd edn. London: Grant McIntyre.

Rimmer, L. 1988. The intra-family distribution of paid work, 1968-81, in *Women and paid work*, A. Hunt (ed.). London: Macmillan.

Rimmer, L. & J. Popay 1982. *Employment trends and the family*. London: Study Commission on the Family.

Roberts, H. & R. Barker 1989. What are people doing when they grade women's work? *British Journal of Sociology* 40.

Robinson, O. 1988. The changing labour market: growth of part-time employment and labour market segmentation in Britain, in *Gender segregation at work*, S. Walby (ed.). Milton Keynes: Open University Press.

Roos, P. A. 1985. *Gender and work: a comparative analysis of industrial societies*. Albany, NY: State University of New York Press.

Routh, G. 1980. *Occupation and pay in Great Britain 1906-79*. London: Macmillan.

Rowbotham, S. 1979. The women's movement and organising for socialism, in *Beyond the fragments*, S. Rowbotham, L. Segal, H. Wainwright. London: Merlin Press.

Rowbotham, S. 1981. The trouble with "patriarchy", in *No turning back*, Feminist

Anthology Collective. London: The Women's Press.

Royal Commission on the Distribution of Income and Wealth 1978. Report No. 6, *Lower incomes*. London: HMSO.

Royal Commission on the Distribution of Income and Wealth 1978. *Selected evidence submitted to the Royal Commission for Report No. 6*. London: HMSO.

Rubery, J. (ed.) 1988. *Women and recession*. London: Routledge & Kegan Paul.

Rubery, J. & R. Tarling 1988. Women's employment in declining Britain, in *Women and recession*, J. Rubery (ed.). London: Routledge & Kegan Paul.

Rubin, G. 1975. The traffic in women: notes on the "political economy" of sex, in *Toward an anthropology of women*, R. Reiter (ed.). New York: Monthy Review Press.

Ruggie, M. 1985. *The state and working women*. Princeton, NJ: Princeton University Press.

Ruggie, M. 1988. Gender, work and social progress, in *Feminisation of the labour force*, J. Jenson et al. (eds). Cambridge: Polity.

Sayers, J. 1979. On the description of psychological sex differences, in *Sex-role stereotyping*, O. Hartnett, G. Boden, M. Fuller (eds). London: Tavistock.

Scott, A. 1986. Industrialization, gender segregation and stratification theory, in *Gender and stratification*, R. Crompton & M. Mann (eds). Cambridge:Polity Press.

Scott, A. & B. Burchell (forthcoming). And never the twain shall meet? Lifetime segregation of working men and women, in *Gender segregation in British labour markets*, A. M. Scott (ed.).

Sedley, A. & M. Benn 1982. *Sexual harassment at work*. London: National Council for Civil Liberties.

Segal, L. 1987. *Is the future female?* London: Virago.

Sen, G. 1980. The sexual division of labour and the working-class family: towards a conceptual synthesis of class relations and the subordination of women. *Review of Radical Political Economics* 12.

Siltanen, J. 1985. Employment and parenting: variations in experience. PhD manuscript, University of Cambridge.

Siltanen, J. 1986. Domestic responsibilities and the structuring of employment, in *Gender and stratification*, R. Crompton & M. Mann (eds). Cambridge: Polity Press.

Siltanen, J. 1990. Social change and the measurement of occupational segregation by sex. *Work, Employment and Society* 4.

Siltanen, J. & Stanworth, M. 1984. The politics of public man and private woman, in *Women and the public sphere*, J. Siltanen & M. Stanworth (eds). London: Hutchinson.

Siltanen, J., J. Jarman, R. M. Blackburn, 1992. *Gender inequality in the labour market. A manual on methodology*. Geneva: ILO.

Smith, D. J. 1977. *Racial disadvantage in Britain*. Harmondsworth: Penguin.

Stanworth, M. 1984. Women and class analysis: a reply to Goldthorpe. *Sociology* 18.

Stewart, A., K. Prandy, R. M. Blackburn 1980. *Social stratification and occupations*. London: Macmillan.

Stewart, M. & C. Greenhalgh 1982. Work history patterns and the occupational attainment of women. University of Warwick Economic Research Papers.

Stewart, M. B. & C. A. Greenhalgh 1984. Work history patterns and the occupational attainment of women. *Economic Journal* 94.

Stewart, A. et al. 1985. Gender and earnings, in *New approaches to economic life*, R. Finnegan, D. Gallie, B. Roberts (eds). Manchester: University of Manchester Press.

213

Stoller, R. 1968. *Sex and gender*. New York: Science House.

Townsend, P. 1979. *Poverty in the United Kingdom*. Middlesex: Penguin.

Townsend, P. & D. Gordon 1989. *Memorandum laid before the Social Services Committee on Minimum Income*. London: HMSO.

Treiman, D. J. & H. J. Hartmann (eds) 1981. *Women, work and wages*. Washington DC: National Academy Press.

Treiman, D. J. & P. A. Roos 1983. Sex and earnings in industrial society: a nine-nation comparison. *American Journal of Sociology* 89.

Tresemer, D. 1975. Assumptions made about gender roles, in *Another voice*, M. Millman & R. M. Kanter (eds). New York: Anchor Books.

Wainwright, H. 1978. Women and the division of labour, in *Work, urbanism and inequality*, P. Abrams (ed.). London: Weidenfeld & Nicolson.

Wajcman, J. 1983. *Women in control*. Milton Keynes: Open University Press.

Walby, S. 1986. *Patriarchy at work*. Cambridge: Polity Press.

Walby, S. 1988. Introduction, and Segregation in employment in social and economic theory, in *Gender segregation at work*, S. Walby (ed.). Milton Keynes: Open University Press.

Watson, T. 1980. *Sociology, work and industry*. London: Routledge & Kegan Paul.

Watt, I. 1980. Linkages between industrial radicalism and the domestic role among working women. *Sociological Review* 28.

Webb, M. 1982. The labour market, in *Sex differences in Britain*, J. Reid & E. Wormald (eds). London: Grant McIntyre.

Wedderburn, D. 1983. Policy issues in the distribution of income and wealth: some lessons from the Diamond Commission, in *The wealth report – 2*, F. Field (ed.). London: Routledge & Kegan Paul.

Weir, A. & M. McIntosh 1982. Towards a wages strategy for women. *Feminist Review* 10.

Whitehead, A. 1981. "I'm hungry, mum": the politics of domestic budgeting, in *Of marriage and the market*, K. Young, C. Wolkowitz, R. McCullagh (eds). London: CSE Books.

Willis, P. 1979. Shop floor culture, masculinity and the wage form, in *Working class culture*, J. Clarke, C. Critcher, R. Johnson (eds). London: Hutchinson.

Wilson, A. & A. Harris 1983. Dial "v" for victimisation. *New Statesman*, 13 May.

Witherspoon. S. 1988. Interim report: a woman's work, in *British Social Attitudes – the fifth report*, R. Jowell et al. (eds). Aldershot: Gower.

Women's Studies Group (Centre for Contemporary Cultural Studies) 1978. Introduction. *Women take issue*. London: Hutchinson.

Wood, S. 1981. Redundancy and female employment. *Sociological Review* 29.

Yantz, L. & D. Smith 1983. Women as a reserve army of labour: a critique. *Review of Radical Political Economics* 15.

Yeandle, S. 1982. Variation and flexibility: key characteristics of female labour. *Sociology* 16.

Yeandle, S. 1984. *Women's working lives*. London: Tavistock.

Young, I. 1980. Socialist feminism and the limits of dual systems theory. *Socialist Review* 10.

Young, M. & P. Willmott, P. 1973. *The symmetrical family*. Middlesex: Penguin.

Zabalza, A. & J. Arrufat 1985. The extent of sex discrimination in Great Britain, in *Women and equal pay*, A. Zabalza & Z. Tzannatos (eds). Cambridge: Cambridge University Press.

Index

215

For Product Safety Concerns and Information please contact our EU
representative GPSR@taylorandfrancis.com
Taylor & Francis Verlag GmbH, Kaufingerstraße 24, 80331 München, Germany

www.ingramcontent.com/pod-product-compliance
Ingram Content Group UK Ltd.
Pitfield, Milton Keynes, MK11 3LW, UK
UKHW020956180425
457613UK00019B/719